GLISSANT AND THE MIDDLE PASSAGE

for Catherine,

in friendship and respect

—John

D1557364

Thinking Theory

GRANT FARRED, SERIES EDITOR

Glissant and the Middle Passage: Philosophy, Beginning, Abyss
John E. Drabinski

Curating as Ethics
Jean-Paul Martinon

Glissant and the Middle Passage

Philosophy, Beginning, Abyss

John E. Drabinski

Thinking Theory

University of Minnesota Press
Minneapolis
London

The University of Minnesota Press gratefully acknowledges financial support for the publication of this series from Cornell University.

Excerpts from *Fastes*, "The Great Chaoses," and "The Indies" from *The Collected Poems of Édouard Glissant*, ed. Jeff Humphries, trans. Jeff Humphries with Melissa Manolas (Minneapolis: University of Minnesota Press, 2005); originally published in Édouard Glissant, *Poèmes complets* (Paris: Éditions Gallimard, 1994), copyright 1994 Éditions Gallimard. Excerpts from Édouard Glissant, *Black Salt*, trans. Betsy Wing (Ann Arbor: University of Michigan Press, 2001), reprinted by permission of Betsy Wing; originally published in Édouard Glissant, *Le sel noir* (Paris: Éditions Gallimard, 1983), copyright 1983 Éditions Gallimard. Excerpts from "The Sea Is History" reprinted from Derek Walcott, *Selected Poems*, edited by Edward Baugh (New York: Farrar, Straus and Giroux, 2007), copyright 2007 by Derek Walcott; reprinted by permission of Farrar, Straus and Giroux. Excerpts from Aimé Césaire, *Notebook of a Return to My Native Land*, trans. Mireille Rosello and Annie Pritchard (Newcastle upon Tyne: Bloodaxe Books, 1995) reprinted by permission of Présence Africaine Editions.

A portion of chapter 4 was previously published in "Aesthetics and the Abyss: Between Césaire and Lamming," in *Theorizing Glissant: Sites and Citations*, ed. John E. Drabinski and Marisa Parham (London: Rowman and Littlefield International, 2015), 139–64.

Copyright 2019 by the Regents of the University of Minnesota

All rights reserved. No part of this publication may be reproduced, stored in a retrieval system, or transmitted, in any form or by any means, electronic, mechanical, photocopying, recording, or otherwise, without the prior written permission of the publisher.

Published by the University of Minnesota Press
111 Third Avenue South, Suite 290
Minneapolis, MN 55401-2520
http://www.upress.umn.edu

ISBN 978-1-5179-0597-2 (hc)
ISBN 978-1-5179-0598-9 (pb)

A Cataloging-in-Publication record for this book is available from the Library of Congress.

Printed in the United States of America on acid-free paper

The University of Minnesota is an equal-opportunity educator and employer.

UMP BmB 2019

Contents

Abbreviations   vii

Preface   ix

Introduction: Between Europe and the Americas   1

1. Origins I: Memory, Root, Abyss   23

2. Origins II: Memory, Future, Abyss   61

3. Ontology of an Abyssal Subject   99

4. Aesthetics of an Abyssal Subject   137

5. Thinking and Building: What Is an Intellectual?   183

Acknowledgments   213

Notes   217

Index   233

Abbreviations

Works by Édouard Glissant

BS—*Black Salt*. Translated by Betsy Wing. Ann Arbor: University of Michigan Press, 2001.

CD—*Caribbean Discourse: Selected Essays*. Translated by J. Michael Dash. Charlottesville: University of Virginia Press, 1989.

CL—*La cohée du Lamentin*. Paris: Gallimard, 2005. All translations are my own.

CP—*The Collected Poems of Édouard Glissant*. Edited by Jeff Humphries. Translated by Jeff Humphries with Melissa Manolas. Minneapolis: University of Minnesota Press, 2005.

FM—*Faulkner, Mississippi*. Translated by Barbara Lewis and Thomas C. Spear. Chicago: University of Chicago Press, 1999.

IPD—*Introduction à une poétique du divers*. Paris: Gallimard, 1996. All translations are my own.

MT—*Monsieur Toussaint: A Play*. Translated by J. Michael Dash. Boulder: Lynne Rienner, 2005.

NRM—*Une nouvelle region du monde*. Paris: Gallimard, 2006. All translations are my own.

PhR—*Philosophie de la relation*. Paris: Gallimard, 2009. All translations are my own.

PR—*Poetics of Relation*. Translated by Betsy Wing. Ann Arbor : University of Michigan Press, 1997.

TTM—*Traité du tout-monde*. Paris: Gallimard, 1997. All translations are my own.

WS—"A Word Scratcher." Translated by Linda Coverdale. In *Chronicle of the Seven Sorrows*, by Patrick Chamoiseau, 7–9. Lincoln: University of Nebraska Press, 1999.

Preface

THIS BOOK IS A LONG MEDITATION on and philosophical treatment of the work of Édouard Glissant, with special attention to the poetics developed in his nonfiction writings. A bit has been written recently on Glissant and philosophy in French, but English-language commentary has been of a decidedly different character. This is a critical gap in the literature.

Glissant's work is profoundly philosophical. There can be no doubt about this, and it makes the gap all the more noteworthy. As well, Glissant's sustained engagement with the central trends of Atlantic thought—from Négritude to various kind of existentialism to ethical-political critiques of modernity to the poststructuralist moment—places him at the center of many debates. I want to argue in part across this book that Glissant's conscious and deeply critical movement across both the north and south Atlantic intellectual worlds makes him a uniquely important figure. The engagements are always critical; central, for Glissant, will always be Caribbeanness considered on its own terms. But the terms of the Caribbean are always unstable, chaotic, and fractal in character, which delinks Glissant from any number of iterations of intellectual nationalism around region, race, history, or memory.[1] Rather, and this is Glissant's final and most emphatic concept, the Caribbean is simultaneously local—hemispheric, specifically historical, particular in its memories—and global—the crossroads of the world, from the beginning. That is, Caribbeanness is *tout-monde*, not as an aesthetic or ethical idea or ideal, but as a direct description of the material histories and memories of the archipelago. Contact is beginning, however violent, and the aftermath is the ambivalent mixture of unthinkable sadness and world-changing depth of meaningfulness. The shoreline of the Caribbean. Landscape of pain, landscape of beauty. *Black salt.*

In terms of the trajectory of Glissant's thought, it is worth noting that my own reading of his poetics works from the insight into *tout-monde*, something largely elaborated in and after *Poetics of Relation*, backward to and through his notion of Caribbeanness. The early treatment of the

Caribbean as a rhizome, most clearly described in the essays collected in *Caribbean Discourse* and further refined in a creolization of Gilles Deleuze and Félix Guattari in *Poetics of Relation* and *Introduction à une poétique du divers,* is on my reading akin to a metaphysics of Antillanité that later becomes an ethics, politics, and aesthetics of globalized cultural contact. As a site of irreducible mixture and creolizing work, Caribbeanness is not strictly speaking a theory of global cultural contact, Relation, and fecundity. And yet it is. So, in what follows I most surely mix vocabularies that are not contemporaneous. For a certain kind of scholar, I imagine that will warrant a pause or two, but ultimately the argument of this book, however quietly so (let me announce it here), is for a continuity across Glissant's work—a continuity we see when reading with the frame of loss, trauma, memory, and ruins. Thinking in ruins, which is productive rather than (solely) melancholic, is already thinking the archipelago as a geography of the globe and the geography of thought. The archipelago is already the crossroads of the world, so the Caribbean of Caribbeanness is already *tout-monde* in memory, history, and experience, if not word and concept.

But that is to have-thought. There is first the question of beginning. We start with the abyss. This is Glissant's founding thought. The abyss is an irretrievable sense of loss. The Middle Passage has no representation. Rather, the Middle Passage is simultaneously the evacuation of meaning and the beginning of being, becoming, knowing, and thinking.

How does philosophy think in this space, which is neither simply paradoxical (it resolves in Caribbeanness) nor ambivalent (Caribbeanness is neither backward nor truncated)? I think this is Glissant's most challenging question to us, and it is not one that, to my mind, has been systematically treated in a philosophical register. I want to move the question of the Middle Passage to the center of philosophical thinking about language, time, history, memory, embodiment, subjectivity, aesthetics, and the very idea of the task of thinking itself. Glissant's poetry and poetics comprise decades of testimony to the centrality of the Middle Passage and demonstrate how thinking at the shoreline, the site of arrival and memory and futurity, makes Caribbeanness a distinctive intellectual force. For philosophical thinking, in the context of the Americas and more broadly across the globe, this motif and Glissant's work generally remain a relatively new proposal. While questions of race and racism have slowly moved onto the horizons of white European and American philosophy, we have not seen the experience of mass displacement, death, and forced migration taken

seriously as founding philosophical moments, concepts, and revolutionary reconstructions and deconstructions of meaning. That is the global
context. But beginning with the Middle Passage is also a revision of the
anticolonial and postcolonial prerogative of so much midcentury francophone thought in the Caribbean and Africa—Frantz Fanon, Léopold
Senghor, and Aimé Césaire, in particular. Rather than resistance to domination and visions of futurity that flow from anti- and postcolonial visions,
abyssal beginning is a story about the intersection of traumatic loss and
world-making. Creolization rather than new humanism, as it were. Afro-
Caribbean world-making, rather than genealogies of ideas of race and
their decimating after-effects. There is already beginning and world. Here,
Glissant breaks from the midcentury moment. Here, creolization makes
créolité possible.

In a certain sense, and broadly speaking, we could say that philosophy
as such—understood as engagement with the conditions of knowing,
being, and creating in the mode of the interrogative[2]—has not yet fully
reckoned with the transformative experience of trauma and its disruption
of all conventional understandings of history, memory, and language. No
matter the geography, the character of philosophy, especially in its white
Western register, has in many ways aspired to be outside the vicissitudes of
cultural and political life. That purity, which is its own kind of imperial cultural imagination and political conservatism, insulates much of philosophy from one of thought's greatest enigmas: How do we come to terms
with the wreckage of history, as Benjamin put it, and how do we think
responsibly and attentively after catastrophe? Postwar Jewish philosophy
has of course taken on this very question. After the Shoah, what remained
for thinking? How do we think the remains, such as they are, of disaster?
This is the question of trauma. But what is the philosophical significance
of traumatic beginning in other geographies? For every reason, every
thinking, is geographic. We begin *in place*. Caribbeanness names beginning in the archipelago, a site of traumatic beginning and life after. What
is the Middle Passage, thought as traumatic memory and traumatic after-
affect/-effect, to philosophical thinking?

The emergence of trauma studies in the late 1990s changed so much
about how we understand memory and history in the Western context. Fantasies of transparency, iterability, and cohesion in representation were halted
by reflection on the historical experience of catastrophe. Coming to presence in representation, the argument begins, bears an important relation

to memory. When memory functions, representation functions. But when memory is confounded, dissociated, and disoriented by traumatic experience—catastrophic historical events being exemplary cases—we can no longer conceive representation on the conventional model or models. Perhaps representation itself poses the wrong question, labors with the wrong logic and the wrong aspiration. Thus, the problem of the unrepresentable, saturated with so many ethical, epistemological, and aesthetic enigmas, quickly becomes the central problem not just of memory studies but of an ethics of historical study and historiography. What, indeed, is the West's long twentieth century if not a long story about trauma? Altering the meaning of memory, history, and representation alters the very significance of thinking and culture—*meaning itself.* Perhaps the fantasy of "conventional" memory is the problem. Perhaps traumatic memory is the convention, the common, and the shared.

In the white European tradition, there was of course a ready-made audience and seat for the interpretation and extrapolation of traumatic memory. Not only the Shoah but also the frenzy of trench warfare in World War I had already prepared European sensibilities for rather bleak figures of memory and history. This is reflected in a cluster of intellectual trends concerned with authoritarianism, eliminationist violence, and the complicated work of mourning. Indeed, beginning with the early Frankfurt School—Walter Benjamin's essays in particular, but also Theodor Adorno and Max Horkheimer's groundbreaking work on anti-Semitism—white European philosophy discovered how deeply transformative and destructive the transmission of historical pain proves to be for notions of time, space, subjectivity, and community. This is no philosophical niche or special science. Philosophy as such can never be the same after registering this sense of historical experience, an experience in which the ethereal character of theoretical reflection and rhetoric about "the tradition" is put in question by the other or Other's history of cultural and political practices. Since tradition is historical, and history bequeaths, in an essential pairing, pain with its ideas, the very notion of a tradition is implicated in traumatic experience. So, to put it wholly immanent to "the tradition," the passage of ideas and values—so prized by intellectual communities concerned with reproducing themselves—is suddenly disrupted by alternative, even absolutely contradictory experiences of the lifeworld. These experiences are the sorts of individual and collective experiences that comprise the foundations of philosophical discourse. One can see here how so much of the work of Emmanuel Levinas, Maurice Blanchot, Jacques Derrida, Jean-François Lyotard, and others reflects a post-traumatic reinvention of European philosophy. And one can also see how such critical interventions, rooted as they are in the pain and loss of historical violence and exclusion, might claim to have upended the loftiest pretensions of the white West and exposed its central myths of presence, transparency, and, in the end, *universality*.

Two features of this discourse stand out for me. First, such discourse has rarely, if ever, displayed humility around, or even qualification of, claims regarding singularity, "history and memory," and related problems of coming to terms with traumatic experience in theoretical study. Even as works on melancholia, loss, failure of representation, and the like were posed as contestations of white Western delusions of presence, Hegelian history, Platonic forms of knowing, and the troubling hegemonic functions of language, many of the same motifs were smuggled in quietly, functioning still in the foundations of the conclusions drawn. Are we really talking about the end of *history* as such? Or are we talking about the end of a certain conceptions of history, and therefore certain forms and figures of ethno-racialized historical experience and transmission that, in the end, are bound by a specific geography? These questions, even if rarely asked, are crucial for the sincerity of philosophical work. In fact, they place issues of colonialism and imperial habits of thinking at the center of philosophy. Second, broadly philosophical writing on traumatic experience and its destructive and deconstructive power has rarely taken the history of the Americas seriously, but have instead been content to universalize white European experiences. In this way, the Americas, particularly in the Afro-Caribbean tradition, have functioned as a kind of counter-modernity, to use Paul Gilroy's characterization of black Atlantic thinking. This narrow resonance in trauma studies, its failure to turn close attention to the Americas, is surely peculiar (to put it generously), for even just the name of the continent and its archipelago carries (or outright says) loss, trauma, and all of those challenges to thinking. And it is not as if the Americas lack such discourse. In fact, in the Caribbean context, thinkers from the middle of the twentieth century (and certainly before) initiated a long and varied meditation on the meaning of the Middle Passage, colonialism, and the postcolonial moment for all the very same issues and others: space, time, subjectivity, memory, history, and, perhaps most decisively, the meaning of a future forged without deep and long-held roots. Forced migration (the Middle Passage) and enslavement (the plantation) radically alter all senses of relation to the past, and so too any sense of future. This experience demands exploration on its own terms. The radical alteration enacted by forced migration, then the centuries of experience of plantation slavery, carries both figures and claims of loss that are particular to the Middle Passage. One of the lessons of trauma studies generally is that interventions in the problem of memory cast a long shadow, transforming foundational concepts of the human and its possibilities, then realities. What sort of theoretical leisure, intellectual imperialism, or philosophical conservatism has white Western philosophy won for itself by turning away from, in willful ignorance of, the traumatic experiences embedded in the terms *Americas* and *the New World*? And so, too, in that turning away, embedded itself in the whiteness of the West and "the West" as (in Glissant's turn of phrase) not a place but a *project*?

This question already asks so much. Indeed, the very idea of Europe is in question—namely, whether or not one can conceive this peculiar entity "Europe" without ethically, epistemologically, and metaphysically accounting for its global entanglements. It seems plain to me that the name "Europe" is inextricably woven into the pains and pleasures of global histories, not just as a victim of its own internal violent frenzies or beneficiary of profound intellectual traditions but, at least with the emergence of modernity (and arguably well before), also (if not firstly) as the perpetrator of global violence and participant in destructive, genocidal, and world-changing cultural contact.[3] Perhaps this sort of questioning is unwittingly another case of Eurocentrism, where even the effort to "call European ideas into question" ends up reifying the centrality of the European experience of language and history. In that respect, I would say, trauma studies and companion discourses join a long list of allegedly radical critiques that fail to abandon what is so conservative about the institutions of white Western philosophy and related theoretical disciplines: a deep, often unconscious reliance on European models of experience and presumption of their universality. Against this, I argue throughout the present work that traumatic experience must be thought in relation to a *geography of reason*. Trauma, like all constitutive concepts, and indeed the concepts that flow from traumatic beginnings, must be thought in terms of the specificity of *place*. Beginning with and from specificity means reading and rendering ideas (*reason* in the widest sense) in relation to the contexts in which they emerge. Historicity as *this* history, rather than history *as such*.

I came to this project in response to this question of models of experience and how they quietly reify colonial habits of measure. In particular,
I am thinking of how Glissant's notion of archipelagic thinking, a figure
and metaphysics of Caribbeanness, shifts our theoretical vocabulary and
reveals, in one swift motion, how important it is to break with the figure
and metaphysics of continental thinking—a movement, essentially, from
unity to fragments. With this notion and all of its attendant shifts, Glissant marks a decisive and genuinely singular postmodern turn in Caribbean theory. It is decisive because he upsets so many habits of thought
in the Atlantic world with an embrace of fragmentation, and genuinely
singular because the origins of this embrace of fragmentation, unlike the
sorts found in poststructuralist theory in the United States and France,
lie in the specificity of the Caribbean experience of the Americas. Glissant's point of contrast with *archipelagic thinking*, what he calls *continental
thinking*, initiates a distinction that, as I hope to show in the pages that
follow, fundamentally overturns the meaning of philosophical thinking.
Michael Wiedorn has demonstrated how this figure of the archipelago
structures Glissant's later work, and especially how we can read his literary production as a deep rendering of the archipelago.[4] Wiedorn's notion
of the paradox is important here, too: Glissant's figure of the archipelago
is a contradiction—a unity out of difference that becomes difference and
disunity, then unity, or what Antonio Benítez-Rojo called a "repeating
island"—that nevertheless produces a world. What are the ontological,
epistemological, and aesthetic implications of this paradox? And what are
its origins in the abyss? From memory to philosophy, the genesis of a paradoxical sense of paradox.

Again, Glissant's shift from the continent to the archipelago as a condition and figure of thinking marks his work with a quick, decisive decolonization of thought. With this distinction, Glissant is able to produce a
figure of thought that explains what is to my mind a nascent conservatism
in so much "radical" theory coming out of Europe and parts of the United
States, as well as much of the midcentury Caribbean tradition. Perhaps,
to say it again, in critiquing the pretensions of the European tradition,
critics—postcolonial, decolonial, or anti-racist—have (at times, at least)
unwittingly reified the idea of Europe with an oblique, even unconscious
fidelity to *pensée continentale*. Fragmentation means loss of meaning. Critique proceeds from there. Glissant's fidelity to Caribbean specificity,
however, exploring all of the consequences of thinking the New World on

its own terms, operates largely outside the internal logic of the Western tradition. The anti-reification of *pensée archipélique*. Fragmentation means creation of meaning. Critique proceeds from there.

And yet Glissant's critical transformation of what we might mean by "philosophy" and its central categories is also immanently engaged with Europe, the United States, and the white Western tradition *at the very same time* that he interprets and puts himself in dialogue with fellow Caribbean writers. This engagement happens at two levels. At a first and largely philological level, close readings of Glissant's texts reveal long-standing and complex critical conversations with Caribbean intellectuals from Aimé Césaire to Frantz Fanon to Derek Walcott to Linton Kwesi Johnson and others alongside a whole cluster of white European theorists, most prominently the work of Gilles Deleuze and Félix Guattari, but also more quietly with Martin Heidegger, Jacques Derrida, and others. This subtler engagement is a second level at which we must read Glissant's transformation of philosophy. In his elaborate and complicated critique of various ideas of Being, time, and the Other, Glissant forges an implicit but utterly crucial relation to those philosophers at the forefront of so-called postmodernism and its poetic and ethical manifestations. Glissant's explicit and implicit engagements with philosophers and philosophical ideas demonstrate one of his greatest innovations as a thinker: creolization as a first principle of reading and interpretation. The first position of creolization eliminates the terms that usually haunt the study of such cross-Atlantic relationships, namely, the colonial specters of *comparison* and *measure*. The concern, even anxiety, is that white European thought either overwhelms or is used as a way of justifying the legitimacy of black Atlantic thought. Anticolonial reading, of course, jettisons this kind of relation and affirms the legitimacy of black Atlantic thought on its own terms. And this is surely Glissant's starting point as a thinker. The Caribbean tradition needs no outside cosign. At the same time, his relation to cross-Atlantic thought, crossing old colonial boundaries, is anything but anxious, for creolization is always already a method of *appropriation* in the best and most fecund sense. In place of measure, creolization puts excess. Glissant's relation to white Western philosophers, and indeed philosophy more broadly, is precisely that: the movement from measure to excess, a writerly embodiment of what he comes to call the thought of *tout-monde*. Excessive thought, excessive relation and Relation, is not threatened by its Other, even the colonial Other. I think Hugues Azéradt gets it right when he writes that "Glissant does not reject the principle of influence, he turns it into a principle of relation."⁵ This is Glissant's second wave of decolonization, I would argue, a wave that re-addresses what had, in the first wave, been jettisoned in the name of self-authorization and self-authoring. Paradox can only begin to describe this relation. Paradox produces abundance, rather than paralyzing or confounding contradiction. As Wiedorn's title has it, Glissant calls us to *think* like an archipelago, not just frame thought *as* an archipelago. Relation is therefore dynamic, productive, dangerous, and alive with fecund engagement and appropriation. It is the sort of eventfulness, the sort of excessive excess, that underlines Alexandre Leupin's argument that Glissantian philosophical thinking gives way, or ought to give way, to poetry—the language of *tout-monde*, the language of archipelagic thinking, the language of paradox that resolves and dissolves.⁶ Anxious relations become relations of Chaos. The *monde* of *tout-monde*. Critical Atlantic relations are transformed.

In this context, we can begin to understand why, in *Introduction à une poétique du divers*, Glissant characterizes his work as a *para-philosophy* (IPD, 82), a characterization noted and expanded upon by Georges Desportes in his short book on Glissant.⁷ Much of the meaning of that sense of philosophy—the logic and economy of *para-* as a decisive supplement and hyphen—will be demonstrated as the chapters below unfold, but a word or two can be said here. To begin, Glissant's self-articulation and self-portrait, which get even more explicit and compelling treatment in *Philosophie de la relation*, give important textual credence to my claim in the present project that Glissant ought to be read as a philosopher. In *Introduction à une poétique du divers*, for example, Glissant defines the philosophical sense of his work in terms of his dedication to the science of Chaos and its mergence with *tout-monde*. I take this programmatic—or even summary—statement as a broad claim that *pensée archipélique* intervenes in the meaning of metaphysics, epistemology, ethics, and aesthetics—and even logic, if one reads Glissant's reflections on contradiction and paradox in that context. Put another way, a poetics of *tout-monde* changes everything about philosophy. As well, and this is one of the interesting effects of the mixture of opacity and creolization in the poetics of Relation, the addition of *para-* to *philosophy* loops the term back into itself. So much is at stake in this loop. With the Caribbean and experience of the New World as an interpretative frame and stage for thinking, one can read para-philosophy as a defense of a poetics of Relation and other

of Glissant's motifs *against* white Western philosophy and its pretensions
or efforts to neutralize the geography and universalization of historical experience. *Para-philosophy as an anticolonial defense of place.* Or, in a second
moment of a double reading of the term, para-philosophy can (also) be
read as warding off those temptations precisely insofar as para-philosophy
becomes philosophy. Rather than warding off philosophy with a poetics,
then, para-philosophy becomes philosophical in the distance it gains from
the currency of *pensée continentale,* that stock-in-trade of the white West's
"love of wisdom." *Para-philosophy as a postcolonial articulation of place.*
    These are promissory notes, of course.

The Introduction and chapters that follow are nearly exclusively concerned with Glissant's theoretical work, an interpretative choice that both
brings out the philosophical nuances of his thought most clearly and limits the scope of my claims. Much has been written about Glissant's literary work by authors such as J. Michael Dash, Celia Britton, Bernadette
Callier, Valérie Loichot, and others. My debt to those careful studies of
Glissant cannot be overstated, and I do not pretend to advance their interpretations of his creative output. In drawing attention to his theoretical work, my work here offers a philosophical interpretation, treatment,
and appreciation of Glissant's work on time, space, subjectivity, aesthetics, and the nature of intellectual responsibility. In taking up these issues,
Glissant's metaphysical and epistemological sensibilities emerge as foundational to his claims about history, the poetic word, and so many other
ideas that cluster to the poetics of Relation. My strategy for demonstrating
this philosophical dimension of Glissant's work is rooted in textual expo-
sition and close reading of crucial passages from his theoretical writings.
This is a modest aim, really: render the theoretical implications and foundations of Glissant's claims from the texts themselves. Such a commitment to primary texts means that critical assessment is largely set aside
in favor of the clarification of ideas. A systematic treatment of Glissant's
philosophical dimension, to my mind, warrants such a commitment; the
texts are that complicated and need exactly this sort of careful interpretative attention. At the same time, the hermeneutic exercises undertaken
in each chapter frame a reading of Glissant with companion discourses,
discourses that are often in instructive tension with his work. Juxtaposition clarifies. Thus, figures such as Heidegger, Césaire, Fanon, Deleuze,
Benjamin, and others function below as interlocutors whose ideas either

clarify by way of contrast, are explicitly present in the text, or are evoked, often quietly, in the course of Glissant's slow development of ideas. In that sense, I want my interpretative frames to make the creative dimension of reading of Glissant's theoretical work clear and evident, the part of interpretation that engages from particular, explicitly articulated critical angles, and with, one hopes, incisive queries. Glissant's articulation of the process of cultural contact—which in this context is another name for reading and interpretation—requires, at the very least, the hermeneutic honesty of making the conditions of that reading and interpretation explicit.

In all, this book moves back and forth across its own title. The Middle Passage and the abyss are problems of beginning. Beginning is perhaps philosophy's most persistent and enigmatic question. How do we commence thinking? How is the commencement of thinking related to historical experience and complicated intellectual geographies? These questions have dominated much of post–World War II white European philosophy, to be sure, but are also constitutive of the very meaning of Caribbean theory since that same period. The difference between these sites of resonance marks the very meaning of philosophy. *Glissant, Philosophy, and the Middle Passage*—if historical experience initiates and structures the movement of thought, movement in and from *beginning*, then Glissant's beginning, as with any sense of beginning in the Americas, begins with the trauma of arrival and the Middle Passage. This arrival, as we will see, builds an abyss into beginning, an abyss that is further doubled in what I call a *shoreline thinking* that is sited, cited, and caught sight of between the Middle Passage and the composition of composite cultural forms. The Middle Passage renders beginning abyssal. Glissant's poetics makes philosophy out of this beginning. It is witness to water, sand, sun, death, and life.

Introduction

Between Europe and the Americas

*"That there is your first name . . . an' you're inside it!" he revealed,
with a wizard's mocking grin.*
*Wo yoyoy! . . . Jojo the Math Whiz had just plunged the little
boy into a fine predicament: he saw himself there, captured whole
within a chalk mark.* Which meant he could be erased from the
world! *Pretending he wasn't scared shitless (which would have
tickled Jojo), he began to copy out his first name a thousand times, in
order to proliferate and avoid a genocide.*

—Patrick Chamoiseau, *School Days*

IN THE PAGES THAT FOLLOW I pursue a single question: What does
the work of Édouard Glissant tell us about the relationship between philosophical thinking and the history and memory of the Middle Passage?
That is, how does the historical experience of the New World alter conceptions of knowing, being, creating, and acting? Glissant's essays and poetry are resolutely philosophical, and the systematic reading in the pages
that follow offers a rigorous appreciation of that philosophical dimension.
Glissant's contribution to our understanding of modernity, postmodernity, and questions of language, nation, and race is utterly singular. What
might this mean for philosophy and philosophical thinking?

The present reflections on the problem of beginning, philosophy, and
the Middle Passage are at once modest and ambitious. The modesty here
lies in the focus on the work of a single author: Édouard Glissant. His
sustained theoretical treatment of the problem of difference, historical
experience, and how traumatic memory fundamentally alters the basic
categories of philosophy is crucial for any notion of future philosophical thinking attentive to place. As well, Glissant's critical, creolizing, and

fundamentally transformative engagement with the central motifs of European philosophy—a transformation that overturns and confounds notions of center and periphery, of influence and cultural contact—critically situates his work at the heart of contemporary philosophizing in Europe and the Americas. One thinks here, perhaps firstly, of his provocative interpretation of the work of Gilles Deleuze and Félix Guattari, which transforms concepts of nomad and rhizome with the experience of the Americas while simultaneously marking the metaphysical, epistemological, and aesthetic irruption of Caribbean identity into its own kind of modernity and postmodernity, and which, in a further turn, locates the European account of the same in a subconscious, unthematized colonial logic. *Critical and productive in one gesture.* Glissant's readerly and theoretical practice is a dynamic paradox. Or, one can think of how his preoccupation with beginning and *poiesis*—the problematic that underwrites so much of the present work—brings Glissant into a curious and complicated dialogue with Martin Heidegger's work on language, history, and being, and thereby reworks familiar notions of double consciousness we find in W. E. B. Du Bois, Ralph Ellison, Richard Wright, and the early Afro-surrealism of René Ménil. And yet, Glissant's reflections on these and related matters have barely, if at all, registered in philosophy outside of francophone Caribbean scholarship. The chapters that follow respond to that gap by initiating a sustained meditation on the meaning of his work for theories of how memory, subjectivity, aesthetics, and the future of intellectual work are transfigured through contact with the intractable character of difference. The modesty of the present project, then, focuses on the trajectory of Glissant's reflections on such issues and offers a depth of appreciation that only such focus can yield.

But there are also larger ambitions in the following pages. Glissant's contribution to philosophy transforms so many concepts of difference by thinking the irreducibly fragmentary character of difference in a New World context. The relation between place—by which I mean the blend of geographical space and historical experience—and philosophical thinking is paramount, and Glissant's notion of Caribbeanness makes this theoretically evident and creates a radical critical method. The New World context and how the geography of thinking is there transformed elevates reflection on Glissant's work above mere philological or textual concern. Such a context urgently infuses philosophical reflection with questions of race, marginality, and the metaphysical and epistemological effects of the global entanglements of empire. Glissant's careful and radical re-articulation of the Caribbean context puts such effects at the center of thinking. If thinking is always generated in relation to place, then the Caribbean context, defined as it is by the experiences of race, marginality, and empire, contends with such issues in philosophy's foundational experiences and structures: language, world, and history. To wit: the name "Americas" carries these entanglements all by itself, evoking the creation of empire and race, which then produced and reproduced the center-margin structure of the world-system.

And yet, for Glissant, the Caribbean cannot simply be mapped on to a wider, generalizing discourse about race and the problem of marginality. Indeed, to map the Caribbean inside that discourse misplaces the problem of place and concedes too much to a colonial logic in which the metropole dictates the terms of relation. This is the difficult nuance of Glissant's thought. Rather, he argues, if we attend to the specificity of the Caribbean context—in particular, the abyssal and composite character of language, world, and history—then the language of race itself is fundamentally transformed and de-essentialized, reconceived on a creole model that places difference and becoming at the heart of questions of identity, displacing or replacing largely fixed notions of Africanness (Aimé Césaire) and the epidermal racial schema (Frantz Fanon).

Such a shift emphasizes the peculiar work and productive sense of what Glissant calls a *pensée archipélique*. The entanglements of empire are as metaphysical as they are political; reality itself is transformed by empire, not just the terms of economy and political representation. This insight puts him in the very same discussion as Césaire and Fanon, his anticolonial intellectual predecessors. Césaire's apocalyptic tone in *Notebook of a Return to the Native Land* and Fanon's enigmatic appeal to a new humanism in the closing pages of *The Wretched of the Earth* give testimony to the metaphysical by calling for a complete break with the present and colonial past. But Glissant's advance on Césaire and Fanon lies in the complexity with which he engages global entanglement, relations that not only express the pathologies of postcolonial life—a moment of overlap with his predecessors—but also produce the differences and tensions that drive the composite processes of creolization—a sense of cultural production we do not find in Césaire and Fanon. This saturates Glissant's work with the aporetic fold of the sadness and the pleasures of life that *goes on*, creates itself, and so makes language, world, and history out of abysses and traces of the traumatic past, rather than retrieving (Césaire) or breaking with (Fanon) that past. This shift to the present (vernacular culture) and a critical engagement with the traumatic past (abyssal beginning) also locates his work between all fixed figures and elements of space and time—in a word, *becoming*, against *being*. Glissant's is a sense of becoming in which roots are (or become) unrooted, territories are deterritorialized, and linguistic and cultural grammars are fractured and disrupted with both anxiety and creative ecstasy. *Glissant between Europe and the Americas.*[1] In the end, this means theorizing and reading Glissant's Americas with all of their peculiar, singular, unprecedented, and fundamentally enigmatic senses of past and future. The archipelago, in Glissant's hands, figures this sense of future nicely and, in that figure, transfigures so much of how we think about history, memory, and beginning. Transfiguration between Europe and the Americas—in which *between* names not a third space but a site of creolizing transformation—is where an abyssal beginning gives birth to Glissant's theorizing philosophy and the Middle Passage.

So, a first question: How do we begin thinking between Europe and the Americas? The entanglements we call "empire" render this "between" constitutive, rather than a forged, then blended, relation between existing identities. Creolization, Glissant reminds us, is not *métissage*. Colonialism puts mixture at the center of meaning for both the colonizer and the colonized. This is how violence works outside the militarism of political life and inside the psyche and culture of the colonial. In a twist on Césaire's insight in *Discourse on Colonialism* that colonialism dehumanizes both colonizer and colonized, perhaps we could say that, for Glissant, global entanglements dismantle the humanism of humanity for both colonizer and colonized. The universal of the human, the generalization of experience, and so the appeal to the non-place of theory and philosophical thinking—none of this can survive empire's entanglement. However, this is not to conflate two very distinct experiences. Although entanglements transform all who are therein implicated,[2] the senses of colonial and postcolonial identity emergent from mixture remain profoundly different, and that difference is instructive. Articulating that difference is crucial for Glissant's thinking the between of thinking between Europe and the Americas in the Caribbean context. This is fundamentally a question of identity.

What can we say about philosophy and the problem of identity? Contemporary white European philosophy, at least since Immanuel Kant, tells a long story about the precarious character of identity. With Kant, the idealism of transcendental philosophy—initiated in that fabled distinction between the phenomenal and the noumenal, between what we know and what is forever beyond our grasp—is in a strange, unexpected way testimony to the crisis of knowing rooted in identity thinking. Kant's concession, and it surely is one, to the finitude of knowing is tantamount to saying that identity thinking has lost the long fantasized power of its reach and scope. The fantasies of traditional metaphysics sustain a near fatal blow when Kant puts identity's reach in question; after Kant, we know *as humans*, finite and limited, so never grasp reality outside that finitude. From Hegel through Heidegger and Derrida and after, European philosophy unfolds as a deepening critique and sense of crisis around identity thinking. The long twentieth century is therefore in many ways a story about the supplanting of identity by a (increasingly radical) sense of difference. Difference dismantles the edifice of metaphysics and, with it, also one of the defining pieces of the Western imagination. No matter the long recurrence (explicit and implicit, witting and unwitting) of identity thinking—fantasies of a total thinking die slowly—and no matter the pleasure of being liberated from the calcifying effect of tradition: the interruptive force of difference creates two centuries of fraught European intellectual space. The vicissitudes of difference demand careful, nuanced thinking. Anxious thinking for Europe, no doubt. Uprooting a long-held, much-treasured sense of the past transforms senses of home into, as Heidegger says in a reading of Novalis, perpetual homelessness in one's language and world.[3]

There are many frames for and threads with which to tell this story, and perhaps the most significant among them concerns the problem of history. Historical experience, especially in and after Heidegger's work, moves to the center of philosophical thinking in Europe after World War I. Prompted by the human disaster of that war, the initially metaphysical question of difference and loss of identity, abstract and caught in the intersection of theorizing knowing and being, suddenly becomes urgent, intimate, and wholly existential. That is, historical experience moves from being an element of cultural reification and reproduction to the catastrophic, terrifying condition for the possibility of thinking *after disaster*. Historical experience, in Heidegger's work, comes to describe the complex sense of how being and knowing are structured by long trajectories of modes of thinking sedimented in language. Philosophy and its expression are not *sui generis*. The very words we use to describe ourselves and our world, and even to account for the nature of words themselves, are assigned or assign a sense before we come to consciousness and conscious life. Indeed, consciousness itself is spoken for before it speaks, which is to say that, in Heidegger's famous and nicely blunt statement, *language speaks.* Our activity as thinkers, we could say, is forestructured (though not determined) by the active-passivity of historical experience. Being draws from the peculiar, primordial sense of (historical and memorial) becoming.

Two insights are to be drawn from this. First, there is the intimacy of language and subjectivity—an intimacy, we shall see, that is critical for Glissant's work.[4] When Heidegger famously writes in "Letter on Humanism" that "language is the house of Being," we ought to see in that claim the very meaning of subjectivity as finitude. The subject makes its home in language. Subjectivity does not generate or create language; we are not the home of language, language houses us. Language itself is therefore creative, not solely because we enact transformations of it (that is surely true of the poet) but also, and maybe firstly, because the intimacy of language and subjectivity reveals us as *creaturely.* We are created. Our creator is language, and that is our home, both as a possibility (the world becomes meaningful in the word) and as a limit (the threshold of the home opens upon what exceeds the word). In white European theory, this has proven to be an exceptionally destructive and fecund insight. No matter the variations—and they are enormous, with important consequences—Heidegger's account of language sets out the path of what we now call "the postmodern," seen in its perhaps most provocative form in the ethical and political works of Levinas and Derrida, where the word of creation is uttered by the utterly enigmatic "Other." In this moment, the negotiation of difference in historical experience becomes constitutive of identity, overturning the Kantian regulative ideal—that last and most hopeful gasp of identity thinking. The infinity of difference rather than identity, in a strange reverse of Kant's ideal, regulates the finitude of identifying articulation and expression. Nothing in European philosophy thereafter looks the same. "Difference" and "the Other" move from margin to center, then explode the very ideas of center, hegemony, and meaning without gestures or efforts of repair. The modern is dismantled by, insofar as it becomes, the postmodern. We should not be surprised, then, that the most radical formulations of this deconstructive difference—namely, Levinas's and Derrida's—have proven fertile for a whole range of anti- and postcolonial theory.

The second insight to be drawn from Heidegger, one that builds on the first, is how historical experience transforms and adds nuance to a general theory of the sign. How does the sign become readable? And what does its readability (or lack thereof) tell us about the world, subjectivity, language, and the entwinement of all three in historical experience? Heidegger's account of language embeds the sign in historical experience, and it yields quirky results. Heidegger's work certainly does not lack nostalgia, which is often expressed in the contention that language preserves and bears the meaning of the past within itself, holding fast to it across massive shifts of time. In *Identity and Difference*, Heidegger writes: "The criterion of what has not been thought [in historical texts] does not lead to the inclusion of previous thought into a still higher development and systemization that surpass it. Rather, the criterion demands that traditional thinking be set free into its essential past which is still preserved."[5] In this passage, Heidegger reworks claims about history and language that derive from both Hegel's philosophy of history and Edmund Husserl's 1936 essay "The Origin of Geometry," resulting in a genuinely potent hybrid theory of the memorial sign. Whatever its lofty rhetoric and aspiration, and Heidegger never hesitates to elevate the stakes, this is not in the end an altogether strange claim. In fact, in a certain sense it is rather banal. We presume to enact exactly what Heidegger describes as readers of history, habitually and constitutively reactivating (we hope) the essential meaning of the past when we read history's words. This sort of thing is fairly banal in the case of, say, reading a theorem from Euclid's *Elements*. In that act of reading, we think the same thought as the master geometer, share his insight, and, across history in the sign that remembers, we enter into a relationship of identification: I see as Euclid saw, I know as he knew. But beyond the banal, there is also the massive ambition of something like Heidegger's reactivation of words for Being in his readings of Presocratic Greek philosophers. *That* ancient Greek, the letter and word, is *an experience of Being,* not just a report of sense or referent in a sign. There is genuine power in Heidegger's most speculative meditations. With such ambition, Heidegger is able to forge important new conceptions of historicity and of the transcendence of language.

At the same time, for all the aspiration to full presence, Heidegger is plenty aware of how historical experience might build irretrievable loss into the sign, how the sign might be loss itself (and so not just an expression of loss). In Heidegger's sense of loss, what ought to gather to the word does not come. And so the reader of the sign of loss is always an interpreter who comes too late and finds little or almost nothing at the heart of a given signification. In a well-known example from "Origin of the Work of Art," Heidegger brings this sense of historical experience—loss, reactivation, presence, and radical absence—to bear on the encounter with the Greek temple. It is always the Greeks with Heidegger. Always. What once summoned the gods and provoked religious ecstasy in the pagan reveler is now, for the interpreter come too late, a *ruin*. The temporality of ruin is enigmatic, precisely because it functions as some kind of presence— the remains remain and show themselves—and yet what is present has already retreated in some fundamental way. Thus, the ruin brings to presence only the failure to come to presence—a strange economy. Heidegger writes: "The temple, in its standing there, first gives to things their look and to men their outlook on themselves. This remains open as long as the work is a work, as long as the god has not fled from it."[6] The god has fled, so we stand in the temple as a ruin. That is, the temple is a ruin (a trace, if even that, of another past), and we are ruin*ed* by the temple (we become a trace, if even that, of the historical experience that is *not* gathered to the site). When the work ceases to work, the sign is closed and only signifies its closure. Heidegger's reflections on the word and the temple, then, bear witness to historical experience in the fullest and most honestly tragic sense: the promise of reactivation (anticipation and openness to presence) and the failure of gathering (disappointment, radical absence). Even just as the site of juxtaposition, the temple's roots persist in the constitution of the meaning of failure. The temple in ruins does not cease to remind us, if we are the ones authorized to gather to it as a site of absence, the ones who read silence as the unworking of work and the closure of the sign, that we are of this heritage. Even in loss and failure, we can say that Heidegger's thought is precisely what Glissant calls a *pensée continentale*: thought committed to the presencing of roots, even in the experience of absence.

Heidegger's ambivalence about the sign of historical experience, the sign that is inextricable from our relation to it in (collective and idiosyncratic) memory, says everything about the long twentieth century in Europe and its capacity to think loss as a form of presencing. Nostalgia for the past's redemptive power bears witness to the same problematic, as does Heidegger's mournful approach to absence: in each instant, philosophy reckons with a crisis initiated by loss. Whether we reactivate the past in language or register the failure of presence in loss, nostalgia and roots *forestructure the anticipated (normative) experience of the past.* It is only loss *because we expect connection.* To be sure, loss is unavoidable in any memory work whatsoever. The very idea of memory, of course, presumes retreat from presence and a loss of fullness. But after so much internal violence, after so much wreckage of history, loss takes on the character of *crisis* in European theory in the second half of the just-past century. Indeed, it is not a risky claim to say that loss was the defining and inglorious character of Europe's long twentieth century. Poststructuralism, especially in the work of Levinas, Derrida, Blanchot, and others, gives a high and compelling theoretical expression to this sense of loss. It is exemplary rather than unique when, for example, Levinas writes in "Signature" of how work is haunted by mass murder and massive human suffering: the death and genocidal destruction of the Holocaust. *Haunted work, writing, and memory.* This is the other specter haunting Europe. It shapes the meaning of language and being.

For me, this other haunting specter functions as *a* (if not *the*) condition for the possibility of European theory in the twentieth century. Here, I do not simply mean direct engagement with this or that traumatic event. Rather, theory under this specter is called to reckon with the constant presence of mass death and disaster in Europe—a presence, as Césaire noted long ago, that was always present in the colonies and never provoked serious discourse or crisis—as a broken connection or disconnection with the past. A *broken* connection—perhaps, to put it in the language of trauma, brokenness is a crisis because the violence of the last century-plus places the promise of the white West in such profound doubt (should it not have always been in crisis? was it not always a machine of pain and death?) and bequeaths, as a *foundational* gift, the unintelligible to historical experience. European experience in the long twentieth century begins with trauma, and trauma, rendered in memory, constitutes a decisive break with the past. Or maybe "decisive break" is better put as "broken *disconnection.*" Every interval of time, after all, is the break of the present from the past. This is what one means by change. So, we could say, disconnection is constitutive of the meaning of time as what moves and flows. The specter of pain and catastrophic loss, however, changes the character of movement, flow, and disconnection by breaking apart the progressive or chronicling *story* of disconnection; stories of loss, in the end, are always a way of connecting across breaks and cracks with some sort of metanarrative. *Broken disconnection,* however, captures more exactly this breakdown of the logic of historical time, separating conventional disconnection-as-change from the catastrophic disordering of disconnection after traumatic violence. The painful, traumatized, and traumatizing past disconnects us from disconnection, leaving something we might be tempted to call an abyss. At the same time, as we shall see in the opening chapter below, even a catastrophic past cannot break European time from the model of connection-disconnection-change.

In considering the meaning of historical experiences of loss, we can see how the legibility of the sign is ultimately at stake. Whatever his wider legacy (and even infamy) as a person and thinker, this is Heidegger's enduring insight. Indeed, his conception of reactivation—whether felt in its intensity of presence or in the rift of absence—is ultimately a description of how historical experience renders a sign legible or illegible. It may be the case that forgetting transforms the sign into a mere scribble, as when we become (or imagine becoming) uncertain of our ability to decipher across the rifts of history. We cannot come up with words for pain, we do not write, we only make shapes and hint at the word. Traumatic experience, this haunting of the present, ciphers or threatens to cipher the sign. This is surely what prompts Heidegger to ponder our finitude at the Greek temple, or what warrants Theodor Adorno's caution against poetry after the Holocaust. And many other examples. Where there are no words, there is always the illegible sign. The word fails to speak itself, and we are left without language. But, still, we are left with an illegible sign. This is what we mean when we say that there are no words, yet we speak to the unspeakable. The gods fail to gather at history's breakup, to write Heidegger's singular reflection on the temple large. Whether this is some long overdue self-reckoning on its part or the consequent trauma of a particularly and emphatically violent century, the white West, in this account, begins with barely legible (or even allegedly illegible) signs of the past, not *as* past, but as the condition of the possibility of any future whatsoever. An interval. Nostalgia for the past might motivate the ambitious labor of reactivation, or illegibility might appear as a profound pessimism—which, in its own way, still *expects* memory and reactivation to work. Ambition and pessimism operate with the same presumption about reactivation. Philosophy therefore becomes a kind of theory of disappointment. Wanting to say, but unable to say; language is frustration, deconstruction an expression of the disappointment built into discourse itself. By way of anticipation, however, let us note here that Glissant's is not a philosophy of disappointment; there is no nostalgia, and thus no condition for the possibility of disappointment. This difference tells us everything about the distinction between *pensée continentale* and *pensée archipélique,* and so something about the foundations of thinking philosophically in relation to loss and memory.

Of course this story about Western thought and historical experience is rarely told, by those thinkers, with any sort of specificity. Narratives of loss, memory, and history typically lack a qualifier, are rarely named as "Western" or "European," let alone the racial qualifier (not all occupants of "the West" or "Europe" are white, it's worth noting). Instead, these narratives, these traditions of thought, go instead by the word *history* alone. Poststructuralist interventions—from Levinas's ethics to Derrida's *différance* to Foucault's disorienting practice of genealogy—are therefore often read as disruptions of the historical as such. And as we recall this compulsion, colonial through and through, mindful of how central it is to the self-understanding and inner-constitution of European philosophy, we should also recall a short remark Gayatri Spivak makes about the rhetoric of crisis. On this occasion, in "Subaltern Studies: Deconstructing Historiography," Spivak writes about how Foucault's genealogical method initiated a crisis in "thinking history." But the specificity of this crisis means everything. She writes plainly: "The Foucauldian example being considered here, for instance, can be seen as marking a crisis *within* European consciousness."[7] Spivak's locating of crisis *in* consciousness *as* geography, while seemingly uncontroversial and even obvious, actually upends the rhetoric of nearly all European theory in a single turn of phrase. Crisis is enveloped, contained, and entered into with certain forms and orientations of thinking.

How are we to think this form and orientation? With Spivak's remark as prompt, we can give an initial characterization of thinking: geography of reason. I borrow the spirit of this phrase from a slightly different context—Walter Mignolo's manifesto *The Idea of Latin America*—in order to draw on Mignolo's insight that a geographic conception of reason "decolonize[s] knowledge and being from the concept of knowledge and being that places in an inferior position."[8] Thinking from a certain location overturns or "de-links" the (putatively) non-located measure of imperial reason—which, as Spivak notes, must also be located in the process of decolonization. The notion of a geography of reason posits the necessity of specificity in any account of thinking, rooting, as it were, the meaning of intellectual work and reflection in a specific place. Place, that is, in the sense of the weave of space and time infused with historical experience—historical experience thought, not as such, but always by these people, in this site, with this sense of language and in this element of transmission. In our context here, the geography of reason raises the question of the legibility of the sign in a new register, asking not how the sign keeps company with the legibility of historical experience *as such*, but rather how *certain* experiences form certain senses of legibility. And so, for example, the geographics of thought ask how the European experience of history and its (constant) reinvention might imbue Heidegger's encounter with the Greek temple with mourning, a mood that, as we have seen, has a very specific legibility deriving from (imagined or otherwise) theories of origin. Heidegger's mourning of the loss of the gods at the temple, in its moment of complexity, turns on the legibility of the *absence of the sign*— the disappointment generated by the expectation of presence. Such disappointment and the legibility of the (absent) sign it makes possible is situated within a specific, non-universalizable geography of thinking. In this history, in this place, certain things become readable, even in their illegibility. This is in many ways the presence of imagination in cultural politics.

The motif of legibility provides an important frame for reading Glissant's theoretical work between Europe and the Americas, as well as, if we were so inclined, his very peculiar relationship to Africa and fragments from the continent.[9] In particular, the question of the legibility of the historical sign is crucial, and each of the chapters below is in one manner or another directly addressed to this problem. Now, it should be said that Heidegger is by no means a theorist of pure presence. He does not claim that the full significance of the past gathered into the present. To the contrary, he is a theorist of loss. But this sense of loss is always measured as an excess of absence. Absence exceeds the pulsations of presence and in that way disappoints the attempt to read the sign. Absence therefore bears a debt to the logic of reactivation. That is, absence is the *failure of reactivation*, a failure made legible in Heidegger's mournful reflection on the Greek temple in "Origin of the Work of Art." So begins, in and well after Heidegger, a long story in European philosophy about traces. The speed and intensity of modernity, the disasters of the twentieth century, and a sustained reckoning with hatred, exclusion, and violence inside Europe's borders initiated (and still initiates) a skepticism, begun perhaps by Heidegger, about retrieving the full presence of the past. Traces help reckon with that loss by offering sites and citations for mourning. The trace still bears a debt to reactivation. The trace *wants to say*, it is *vouloir-dire*, and so therein has its meaning.

Glissant will also tell a long story about traces and the ruins that inform and are informed by the historicity of the New World. However, his is a story with a very different account of the experience of legibility and the conditions under which the illegible is formed and deformed. Against the European experience of legibility as a kind of mournful absence, Glissant will pose (not appose, as is his typical strategy)[10] what he calls the "right to opacity." This phrase occurs on multiple occasions in Glissant's work, featured prominently in an opening essay in *Caribbean Discourse*, then repeated in *Poetics of Relation* and *Introduction à une poétique du divers* in order to make critical arguments about Caribbean poetics. Let us take this phrase seriously: *the right to opacity*. The phrasing is both peculiar and critical. It is a peculiar phrase because Glissant's work on creolization and Relation insists on the (possible) *fecundity* of cultural and linguistic contact, chaotic to the point of transfiguring our very concept of world, rather than emphasizing inherent violence and degradation. Contact suggests that the visibility of signs across geographies is a precondition of productive contact. Yet, and this is where Glissant's turn of phrase takes on important critical dimensions, it is precisely the resistance to visibility, this irreducible opaqueness, that keeps creolization and Relation in motion. Opacity is both an ontological and epistemological concept, insofar as it sustains the rhizomatic and nomadic character of subjectivity, intersubjectivity, and so the constant reinvention of not just meaning, but the meaning of meaning in the New World, now become the *tout-monde*. In that sense, opacity would appear to be precisely outside the logic of possession; contact is very different from trade or exchange. What does it mean to have a *right* to opacity?

The critical sense of this phrase—*the right to opacity*—lies in its anticolonial force, and therefore its resistance to certain senses of knowing and understanding that would seek to absorb, reactivate, and possess; it is resistance to the dialectic of legibility and illegibility. The right to opacity is a right to be, even if that being is saturated with the unknowable and characterized by its withdrawal from economies of visibility. In *Caribbean Discourse*, Glissant writes:

> An "intellectual" effort, with its repetitive thrusts (repetition has a rhythm), its contradictory moments, its necessary imperfections,

its demands for formulation (even a schematic one), very often obscured by its very purpose. For the attempt to approach a reality so often hidden from view cannot be organized in terms of a series of clarifications. We demand the right to opacity [*le droit à l'opacité*]. Through which our anxiety to have a full existence becomes part of the planetary drama of Relation: the creativity of marginalized peoples who today confront the ideal of transparent universality, imposed by the West, with secretive and multiple manifestations of Diversity. (CD, 2; translation altered)

Opacity does not seal identity, nor does it secure a sense of being or Being. This is the enigma of Glissant's thought, worked out through a paradoxical sense of the opaque. Rather than closing off or setting limits, opacity opens horizons that are situated at one and the same time inside colonial experience, anticolonial struggle, and post-colony cultural life. *Pensée archipélique*, the play and creative space of rights to opacity in contact, the repeating island(s), begins precisely with this movement: away from the transparency of the universal, toward the irreducible difference—sustained by opacity—that Glissant calls Diversity.

That is the argument in *Caribbean Discourse*. Just a decade later, with a slight revision in *Poetics of Relation*, Glissant recalls this evocation of the right to opacity. Legibility appears in *Poetics of Relation* under the rubric of communication, responding to the criticism that opacity makes knowing and contact impossible. Glissant confirms the right to opacity as a right to difference, and this right makes Relation and creolization an infinite process of becoming. He writes:

Several years back, if I made the statement, "We demand the right to opacity," or argued in favor of this, whomever I was speaking to would exclaim indignantly: "Now it's back to barbarism! How can you communicate with what you don't understand?" But in 1989, and before very diverse audiences, when the same demand was formulated, it aroused new interest. Who knows? Maybe, in the meanwhile, the topicality of the question of differences (*the right to difference*) had been exhausted. (PR, 189; my emphasis)

For Glissant, of course, differences are not exhaustible and in contact reproduce forms of opacity. And so he follows this with a short comment on the problem of difference with a simple proclamation that "the theory of difference is invaluable" (PR, 189). Invaluable, however, does not mean that difference is not made precarious at nearly every turn. The problem of difference traffics in language, conceptuality, crosses our worldly being, and thus can be articulated in such a manner that *difference itself* becomes clear and distinct, beholden to the gaze, fixed in a schematics that compromises the radicality—the invaluable of its value—of difference. (Glissant has in mind here his long-standing complaint against ethnography, which affirms difference without eschewing comprehension.) "Difference itself," he writes, "can still contrive to reduce things to the Transparent" (PR, 189). The movement from difference to transparency, colonial and imperial through and through, represents a failure of what Glissant calls the imaginary—the ability to imagine forms of contact in which difference is sustained rather than dissolved. Barbarism, then, lies not in opacity and its resistance to all absorbing notions of identity and comprehension, but in the compulsion to contest and surmount difference. When Glissant revisits the question of opacity in *Introduction à une poétique du divers*, he writes, refining further:

> In the encounter of the world's cultures, it is necessary that we have the imaginary force to conceive all of those cultures as exercising at one and the same time and an action that unifies and an action that liberates diversity. This is why I reclaim, for all of us, the right to opacity . . . Today, the right to opacity would be the most evident sign of *non-barbarism*. (IPD, 71–72)

The context of this mention in *Introduction à une poétique du divers* concerns the status of knowing, the deeper sense of comprehension as a grasping or possessing of the thing known. Glissant here (as elsewhere) explores what it means to say we *know* another, know what is other in the broadest sense, and what sorts of cultural and political consequences come with the encounter with otherness. Opacity and the non-barbaric imaginary it initiates fundamentally transform the structure of knowing and contact, which, in turn, transforms what we might mean by the legibility of material things: memorials, ruins, language, and so on. For Glissant, the transformation of legibility sets the course—which is chaotic, so perhaps only ironically "a course"—of *pensée archipélique*. Michael Wiedorn, for example, renders opacity in this moment as an "ethics of alterity,"[11] which, while entirely correct, also understates or (perhaps) conceals the ontological and epistemological elements of opacity and how it produces movements of being and knowledge; ethical claims flow from this condition, rather than condition being and knowing. Opacity names the materiality of the "*lieux communs* of contemporary thought," the common space of thinking about a radical difference—a non-barbaric imaginary—that refuses to make either the space between or the material sites of contact legible, but rather keeps the opaqueness of the unknown and chaos in motion alongside the known and the ordered. "There is an opacity of the material," Glissant writes, "which, for that materiality, must be reckoned with *and is insurmountable*" (IPD, 75; emphasis mine). Reckoning and insurmountability: ethics, epistemology, ontology in one and the same event.

From these passages, drawn from three different moments in Glissant's critical work, we can glean four fundamental senses of opacity, all of which labor against the sorts of legibility and loss that dominate Heidegger's account of the memorial ruin. The site or non-site of loss is crucial here. With opacity, Glissant is able to begin a long story about how beginning *after* the Middle Passage, this loss become an abyssal beginning that asserts itself *without reference to what precedes*. Reactivation therefore ceases to structure and regulate notions of remembering and forgetting. This assertion, the first sense of opacity, gives shape to the plantation-birth of Caribbean memory, history, and subjectivity. Abyssal beginning, as we shall see, is opaque because it begins in the abyss thought three ways, an originary opacity that gives the future after arrival and out of catastrophic loss. *A shoreline thinking.* Second, opacity functions as an anticolonial strategy for Glissant. Opacity names both how and why meaning and cultural production were historically hidden from the colonizer in acts of resistance, whether in the linguistic and cultural cases of creole and pidgin (*pace* Césaire and Fanon) or, in more complex operations, the development of Afro-Caribbean identities outside the limits of the colonial gaze. The right to opacity carves out a space of resistance to colonialism's waves of alienation and violence manifest in what Fanon called the problem of *comparison.* Opacity functions in this context as an epistemological interruption and marking of a limit, though always a limit that facilitates and transforms knowledge (cultural production), rather than merely destroying its pretensions (critique left as critique). *A revolutionary thinking, creating another world.* Third, opacity structures Glissant's account of creoleness and creolization. In creole languages, meaning is hidden not just from the colonial gaze, but even, in large part, from itself. *Meaning hides from itself while also producing meaning from the position of opacity.* To be sure, Glissant is careful in this context to distinguish his work on creolization from Jean Bernabé, Patrick Chamoiseau, and Raphaël Confiant's notion of *créolité*, developed in their *Éloge de la créolité*, and that is part of his unicity as a thinker. Creole languages, for Glissant, are not *things*, but rather the *activities*, always creolizing. "For me," Glissant writes in *Introduction à une poétique du divers*, "*créolité* is another *interpretation* of creolization. Creolization is a *perpetual movement* of cultural and linguistic interpenetrability" (IPD, 125; emphasis mine). And so opacity is maintained in and through movement and ceaseless knowing-as-becoming, rather than being the sort of thing that fixes itself and sets a single root. *A mixing thinking, a rhizomatic thinking, pensée archipélique.*

Fourth and last, opacity functions as a constituting condition of Glissant's signature idea: Relation. The opacity of meaning refers the sign or expressive medium to two times, and then, through diachronic contact, a third and more critical instant. The opacity of meaning refers both to the knowable and the unknowable of the past and those ways in which they are folded into the present, yes, but opacity, by way of Relation, also opens upon a future without closure. In this way, we can say that Glissant develops the notion of opacity in order to forestall the closure of knowledge, interrupting the movement of comprehension and escaping the grasp of colonized epistemologies. Openness without closure and the surprise of interruption creates a new imaginary space. This new space, this surprise of interruption, surmounts the grasp that possesses and all the terrifying consequences terms like "grasping" and "possessing" might suggest in a New World context. Opacity demands another model of knowing, one that affirms the *right* to opacity (not just the *fact* of opaque meaning-structures), and thus affirms a mode of relation (Relation) that desires, not the Other, but that the Other not cease to be Other. *Radical difference as ethics, ontology, and epistemology, sorted out in affect.*

Through these various manifestations and counter-movements, opacity leads Glissant to propose a kind of relativism in response to the efforts of universality. But this relativism should not evoke the moral or cultural indifference of "difference." Rather, it should recall, and then immediately step a bit beyond, the concluding remark to Fanon's 1956 essay "Racism

and Culture," in which Fanon proposes a paradoxical universality that "re-
sides in this decision to recognize and accept the reciprocal relativism of
different cultures, once the colonial status is irreversibly excluded."[12] *Irreversibly excluded.* This is the critical move for Fanon, and it speaks to Glissant's anxious relationship to the imperative of *tout-monde* and the realities
of global power and cultural politics. Glissant's work begins with this very
same sort of "relativism" Fanon articulates, working from the premise of
a revoked or refused colonial measure. The postcolonial moment in fact
demands it. For, as Glissant puts it in *Caribbean Discourse,* "Caribbean
people should not entrust to others the job of defining their culture"
(CD, 6). Cultural definition, however, is not isolation. Nor is it static. It
is *tout-monde* as origin and destination. Cultural definition is, for Glissant,
the initiation of the notion of Relation as elaborated in *Poetics of Relation,*
a notion that "informs not simply what is relayed but also the relative and
the related" (PR, 27). And further, in an echo of Fanon, "what Relation
relates, in reality, proceeds from no absolute, it proves to be the totality
of relatives, put in touch and told" (PR, 28). Contact and mixed narrative
proceed from the very condition Fanon articulates: *after* the colonial measure, without the absolute. But touch and telling commence creolization;
contact and exposure to the Other begin the Chaos of meaning-making
and meaning-remaking. This shift changes so many terms of discussion.

   Opacity and its production of myriad senses of the relative blend the
known and unknown, confounding distinctions between the legible and
illegible sign. But this blend proceeds with a sense of the unknown other
than that of the object of imperial search: Glissant's unknown is neither
mystery nor a trace legible in its illegibility. For Glissant, rather, this transfigured notion of the unknown emerges at a certain endpoint of (global)
history. In *Poetics of Relation* he describes what we might call a postcolonial sense of the end of philosophy, transforming that much-discussed
claim in European theory that certain forms of philosophizing have closed
out or come to full fruition. The *postcolonial* end, thought as an archipelagic thinking, introduces an important nuance. Glissant's geographic
shift draws from the experiences of the closure of the colonial gaze, which,
in turn, opens up another mode of relation to the Other—and thus new
models of knowing that do not *possess* what is known, but instead *sustain
what remains opaque,* emerging as possibilities and ethical imperatives.
Contact. Relation. *Tout-monde.* A geography of reason suggests this possibility. "The vague feeling," Glissant writes:

that the end of the world had been reached, in the geographical sense, removed whatever element of adventure and perhaps blind belief there had been in the discovery of the other. Since the beginning of this century [the twentieth] the shrinking of unexplored regions on the map of the world has made minds less infatuated with adventure, or less sensitive to its beauty, inclining more toward a concern for the truth of human beings. Understanding cultures then became more gratifying than discovering new lands. (PR, 26)

Glissant will go on to underscore and explore the dangers of "understanding," writing that "the verb *to understand* in the sense of 'to grasp' (*comprendre*) has a fearsome repressive meaning" in both the colonial and postcolonial context (PR, 26), but it is important to also note that the end of the world, the closure of the colonial gaze, produces the *possibility* of another sort of relation to otherness. The problem of opacity intervenes in this opening of possibility in the ways noted above—saying yes to abyssal beginning, vigilant in its anticolonial epistemology, perpetual in the movement of creolization, Relation without closure—and in these ways labors at the end of the world-as-colonial-gaze. Labors, that is, with a wholly other model of the legible and illegible.

Heidegger's critique of presence, gathered with such force in his reflection on the Greek temple, also labors at a certain kind of end, but legibility-as-reactivation remains a point of measure that sets the boundaries of knowing and being. Opacity signifies otherwise. Opacity is not sheer illegibility, of course, for the movement of creolization requires contact and the passage of meaning between transformed and transformative sites—in a word, Relation. Opacity manifests the kind of non-legibility evoked in Chamoiseau's figures of the chalk and name in the epigraph above. In *School Days*, Chamoiseau's little boy sees his identity, in its fullest sense, brought to word in writing his name, but the materiality of expression—and so of identity—makes it all so precarious. Protecting the sign and its fleeting legibility, already as thin as chalk dust, is not just a matter of a particular boy's particular name. Chamoiseau describes the moment as a flirtation with genocide, and we have to take that characterization seriously. Reinscription proliferates in order to keep alive through accumulation, not iteration; the name is always at risk, never secured by an immovable essence of some sort. *Write it again so that it can be read.* Put in more metaphysical terms, this is a precarious legibility because the ultimate reality of what is said or declared in the chalk mark glimpses into, then witnesses the withdrawal of, opacity. Legibility as such risks too much. To make wholly legible is to lose the opacity of the opaque, to lose a crucial site of resistance to domination, to fumble away the challenge of Afro-Caribbean singularity, the repeating island, and how senses of belonging and world-making are *not* subject to a more general economy. That is, legibility puts that which survived trauma and loss, and then formed the cross-cultural contact that makes up Caribbean creoleness and creolization, back into the epistemology of seizing and grasping. But legibility is something very different when structured by and as opacity, with opacity as the condition of knowing, being, and doing.

Opacity is therefore something other than illegibility; History's sign is not unreadable *and that's it.* Glissant's notion of opacity asks us to think outside the binary of the legible and illegible—to think, perhaps, of meaning as simultaneously declarative and precarious, just like the name written over and over in chalk. Accumulation rather than iteration, to put it simply. Erasure, trace, struggle, proliferation, accumulation, knowing, and the unknowable—all at once. *Opacity.* What cannot be read as history—the trauma of birth in the Middle Passage and arrival on the plantation and Plantation—is also what gives New World history possibility, openness, and mixture. Opacity underpins this resistance to the legible. Opacity is *life* that does not make itself legible, refusing a legibility which, *prima facie*, would infect opacity with transparency. Yet, no matter the obvious temptations, Glissant will not associate the non-legible with notions of the unconscious or subconscious. Rather, he insists that opacity, creolization, and Relation are only possible on the basis of a consciousness of consciousness. Thinking at the end of the world, at the end of history as History, fundamentally changes the relation between the known and the unknown, shifting away from the opaque as conquerable mystery and toward opacity as both the core and the residue of Chaos. This is a difficult nuance. Chaotic motion moves Relation toward the unexpected, but always in terms of contact, entanglement, and engagement. And so opacity does not imply or enact a fundamental passivity—a term that, as Glissant says of "seize" and "grasp," has terrifying resonance in the Americas—but rather, with the consciousness of consciousness secured at the end of the world, a kind of vulnerable activity. Vulnerable, that is, because opacity is open to transformative contact, and active because the consciousness of creolizing contact is conscious of its own life.

Consciousness of life, this peculiar Glissantian consciousness of consciousness, is both elaborated in its constitutive elements and constantly at stake in each of the following chapters. Glissant's long meditation on beginning treats this consciousness of consciousness in the tense space between the descriptive and the normative. With the former, Glissant reckons with the Caribbean's particular geography of reason: abyssal beginning and composite cultural forms *describe* the history of Caribbean reality. With the latter, Glissant marks his own work with the deep political and cultural urgency of postcolonial thinking: the Caribbean making its own world, on its own terms, as an ethical and political imperative.[13] Consciousness of consciousness is therefore won through Glissant's coming to terms with the space, time, subjectivity, and aesthetic of Caribbean historical experience. This coming to terms, engaged as it is with Négritude, existentialism, and the postmodern, leads him to the strange intersection of critique and appropriation of so many intellectual sites cited between Europe and the Americas.

CHAPTER 1

Origins I

Memory, Root, Abyss

*How many times, how many days will you offer yourself, abyss, to the
patience of the migrating herd?*

—Glissant, "The Indies"

WHAT IS THE ARCHIPELAGO TO HISTORY? And to memory?
That is, what is the archipelago to the imagination?

Beginning with the archipelago begins with the materiality of space
(the island) and with the quasi-materiality of non-space (the sea), the
related and the enigma of their relation. The sea carries time, or even *is*
time, and that carriage is the mode of relation that makes the archipelago
a formation which is not one. A formation, yes, insofar as the archipelago makes its mark in the geography of history; the Caribbean is a space
on a map and, on that map, a very particular moment of imagination, of
history, and in the making of modernity and postmodernity. The Caribbean archipelago is literally and figuratively the interval through which the
Americas as New World were imagined, then invented, and then inserted
into Atlantic history and memory. Arrival, encounter, conquest—the very
name *Americas* bears the pain of history within itself and is unimaginable
without that pain. *Americas* is perhaps a word for the unspeakable. Indeed,
the name *Americas* can only be uttered *after* so many disasters: conquest,
genocide, slave trade, and colonialism.

What does it mean to be reminded of that pain, whether in the utterance of the word or in the careful, difficult, even impossible work of making an identity after the disasters? This question already asks too much and
is cast too wide. For Glissant, the specificity of discourse—the "geography
of reason," the locating of thinking inside the history and memory of space
and spaces—locates the question of history's pain, not in the region of

the Americas as such, but specifically in the archipelago. A sense of history's pain in fragments, as it were. This nomadic location, a location that disassembles at the very same moment as it assembles, whether through the multiplicity of language or through the multiplicity of uncommon origins, scatters questions of pain and history, trauma and memory, across the many sites of that pain and trauma. Across that scattering is the abyssal presence of the Middle Passage. This abyss does not just offer itself as an item among others, but structures, at some important existential and theoretical level, the entirety of the problem of beginning.[1]

I want to begin with a broad claim: *trauma is for the dead*. In order to appreciate the myriad consequences of this claim, the present chapter explores the relation between Glissant's account of memory, history, and beginning in the context of the Middle Passage. Glissant's account folds the past into the future, but the sense of futurity will be a matter for the next chapter. Before we can discuss the meaning of the Middle Passage for a sense of futurity—a discussion that brings crucial issues of plantation life and creole language into focus—we first need a sense of how Glissant conceives loss and the transformation of the past in that conception of loss. This conception of loss is figurative and functions as a certain kind of regulative condition on poetry and the poetics of memory and history (poetry is always at least in part a form of mourning for Glissant), but loss also underpins so much of what we can call the existential *situatedness* of the Caribbean. The situatedness of the Caribbean—which, for Glissant, produces a *method* and not just a *pathos*—is rooted in the unrooting historical experience of catastrophe. The historical experience of catastrophe, the abyssal beginning, gives birth to the Caribbean as such. Dislocation and dispossession, both from Africa and in the Americas, stretch across the Atlantic as a massive historical disaster and trauma. This loss conditions what Glissant calls "Caribbeanness" (Antillanité).

Caribbeanness, as we shall see, is structured by an *aporia*. "Rooted" in the "unrooting" effect and affect of traumatic memory and the weight of history's pain, Caribbeanness couples a sense of beginning to the abyss. The abyss is produced by a certain kind of *trauma*, and so, in the reflections that follow, I want to critically explore the sense and specificity of this notion of trauma. In pursuit of specificity, I want to consider a site of critical distinction: the European context of trauma, memory, and history, to which Glissant will always, simultaneously, juxtapose and entangle his account of the same. In particular, Walter Benjamin's reflections on the sadness of history will prove to be a crucial point of engagement for Glissant in his development of notions of trauma, memory, and history, especially around reflections on the destruction of Carthage. Carthage, an ancient site and citation of history's sadness between Europe and Africa, provides the following reflections with an important occasion for specifying Glissant's sense of trauma as constitutive of Caribbeanness and beginning. So, in taking what will be a sustained excursus into European discourses of trauma, loss, and history, I hope to focus the specificity of the Caribbean in this and subsequent chapters, as well as to shed some critical light on what goes by the generalized names "memory" and "history" in so much contemporary theory. An excursus into European theory here in no way *authorizes* the Caribbean context, but rather quite the opposite: the Caribbean context, set in contrast, underscores the specificity of the European experience and implicates its formation, even at the site of disaster, inside the position of empire.

Another broad claim: every term and concept is a historical artifact, fashioned in historical experience and appreciated in the aftermath of that experience. At the same time, there is surely some bit of essential character to trauma, a thin but not nothing bit of a thread across experiences of traumatic violence, and so too the effects of trauma on our thinking about memory and history. Put most generally, trauma in its essential bit and thin thread describes the loss of intelligibility in lived and historical experience. The vanishing of intelligibility fundamentally transforms the meaning of memory for the individual, yes, but also for the collective vicissitudes of life. The signature moments of Europe and the black Americas—the former a culmination, the latter a beginning—are settled in traumatized memory as a loss of intelligibility, whether we think here in terms of the lived experience of forced migration (the Middle Passage) and mass murder (genocidal violence) or the sheer number of dead (war, genocide). Trauma in those moments, and also in the aftermath, is carried as memory and is transformative of history. Trauma in its generalized form crosses borders in this narrow sense; disaster springs from the vanishing of intelligibility. But the geography of reason, attentive to the here-ness of a given discourse, requires that we think through a notion like trauma in its specificity. Figures of loss, then, are not just parts of literary technology in the study of disaster. Rather, as kinds of conceptual black holes that suffocate words, such figures gather to them something crucial about the event and the historical experience, and then, in the vanishing function and its after-effect (with complex affects), such traumas bequeath to memory and history (as the mourning of the past and production of the future) the enigma of another beginning. That is, trauma marks not only loss and absence but also, as Glissant figures the slave boat in *Poetics of Relation,* a womb. Place, history, and a people are born. Any discourse that attends to the work of trauma in historical experience must also attend to the interval between sites of loss and sites of birth. *Abyssal beginnings are geographic.* Disaster vanishes intelligibility into nothingness. After that abyss, there is becoming. Pain is fecund, while also just outside the thinkable—a condition of thought that is itself unthinkable. Paradoxical paradox. The imperative is to think both at once, to think how a site can be so saturated with sadness that it drowns expression *at the same time* that one thinks the beauty of inheritance, survival, and creation.

So, driven by this imperative, the present chapter asks about the distinctiveness and specificity of Glissant's discussion of trauma with this cluster of questions in view. If trauma generates ghosts, and trauma is understood only in its specificity, then what ghostly figures dismantle and sustain the Caribbeanness of traumatic memory? How can we understand the Middle Passage as an abyssal origin of those ghostly figures? What does it mean to think abyss as the originary source of memory? What is the meaning of "root" and "rootedness" in this context, especially when met with the paradox of an abyssal root? And so, ultimately, with what meanings—however little, never nothing—and with what obligations—however unbearable, never a burden—does Glissant begin? Only with such matters settled can we pose the question of the future.

The Visible Sadness of Carthage

The question of trauma has been central to various cultural, literary, and philosophical projects over the past two decades, and much of the work on trauma has concerned the European experiences of mass death in the first half of the twentieth-century. Thus, the problematics developed in this conversation typically concern issues gathered around the question of the representation of traumatic experiences of trench warfare, anti-Semitism, and the Shoah. How is one to represent traumatic experience? What sort of ethical and epistemological enigmas are raised in the matter of representing trauma? The stakes are raised for representation precisely for what representation—in the case of the traumatic experience of mass

death—contends with, namely, the dead and those companion experiences of radical absence. The dead cannot speak. Any representation of
the dead, then, puts the precariousness of voice in the hands of the one
forging the representation. For the survivor there is the problem of intelligibility in memory; trauma dismantles the intelligibility of the originary
experience, which, in turn, places intractable epistemological conditions
on the process of recollection and representation. How can we describe
these enigmas, and how might the figures of traumatic memory instruct us
in mapping historical experience on the geography of reason?

In representation, memory forges a relation between the present and
the past. When I recall an object or event, what was past is made present
again, and while there is always a sense of forgetting or fading in any act of
recollection, conventional memorial experience brings the content, shape,
and contour of a past experience back into the present with some measure
of clarity. Indeed, the experience of remembering is measured according
to gradations of vivacity; what is old lacks vividness, what is new or recalled with special intensity increases in the same. The coincidence of past
and present works as a kind of regulative ideal for memory by drawing
both a boundary around—*is this memory or pure fantasy?*—and a placing
certain epistemological constraints on—*does memory inform or instruct,
and do so accurately?*—what counts as memorial experience. That is, memory is *more* like memory or *more* perfectly so if and when the past is perfectly present in a recollecting perception of the past. Memory is therefore
connected, in its conventional sense, to a notion of truth; false memory is
no memory at all, insofar as it departs from precisely what concerns memorial acts. We can say that memory has told the truth when there is a
near coincidence of the past in the present recollection of that past, and
memory deceives us when such coincidence does not obtain or does not
obtain to a sufficient degree.

The experience of catastrophe, however, introduces special problems
for any conventional sense of memory as representation. For good reason.
Trauma marks a wound in time. The wound to time is the consequence
of catastrophic trauma's destruction of the intelligible core of the originary event of memory, an event that overwhelms the subject to the point
of overturning and destroying conventional systems of meaning-making.
This destruction alters not only the formal structure of memory but also,
and most importantly, the very coherence of the subject. There is no
subjectivity without memory—we exist as temporal creatures, of course.

Interruptions in the structure of memory interrupt the life and coherence
of subjectivity. Bessel van der Kolk and Onno van der Hart note in a now
classic essay that the fixed character of a traumatic event prevents the inte-
gration of past and present. "Switching from one's present-day world to the
world of traumatic memory," they write, "does not only imply the simultaneity of two utterly incompatible worlds, of an ordinary and a traumatic
state of mind."[2] Rather, they claim, the traumatized subject is split at one
and the same time into a traumatic past and "the bleached present"—an
irreducibly diachronic existence. Along the same lines, Dori Laub argues
in "Truth and Testimony" that the experience of trauma disassembles the
traumatized subject's relation to truth in two senses. First, there is the
problem of reckoning with one's own experience of the trauma. Access to
the experience that haunts the traumatized subject is blocked, for that subject, by the vanishing of intelligibility in the originary event of memory.
Second, there is the problem of putting such an event into words. It is not
simply that the subject lacks words for an overwhelming trauma, but also
that language itself, dependent as it is upon the intelligibility of experience
and memory, is unable to sustain the transmission of traumatic memory.

> The act of bearing witness at the same time *makes* and *breaks* a
> promise: the promise of testimony as a realization of the truth.
> On the one hand, the process of the testimony does in fact hold
> out the promise of truth as the return of a sane, normal, and con-
> nected world. On the other hand, because of its very commitment
> to truth, the testimony enforces at least a partial breach, failure
> and relinquishment of this promise. . . . The testimony aspires to
> recapture the lost truth of that reality, but the realization of the
> testimony is not the fulfillment of this promise. The testimony in
> its commitment to truth is a passage through, and exploration of,
> difference, rather than an exploration of identity.[3]

If testimony to traumatic experience promises truth yet always takes back
that promise in the failure of memory and words, then time itself is ruptured. The self is divided, perhaps to the point of an irreparable dislocation.
A haunting diachrony comes to structure the time of memory. Time is
split between what is caught, without words, in the originary traumatic
event and what remains after the trauma. Time therefore moves through
the traumatized subject as if limping, as Jean-François Lyotard says of the

discourse of the unrepresentable. This limping, anxious relation to differ-ence within subjectivity wounds time and language with catastrophe. Representation is transformed into the problem of the unrepresentable, which is nothing more than the moment in which the promise of testi-mony and bearing witness is broken, not by, but *against* the subjectivity or subjectivities entwined in the promise-making of memory. What cannot be represented stands outside the very economy of representation, and not in a teleological relation to the work of representing. Thus, the unrep-resentable is not representation's failure to grasp fully, to give enough at-tention, to have enough time, to have the proper orientation in space, or to find the right kinds of words, but rather, and more radically, a category dis-tinction. Representation labors in a wholly different time, one modeled on synchronic temporality, whereas the unrepresentable separates from the temporal flow of memory and storytelling. Any definition of the unrepre-sentable in relation to efforts of representation is a plain category mistake.

Yet there is always a relationship *to* the unrepresentable. No matter the unbridgeable difference at the heart of traumatized subjectivity, no mat-ter the failure of memory *after* catastrophe, there are still the enigmatic relations of affect: loss, melancholy, haunting. What does it mean to relate to the unrepresentable? How does the affective trace of the unrepresent-able change philosophy and theoretical discourse more generally? If we take Freud's reflections on melancholia seriously, then the answer has a certain irreducible ambivalence. That is, if the unrepresentable is where, in Maurice Blanchot's words, "the movement of Meaning was swallowed up,"[4] then traumatic experience establishes a sort of interdiction on coher-ence in its melancholic wake. There is at once the necessity of speaking and describing *and* the encounter with the impossible. What must be said cannot be said. And so the irreducible difference between temporalities produces a melancholic halo around post-traumatic writing and creating.

Traumatic memory fundamentally transforms aesthetic, epistemolo-gical, and ethical questions of representation. But this is not simply a problem for the poet or memoirist, an idiosyncratic dilemma for the solitary writer-survivor or creator of memorial work. Rather, and this is crucial, the problems of memory are also the problems of historiography. Traumatic memory interrupts the writing of history from within histori-cal events themselves precisely because the counter- or simply alterna-tive narratives of victims and other subaltern actors are inextricable from the movement of history. So, when a traumatic event produces traumatic memory—which in turn places the unrepresentable alongside and out-side, but always in relation to, what is representable—historical narrative, as a matter of form, is called into question. The Shoah, for example, be-comes that rupture in "history" which cannot be rendered or retrieved within conventional modes of narrative and didactic representation. Questions of memory are questions *to* history.

The crisis of conventional modes of representation is partly an episte-mological problem, rooted in the fracture of traumatic memory and how it swallows historical meaning in catastrophic experience. Traumatic mem-ory departs from the exchange of knowledge; haunting replaces insight, the diachrony of loss replaces the synchrony of metanarrative. Coupled to this epistemological gap is the ethical problem of representation. How are we to conceive memory and representation in relation to the dead, those who cannot speak yet remain wholly in our hands and at constant risk of oblivion? The crisis of what we cannot put into words becomes emphati-cally ethical at this very moment, where the life of the dead, in their capac-ity to instruct us in their haunting, obligates us without a direct voice. To be sure, every representation of another risks or perhaps always traffics in a kind of violence, but the muted victim of disastrous violence is a particu-larly emphatic case. In representing the unrepresentable, we bear the only traces of life after disaster and we labor with burden against forgetting. Trauma and catastrophe are therefore not simply questions of speaking, writing, and remembering after a disastrously overwhelming experience. Trauma and catastrophe also raise questions of responsibility to a human suffering that is not our own. The burden of this responsibility is perhaps unlike any other, one that might evoke Paul Celan's devastating, obligat-ing turn of phrase: "The world is gone, I must carry you."[5] *He* survives. *She* survives. *They* survive. *We* survive. In this movement across subjects, from one to another to the collective *living after*, catastrophic trauma folds victim, survivor, witness, and witness to the witness into one and the same imperative: never the same poetry, never the same culture, never the same metaphysics, never the same theodicy, never this catastrophe, never any catastrophe, never again.

Trauma, in this shift from the epistemological enigmas of memory and history to the ethical demands of remembering the dead, becomes as much about the living as it is about the dead. Indeed, it is about think-ing the living and the dead all at once, thinking within that mute space of intersection that we call both disaster and survival. And all of these gods must be transformed as we begin *again*. Trauma is about the dead, surely, but it is also *for* the living as a relation to the dead, the living as obligated to the dead with unbearable imperatives, and so always charged with the duties of beginning again from the ruins with a new, renewed history.

How can we address this aesthetic crisis? Surely it is not only a question of rethinking aesthetic strategies—though it is certainly that. The crisis evokes, at the very least, Theodor Adorno's famous remark in "Cultural Criticism and Society," an essay collected in the volume *Prisms*, that there can be no poetry after Auschwitz. In that essay, Adorno's interdiction pauses before the frivolity of the pleasure and enjoyment of words, not to mention their common communicability, for the simple reason that such relations to culture conceal the barbarism and pain of the past. Adorno revises that position in *Negative Dialectics*, published roughly fifteen years after "Cultural Criticism and Society," saying that it was not quite right to place such an interdiction on language. His retraction is partial, though, because the ethical question still remains: What demands are placed on the thinker and writer *after Auschwitz*, after the catastrophic trauma that brought the barbarism of culture to its end in the camps and erased history's moment for its victims and survivors? The thinker and writer are charged with so much: thinking *in* the ashes, thinking *out of* the ashes, thinking *after* the ashes. Figures of loss underpin the meaning of thinking and writing after Auschwitz; figures disassemble writing and demand a different sort of writing. Blanchot's reflections on the ethics of writing are exemplary, especially when, in *The Writing of the Disaster*, he describes "the impossible necessary" as "that which is written in the time outside time."[6] This, I believe, is the fullest sense of Adorno's new categorical imperative: one cannot separate intellectual work from life after the catastrophe. Life after catastrophe is transformed at its foundation. After Auschwitz—a life lived under Adorno's imperative puts language and thinking into question from within historical experience itself.

This sense of imperative finds its European master text in Walter Benjamin's 1939 essay "Theses on the Philosophy of History." The text can be read as a kind of vision of what is to come, a vision of the future. Benjamin's reflections describe, with such uncanny imagery, the very scenes of catastrophe to which white Europe would bear witness in the years following World War II. And yet Benjamin was *not* describing the Shoah. He was, rather, describing the meaning of history and historical experience from the perspective of the subaltern—the dead. In that description,

Benjamin attempts to shift our conception of what a *materialism* might mean for history. Perhaps, he proposes, the materialism of death ought to describe the movement of history, where loss and disaster are not instruments of historical meaning but rather the meaning itself. This is a crucial insight. The experience of the Americas *from the perspective of the dead and those who survive*, a shift Benjamin's essay authorizes, cannot but register history as the enactment of violence. This perspective, a certain *materialism of the Other,* is located in what Benjamin names the angel of history. Benjamin introduces the angel of history in a quirky, moving reflection on Paul Klee's painting *Angelus Novus*. It is familiar in many contexts, but still worth quoting the passage in full:

> This is how one pictures the angel of history. His face is turned toward the past. Where we perceive a chain of events, he sees one single catastrophe, which keeps piling wreckage upon wreckage and hurls it in front of his feet. The angel would like to stay, awaken the dead, and make whole what has been smashed. But a storm is blowing from Paradise; it has got caught in his wings with such violence that the angel can no longer close them. This storm irresistibly propels him into the future to which his back is turned, while the pile of debris before him grows skyward. This storm is what we call progress.[7]

The visionary element of this passage lies in the evocation of wreckage, an evocation that can be coupled with uncanny coincidence to images of the bulldozing of corpses at Auschwitz in, for example, Alain Resnais's *Nuit et brouillard*. And yet, to say it again, Benjamin is not describing this imagery or this aftermath. He is not merely taking note of the violence that accompanies so many other *events* in history, events in which, typically, violence is dialectically subsumed under a matter of wider significance. He is instead and more pointedly describing the significance of history's movement itself. Benjamin's description reminds us of the materialism of any derivative materialism: progress *is* death and destruction. Corpses are manufactured, not in aberrations of history, but as history's very movement. The corpse as efficient cause.

The angel of history plays the role of witness. He does not intervene and he cannot rearrange the meaning of events held under his gaze; this is why Benjamin describes the angel as blown with force toward a future, even as the angel "would like" to redeem history's pain. As a witness, the angel first describes what is seen in the long story of history. In that story, a peculiar revolution happens: what was mute on the slaughter-bench of history, to recall Hegel's famous description from *Lectures on Philosophy of History*,[8] now begins to speak. That is, the dead begin to make us responsible as more than a moment in history, but rather, now, as historical experience itself. What sort of imperative is passed on to us in this historical experience? What does it mean to relieve history's victims of their silence and register that voice? Benjamin's "Theses on the Philosophy of History" largely leaves these questions unanswered, but there is plenty in the essay for thinking about the victim's voice. The essay itself holds two approaches to historical experience under the critical lens: historicism and historical materialism. The former is dominated by the regulative ideal of the chronicler, the one who wants to tell the entirety of history's details, but without any affective or political resonance of those details. The latter corrects the chronicler with its attention to the significance *signaled* by historical detail and the minutiae of shifts in culture, but always with the risk of condemning the victims of history to oblivion. Situated between or alongside (Benjamin is not clear on this matter) historicism and historical materialism is the *affect* that survives the story of history—what we described above as the melancholic effect of traumatic memory. This affect, which is only enacted at the moment that the angel's gaze is turned toward the human wreckage of progress, is depicted as the sadness of history within history's own problematic invitation to empathy. Benjamin writes:

> To historians who wish to relive an era, Fustel de Coulanges recommends that they blot out everything they know about the later course of history. It is a process of empathy whose origin is the indolence of the heart, *acedia*, which despairs of grasping and holding the genuine historical image as it flares up briefly. Among medieval theologians it was regarded as the root cause of sadness. Flaubert, who was familiar with it, wrote: *"Peu de gens devineront combien il a fallu être triste pour ressusciter Carthage."*[9]

One should note that Benjamin is no optimist here. The sadness of history, which is carried here by the memory of Rome's destruction of Carthage in 146 B.C. and perhaps also the second destruction in A.D. 698, is a *challenge* to historicism and certain kinds of historical materialism.

Whereas Gustave Flaubert's sentiment points us to the victims of Rome's catastrophic violence, the historian who is animated, then defeated by *acedia* finds a different footing and casts a very different gaze. Maybe the sadness is too much to bear (which Benjamin would seem to indicate with the term *acedia*), or maybe the gaze and sentiments of the historian are drawn to the glory and spoils of historical narrative.

The angel of history speaks against this gaze. The angel cannot make the wreckage of history whole again, so the trauma and loss constitutive of history's meaning is unredeemed, but the prophetic voice is still needed against the story or stories of history. Benjamin's mythical historian, the angel's foil, finds a comfortable identification in history's victorious movement:

> The nature of this sadness stands out more clearly if one asks with whom the adherents of historicism actually empathize. The answer is inevitable: with the victor. And all rulers are the heirs of those who conquered before them. Hence, empathy with the victor invariably benefits the rulers. Historical materialists know what that means. Whoever has emerged victorious participates to this day in the triumphal procession in which the present rulers step over those who are lying prostrate.[10]

This procession runs against the direction of the gaze of the angel of history. But Benjamin's address is not just to the art of historiography. Indeed, his aim is to remind one of how history is written into—and even ultimately by—the very physicality of culture: the treasures and artifacts of a civilization or people. Cultural treasures do not appear from the work of genius alone. Understanding cultural objects in terms of the fantasies of a creative genius would place one's empathy with the victors. Cultural treasures are born from struggle and conflict, and so their trafficking across time follows the same disastrous passage as history as such:

> According to traditional practice, the spoils are carried along in the procession. They are called cultural treasures, and a historical materialist views them with cautious detachment. For without exception the cultural treasures he surveys have an origin which he cannot contemplate without horror. They owe their existence not only to the efforts of the great minds and talents who have created

them, but also to the anonymous toil of their contemporaries. There is no document of civilization which is not at the same time a document of barbarism. And just as such a document is not free of barbarism, barbarism taints also the manner in which it was transmitted from one owner to another.[11]

In this last remark, Benjamin underscores an unsettling feature of cultural transmission. It is not simply the case that barbarism lies in the original event of the object. The culture that receives the object and reifies it as a treasure in the reproduction of meaning and significance reproduces barbarism in that reception and act. That is, civilizations are historical and *ideological* in the sense Louis Althusser gave the term.[12] As historical, civilizations maintain themselves in the reproduction of meaning and significance. Reproduction is essentially historical experience, which is to say, there is no civilization without the cultural objects—even the ruins of them—through which historical experience passes. The barbarism of the past is therefore concealed not just by fantasies of progress that blind us to history's wreckage, but also in what a culture holds most precious in acts of reproduction: treasures.

We can recall familiar stories about the Roman Empire, referring comfortably to its literature, philosophical contributions, religious revolutions, and the ruins of majestic architecture. Works of genius, to be sure, yet the very same empire razed the city, enslaved tens of thousands, murdered so many, and was long reputed to have salted the earth to ensure that life remain unsustainable. The wreckage of Roman history. And so there is also the sadness of Carthage. What is our relation to the destruction of Carthage as we contemplate the cultural treasures of Rome? What is Carthage to us? In the passages above concerning both the angel of history and Flaubert's short remark on historical empathy, it is clear that Benjamin's peculiar historical materialism wants to sever historical narrative from itself by registering the trauma of mass violence. This register is at once memorial and perceptual, for both are folded into any civilization and any cultural treasure. Benjamin *reminds us* of the unrepresentable, the silent, at the heart of any representation of historical experience. How can we begin thinking through this rem(a)inder?

A number of items are key for thinking about Benjamin's contribution to our thinking about history, memory, and catastrophe between Europe and the Americas. There is a deep lesson to be drawn, then transformed

or creolized by Atlantic routes. Philosophy of history cannot be the same
after Benjamin, and his decisive contribution to the critique of historical
metanarrative is clear. The angel of history functions as the conscience
of thinking. If paired with the allusion to thinking historical empathy—
and so historical experience more broadly—in terms of the sadness of
Carthage, then philosophy of history is akin to a memory project. And
wholly ethical. That is, the conscience of philosophy of history fundamentally overturns the gaze of the historian. We can no longer behold cultural
treasures without seeing the immense suffering set within the surface and
sheen of genius and interpretation, just as, say, Karl Marx's critique of the
commodity changes our perception of products of alienated labor. The
victim moves from oblivion to center in historiography and the imagina-
tions of memory, and so the effect of trauma is registered in each and every
way we think about historical experience. The wreckage of history and the
sadness of Carthage build trauma into our historical imagination and any
sense of connection to and representation of tradition.

    Yet, this traumatic register in historical imagination and representation
is split in an important way across Benjamin's sites of memory. In this split,
we can glimpse the problematic of visibility: How visible is history's victim? Benjamin's figures bear a certain ambivalence. On the one hand, there
is a failure of visibility; the angel of history cannot gain footing ("This
storm irresistibly propels him into the future"), and the pile of wreckage
builds ever higher. The topology of this fantasy conceals the victim from
even an angelic gaze. As well, the sadness of Carthage remains an allusion
for Benjamin. *Acedia* propels us too, in this case, toward the historian's exhaustion with pain and shift to empathy with the victors. Memory of this
sadness never quite appears. On the other hand, history's victims are visible as *at least* elliptically indicated. While Benjamin's angel witnesses an
ever-increasing pile of corpses, the corpses show themselves. We see the
victim, which is precisely why it is fair to describe the wreckage of history
as *mute*. The victim, with all the aporetic language needed to explain this
peculiar presencing, appears as an absence. Indeed, one need only consider the language of loss, trauma, and representation in those discourses
most dedicated to the historical experience of catastrophe and radical absence. The negative sublime, the cinder, ashes—while each attempts to
perform the impossibility of its own utterance in a word or phrase, it is
important to underscore how they maintain, even in self-dismantling failure, the fundamental visibility of loss and memory of the dead. Benjamin's

meditations disrupt conventional historiography, to be sure, but they also return us to Europe's persistence as visible *even in the wake of disaster*. The legibility of the illegible.

The question of visibility and its legibility even in the illegible is instructive, especially because of how historical experience interweaves memory and history in relation to a (catastrophic or not) present. Our relation to language and world is sustained by the visibility of our past, where transmissions of history and memory give shape, contour, and dimensionality to speaking and acting. Indeed, figures of the negative sublime, cinder, and ashes deconstruct language after disaster in the transmission of history's pain. Benjamin helps make this transmission of the past possible with the angel of history and the question of Carthage and historical empathy. Trauma sustains the language of loss, which is why writers such as Adorno are able to offer interdictions on certain kinds of speaking. And precisely because the question of trauma has, for the most part, been dominated by the European context, the primary concern has been with the relation of trauma to the *rooted* past—the past as manifest in memory, and so the past's problematic, disruptive relation to the present. *The rooted past* conditions the very possibility of the language of loss in European discourse on memory and history.

The Caribbean context alters the terms of this kind of relation to the past and present (and then, of course, future). To wit: discourse surrounding the Shoah always marks the transformation of "our" relation to history. Thus, Adorno articulates the "new categorical imperative," that one ought to "arrange their thoughts and actions so that Auschwitz will not repeat itself."[13] Benjamin's reading of Klee's angel of history in "Theses on the Philosophy of History" marks that same kind of transformation of *a* history, where one no longer sees the march of progress in "a chain of events," but only the repetition of death, destruction, suffering, and sadness at the heart of "progress." Wreckage makes all of this visible. Even if just the manufactured corpse or the ashes of the victim in the Shoah, both of which sustain the precarious language of loss and trace, there is visibility. An important transition and impossible translation inserts itself here if we recall Glissant's opening motif in *Poetics of Relation*: the right to opacity. Where is the wreckage of the Middle Passage? And how might that non-location work opacity against visibility?[14] These companion questions break the Caribbean question of trauma from that of the Shoah in the very first instant, for piles of wreckage are still history, even if an *impossible* history. (Impossibility, after all, is essentially a contest against the possible.) The dead are mute, yet, in their memorial presence, the corpse provokes memory by giving roots to historical experience.

So, there are Glissant's questions: Where are the bodies of the Middle Passage—the memorial sites of loss, however ruined, however dislocated or non-located—in that wreckage? What is the significance of *this* invisibility? How does this shift from the trace-visibility of the cinder to the absolute invisibility of the drown transform the articulation of historical experience? These bodies are not mere literary figures, after all. They are historical experience itself, the conscience of memory, the very condition of memory and the possibility of folding memory into the present, then future. The Middle Passage signifies non-passage for the drowned and an abyssal beginning for those who survived. Drowning is not ashes, water is not earth, and bodies disappear differently. These are two different materialities and therefore two different figures of loss. The future, then, insofar as it can be taken up, offers *less than nothing* as wreckage within which a movement to the future can take root. This is the Caribbean context. "Roots," Glissant writes, "make the commonality of errantry and exile, for in both instances roots are lacking. We must begin with that" (PR, 11). How roots are lacked and precisely what figures *this* sense of the loss of rootedness is decisive for thinking trauma, memory, and the future in the Caribbean context.

The Other Carthage

In the epigraph to *Poetics of Relation,* Glissant evokes the central motif of the book in a citation of the title and central refrain of Derek Walcott's "The Sea Is History." This short poem reflects on the relation of history to the Middle Passage, which, as the title makes plain, figures history *as* the sea. It is an archaeology of the disaster of forced migration, a wandering on the Atlantic Ocean floor in search of, yet failing to find, a wreckage that would gather the past and blow into a future from the awakening of that past. That is, for Walcott, the sea tells a story, gives a history, and so comes to the Caribbean, crashing a cruel and fecund wave, as a collective foundation of sorts for the archipelago. What does it mean for the sea to be history? How does this predication describe a trauma that must be figured otherwise than the corpse and ash of Europe's great internal disaster?

Walcott's poem begins with a question of tribal memory. His questions lay out the stakes of memory nicely, for the naming of the memory "tribal" is as much a question of roots as it is the passage of representations, images, and meanings. That is, the tribal *promises* to situate collective identity in a ground of identifiable—and so passable in language and memory—history. Walcott's gaze turns in the interrogative, wondering about and in search of the monument, ruinous or vibrant, that might function as an outer sign of inner-identity. But it is precisely this that the Middle Passage renders impossible. And so the poem begins:

> Where are your monuments, your battles, martyrs?
> Where is your tribal memory? Sirs,
> in that grey vault. The sea. The sea
> has locked them up. The sea is History.[15]

If the sea is history, it drowns in the "grey vault," locking up memory. The sea cannot give tribal memory to the archipelago. Tribal memory requires a body. Memory must be spoken, even if, as with Benjamin's figure of the angel of history, that speaking speaks, as legible in its muted illegibility, from the slaughter-bench of history. The body is not given in the sea as history. The corpse is not just drowned, but fused to the sea as a space of obliteration and entombment:

> Exodus.
> Bone soldered by coral to bone,
> mosaics
> mantled by the benediction of the shark's shadow,
>
> that was the Ark of the Covenant.

The corpse, lying at the bottom of the sea, is bone and soldered to itself by the coral—that very element which binds the body to the sea's floor. It cannot surface. It cannot be seen. The bone no longer carries the flesh of the body, which for Walcott figures the loss of the Middle Passage as the loss of everything that sustains, everything that might reproduce in body, between bodies. And yet that loss also forms the mosaic Walcott describes as the Ark of the Covenant. The Ark of the Covenant, which Lamentations calls the "beauty of Israel," marks both the depths of loss and the meaning of what might remain. The unfindable beauty that animates life—this is Walcott's reckoning with the drowning of history and memory and its settlement on the ocean floor. The sea is history; it makes what is new even in this pain.

There is always remainder. There is remainder because the sea washes ashore in the New World, leaving salt and sand to form the "only faith" remainder from which "each rock broke into its own nation." An archipelagic vision. Faith alone; the fusion bones. Walcott closes the poem by connecting the problem of history as the faith-alone-remainder with the enigma of beginning. He writes, in one of the most important passages written on the Middle Passage and trauma:

> and in the salt chuckle of rocks
> with their sea pools, there was the sound
> like a rumour without any echo
>
> of History, really beginning.

Walcott concludes precisely where the future begins, so a fuller reading of "The Sea Is History" will have to be postponed. I am here concerned with trauma's relation to the past. But what is important in Walcott's shift in the poem is how history arrives: *without any echo* and *as a beginning*. A first voice. The sea is history; it does not bear a body, corpse, or bone, but only a pool of water amidst a rocky, sandy shore. The first voice is beginning without tribal memory, a "Genesis" of sorts, according to the poem's third stanza, with the sacredness of memory of the dead set as and at the beginning. Memory is traumatic and carries that pain of history in the figure of the sea. The element of recollection, the element of being, the element of knowing. The sea is history is beginning.

Walcott links this sense of beginning to erasure. Erasure leaves and gives traces (every trace is a gift); there is work to do with what remains, and yet that work is never nostalgic, never in flight from or denial of the orphaned status of those who remain in the wake of remainders. Traumatic beginning conditions the being and knowing of Glissant's—and Walcott's—orphan narratives.[16] The trauma of the past, when that trauma is for the dead, pushes immediately toward a future, toward being for the living. But that gets us too far ahead in this moment. We must first register the breaks and breakdowns of a past traumatized to the point of erasure. What remains? The trace. What is the trace to being and knowing? In "The

Muse of History," an essay that draws out so many of the existential consequences of figuring history and memory as the sea, Walcott writes:

> I accept this archipelago of the Americas. I say to the ancestor who
> sold me, and to the ancestor who bought me, I have no father, I
> want no such father, although I can understand you, black ghost,
> white ghost, when you both whisper "history," for if I attempt
> to forgive you both I am falling into your idea of history which
> justifies and explains and expiates, and it is not mine to forgive,
> my memory cannot summon any filial love, since your features
> are anonymous and erased and I have no wish and no power
> to pardon.[17]

If the sea is history, then Walcott here makes that history existential—
bearing on the very being of the Caribbean and Caribbeanness. History is
at once oblivion and new beginning. Oblivion is sealed in the break from a
history with which the archipelago might engage; forgiveness itself is for-
bidden without an essential link between histories. Walcott does not forgo
reparation, complaint, or rage. Rather, he names what beginning looks like
if the sea is history. In that beginning, there is no essential relation or relation of roots. The compulsion to forgive is itself forgiven. Abyssal beginning pardons the pardon.

The sea is History. This begins *Poetics of Relation.* Glissant characterizes
the traumatic movement, passage, and its memory in Walcott's poem as a
dislocation. Dislocation, read alongside the loss of tribal memory, names
the abyss opened up between Africa and the Americas by the Middle Passage. Dislocation disorients, and so the language of trauma emerges at the
moment in which intelligibility vanishes in the sea. Rupture, dislocation.
This "painful negation" shocks continuity and upends philosophies of history. In *Caribbean Discourse,* Glissant writes:

> The French Caribbean is the site of a history characterized by rup-
> tures and that began with a brutal dislocation, the slave trade. Our
> historical consciousness could not be deposited gradually and con-
> tinuously like sediment, as it were, as happened with those peoples
> who have frequently produced a totalitarian philosophy of history,
> for instance European peoples, but came together in the context
> of shock, contradiction, painful negation, and explosive forces.

This dislocation of the continuum, and the inability of collective consciousness to absorb it all, characterize what I call nonhistory. (CD, 61–62)

A theoretical confrontation with Benjamin in this passage is possible precisely around such terms as "deposited" and "sediment." With these terms, Glissant marks the break with European historiography, especially with what he here calls the totalitarian philosophy of history. Beginning *as* dislocation, a history that commences with brutal rupture cannot be absorbed or explained by a master narrative, even a master narrative of generalized loss and a vision of piled human wreckage; neither history's shape and movement nor the details of transmission are sufficient to the traumatic effect of the Middle Passage. Benjamin is an important interlocutor here. "Theses on the Philosophy of History" *wants* to reverse the totalitarianism of philosophy of history with the evocation of the sadness of Carthage against empathy and in the figure of the angel of history. To be sure, Benjamin argues against the simplicity of certain forms of historical materialism and historicism, critiquing both the notion of the chronicler and theodicy narratives that are part of so much philosophy of history. And Benjamin, like Glissant, argues against those narratives on the basis of their totalitarian aims, tendencies, and orientations. So, how does nonhistory *contest* Benjamin's angel? This is a deeply critical, not simply creolizing, relationship. How does the Middle Passage work *outside* the angel of history, his negation, and the refusal of empathy with the victor? Does an orphan narrative ask different questions about loss?

To begin, the critical figure here is visibility. Benjamin's angel *sees*, even as he is blown with back turned into a future, that peculiar and troubling thing called "progress." The angel sees the wreckage of history—history's corpses—as it piles on top of the pile. The corpses are visible, even if the singularity or face of the corpse is concealed by the enormity of loss; Benjamin's account of historical trauma in some ways depends on the tragedy of blurred visibility. A pile of wreckage, after all, is still a remnant of historical meaning and connection. Indeed, it is precisely the visibility of the corpse that gives Europe its sense of loss and the contours of traumatic memory in so much post-Shoah discourse. In the European context, to have lost is to have had (a) history in one's grasp, to have reckoned—even with a cluster of important caveats—with the *roots* of collective memory in a place. This is why figures of ash and cinder dominate so much of the discourse around trauma in European literature, and why the nuance of Benjamin's wreckage is the near erasure and radical fragmentation of history's victims in the Holocaust.

The figure of the sea says so much. What does it mean to describe the sea as history, and thus to figure loss with the watery abyss? How does the sea as history erase otherwise than the wreckage of history held under the angel's gaze, longing as it does for redemption? In *Caribbean Discourse*, Glissant puts it plainly when he writes that "the negative effect of nonhistory is therefore the erasing of the collective memory" (CD, 62). And this erasure is absolute. Benjamin's wreckage, that pile of corpses too foreseeing of Europe's great trauma, and later revisions of the figure of history's traumatizing pain as fragment or cinder or ash, is rooted in collective memory and prior belonging. Loss, in Benjamin's figuring of it, piles on top of those roots, burning and murdering what grew from them. Roots are a necessary condition of this figuration.

This is not to say that the figure of ash is not also present in Glissant's reflections on historical experience. The evocation of ash in Glissant's work, however, does not identify the *body of loss* in the figure, but instead draws us to Benjamin's most enigmatic allusion in "Theses on the Philosophy of History": the sadness of Carthage. For, in figuring history's pain and trauma, there are also the ashes of the incinerated city, set alongside the very potent, in the Caribbean context, image of *salt*. The Romans burned Carthage—not only the city, but also the ruins themselves. Carthage is a site of literal erasure. The Romans then salted the earth in order to seal the loss as unredeemable. In pointing us toward the sadness of Carthage, by way of Flaubert's words, Benjamin means to provoke the possibility of an empathy, perhaps an impossible empathy, that lies with the victims on history's slaughter-bench. In confronting the pain of history, Glissant returns to the story of Carthage, and yet it is a very different Carthage.[18] It is a black Carthage, the African Carthage. What is Carthage to Glissant? How do the figures of loss in Carthage—ashes and salt—come to register in Glissant's work? And so how do those revised, creolized figures of loss describe trauma in the Caribbean context?

To begin, Glissant reads the case of Carthage through the method of what he calls Relation. With Relation, Glissant underscores the transformative effect of reading and theorizing from *inside* the geography of reason, which is simultaneously *outside* the same, and where the tropes, figures, and central metaphors from another shore are reinvented through the act of creative appropriation. Glissant notes in the one of the scattered prose remarks in "Black Salt" that the case of Carthage gathers something importantly global to it. Glissant's provocation: there is not *one* Carthage. Rather, Carthage is in some fundamental sense the experience of a history dislodged from any relation of empathy with the victors. On this account, Benjamin has said perhaps more than his work can contain. Glissant writes in "Black Salt":

> Carthage
>   Salt already on the hands of the gravediggers. The sea's scum, no longer a fragrance, is spread over the conquered city. One forgets the first salt he tastes: behold him trafficking its essence. The world—and today one sees countless more plundered Carthages—feeds this fire within him to conquer, to kill. The docile sea is his accomplice.
>   A people arrives; and is rationed its share of salt upon the labor of its wounds. At last free it laments upon ashes. Salt is forever mixed with the victims' blood and with injured stones that were the toil of men.
>   (CP, 108; italics in the original)

Glissant had already begun a reflection on Carthage as early as "The Indies" (1955), an occasion that Bernadette Cailler has treated in some detail in her *Carthage ou la flamme du brasier*. In "The Indies," Glissant interrupts what is initially a musing on the dreamland visions of the explorers—one of the real complexities of that epic poem lies in its shifting perspectives and voices, which is really about the complexity of the new of the New World—with the stakes of treating the Caribbean as an imaginary, then real (*réel*) landscape. The folds of traumatic memory emerge in parentheses. Parentheses, after all, are where so much memory is written into history. A fatal and decisive supplement to any discourse. Glissant writes:

> Pale with that ash beneath the salt (as in Carthage when it was
>   destroyed!
> As, concealed in the salt of distance, from the Gold Coast to
>   Maracaibo,
> Ash of ship's hold and the storeroom's cane syrup!) I had known the
>   approach of that water. (CP, 72)

This parenthetical interruption, and it has to be read as an interruption of historical flow, places Carthage and the figures of ash and salt in the passage between Africa and the Americas. *Carthage as a diasporic event, dislocated from linear time.* Indeed, naming of the Gold Coast here implicates the figures in the Middle Passage, the point of origin, the lost father who is lost to the abyss and registers only as trace and melancholy when fixed as past. How do Carthage and its companion figures resonate in Glissant's hands?

The salting of the earth in Carthage signifies its oceanic meaning, its proximity to the sea as a history—here, in North Africa, as a supplement to its history, a great good-bye to the past sealed by the impossibility of fertility, loss of land by the dead doubled by the death of the land lost for even the memory of the dead. *Peu de gens devineront combien il a fallu être triste pour ressusciter Carthage.* But Glissant's poem makes that key shift, a shift in geography, letting the salt of Carthage resonate and resound in the oceanic feeling of the Atlantic. The Atlantic, that is, as a site of loss that is also a homeland, an abyss that traumatizes as it gives. Water approaches—first, the washing of water on the Roman ship, the Mediterranean as a passage of mass murder. Water leaves, salt remains. Salt on the earth doubles the pain of genocidal violence. Water approaches— second, the washing of water on the slave ship departing, on the slave ship casting bodies overboard that then form the drowned archaeological non-site of the Middle Passage, Walcott's "Bone soldered by coral to bone," water on the slave ship arriving. The salt mine, the salty air, at every turn a doubling of trauma and loss. Carthage moves across time. It is plunder and murder. That is, Carthage is traumatic loss and the abyssal question of what comes after. Carthage is memory traversing, repeating on island and continent. If salt mixes with the blood of the victim, but the dead become a people, then the bloodline is also salted, forever Carthage but forever more than the post-Roman landscape. Europe does not make the imagination or the imaginary. A wound that does not heal, but a body that makes a world. Melancholy, for sure, but it becomes something more. We can recall Walcott's rage against the very idea of claiming paternity. *I have no such father, I want no such father.* It is the lament of Carthage after the Middle Passage.

The knowing approach of the water.

Departure: cane syrup in the hold.

Arrival: salt in the wounds.

Beginning's Abyss

Where to begin?

Glissant's literary and theoretical work consistently engages with the image and botanical-geographic meaning of the mangrove in order to characterize the poly-rooted, rhizomatic character of Antillanité. J. Michael Dash, for example, argues convincingly that the alteration between figures of stone—whose persistence gives identity, even as they are formed by the elements—and mangrove—the intertidal tree between shore and sea—provides us with the shape and contour of Glissant's conception of archipelagic thinking.[19] The mangrove is particularly suggestive here for the question of beginning. To begin with beginning, the mangrove grows between shore and sea in the intertidal space that functions as the purest site of beginning: neither the abyss nor the fantasied root that persists or is re-rooted upon arrival (this is Glissant's great distance from the Négritude movement). Salt does not destroy the mangrove; salt and life are no longer disjunctive. The intertidal is *interstitial*, a resonance that will become especially important in our account of Glissant's meditations on subjectivity in chapter 4. But here it is important to locate the peculiar and geographically appropriate—in the sense of a botanical geography and of a geography of reason—place of roots in the organic structure of the mangrove. The tropical mangrove, the *Rhizophora*, survives precisely because it is lifted above the sea with special roots. Propped above the tidal pulse, the tree's body is given oxygen, which keeps it alive despite the unpredictable and often violent crashing of salt, time, memory, and waves on the shoreline. Yet, the mangrove is also constantly contested by the sea. *Becoming mangrove* is no easy piece. It survives because the roots have lifted what is essential above the contingent destructive reach of the waves. The mangrove is a border plant. Roots like no other—plural and in no relation of dependency to the One. Difference without identity, yet an identity. The botanical archipelago, the repeating island bordering the island that repeats. Death and life intertwined without melancholy. The fecundity of the *Rhizophora*.

And so we can see quite easily why Glissant in *Traité du tout-monde*, in a powerful turn of phrase, describes the mangrove as "complicatedly obscure, lost in red root branches, the mangrove beginning [*commençait*] at the cemetery" (TTM, 69). The cemetery is the site of an abyssal beginning, but even at this site of trauma and loss there is what sustains life, for the mangrove is sustained by what Glissant figures as the "shore of yellow-upon-blue water, reaching as far as the salted river" (TTM, 69). Glissant gathers a trio of exceptionally rich images here: the sea, the mangrove, and the river's mouth. The sea, this cemetery that feeds or even creates the roots of the mangrove, carries the dead to the shore. Let us not forget that the mangrove lives only because it has generated roots that can sustain the blow of the sea, lives *after* the trauma that conditions beginning from the abyss. We might recall here what Glissant says in "The Indies," prefacing the poetic meditation on the slave trade, where he writes: "*The slave trade. Which shall never be erased from the face of the sea.*" Shall never be erased. With this turn of phrase, Glissant infuses the question of beginning with an ethics beholden to a specter. Traumatic memory recurs as the face of the sea, where the dead, not unlike Benjamin's corpses on the slaughter-bench of history, begin to speak and give life even as they remain only an abyssal presence. Glissant continues in "The Indies":

> *Monstrous mobilization, oblique crossing, Poem of Death. A language of unreason, but which carries a new reason. For it is also the beginning of a Unity, the other part of an agreement finally commuted. This is the Indies of suffering, after the Indies of dream. Now reality is daughter of man truly: born of the contradictions he has lived and brought about.*
> (CP, 86)

The Middle Passage arrives, but crossing remains oblique. The oblique-ness of crossing gathers the notion of traumatic memory into the present. While representational memory of them is perhaps impossible, the dead, who cannot be erased, make the Indies a *place*—a reality saturated with suffering, but still a place.

There is also arrival at the shore, the persistence of life sustained and haunted by what cannot be erased. The mangrove is therefore also a critical figure of *interval*. The time of the mangrove is the time of transition out of, from, and always, because the wave withdraws after it crashes, back to an abyssal past. Life *after* and *in the wake of* this mangrove is sustained and perhaps even flourishes in the mixed site of the river's mouth, where the fresh- and seawater intermingle. *Carthage in the confluence.* The salted river, then, this watery land and geography of the New World Carthage, gives us abyssal beginning as a mixture of life and death. History becomes a story, one that Glissant describes in *Poetics of Relation* as "this Relation made of storms and profound moments of peace in which we may honor our boats" (PR, 8–9). There is an ethics that attends to this beginning, always.

This is no casual affair, of course, the problem of beginning. Walcott's linking of the sea—and so history—with lament and the sacred gives the abyssal character of beginning important depth, profundity, and claim on its children. The dead of the abyss are history as the sea. And they obligate. *Honor our boats.* It is not simply the case that the Caribbean begins with arrival and the singular melancholy of transatlantic passage. That is to imagine a future de-linked from ghosts of and responsibilities to the abyssal past. As well, there is the sanctity of arrival, where the Middle Passage, for Walcott, is also the transmission of the Ark of the Covenant. That is, just as the Ark of the Covenant carried (in the King James translation of Lamentations 2:1) "the beauty of Israel," the Middle Passage carries the sacred event of beginning again. How to write this sacred is one of Glissant's great tasks as a poet, and it is also where he is at his very best as a writer. For example, Glissant closes "The Indies" with violent contradictions, evoking

> this lament of the world that
> inebriates
> The lungs—and yet which traces out hope. (CP, 99)

This mixture of lament and hope—a paradox that is an archipelago become island that repeats—then culminates in the intertwining of time and sadness, the recurrence of beginning, like the shifts of tide and the withdrawal-then-return of crashing waves, in every moment of historical formation and re-formation:

> Rugged calm of the horizon amid an uproar of currents,
> And the eternal fixity of days and tears. (CP, 100)

For Glissant, then, *arrival* is beginning, even if that beginning is at once new and beleaguered by sadness. Beleaguering sadness, eternally fixed as a moment of beginning, inscribes the abyss in time as such. The temporality of the archipelago is not simply the chaos of movement across islands, that Benítez-Rojo motif of repetition, but the recurrence of beginning—the making of "one vast beginning." Glissant writes:

The next abyss was the depths of the sea . . . these lowest depths, these deeps, with their punctuation of scarcely corroded balls and chains. In actual fact, the abyss is a tautology; the entire ocean, the entire sea gently collapsing in the end into the pleasures of sand, make one vast beginning, but a beginning whose time is marked by these balls and chains gone green. (PR, 6)

These "melancholic transatlantic crossings" (PR, 6) are sites of birth. The slave boat is a womb. Walcott forswears paternity. Glissant begins with maternity.[20]

Beginning is nothing other than orientation toward the future, though the grounds or non-grounds of that orientation are of ultimate significance. Intellectual work toward the future—this work is always some form of historiography. The act of creation in the Caribbean context is marked by history, no doubt, but in a different manner. Creation is always geographic. In *Caribbean Discourse,* Glissant writes that

the language of the Caribbean artist does not originate in the obsession with celebrating his inner self; this inner self is inseparable from the future evolution of his community.

But what the artist expresses, reveals, and argues in his work, the people have not ceased to live in reality. The problem is that this collective life has been constrained by the process of consciousness. . . . That is why he is his own ethnologist, historian, linguist, painter of frescoes, architect. (CD, 236)

The Caribbean organic intellectual is his own—everything. What does that make of beginnings? What kind of subjectivity begins at the shores of arrival, in the wake of a specific kind of *less than loss* that drowns, rather than burns, history?

A first clue. Glissant affirms (with all due caveats) the Deleuzian notion of nomadic subjectivity in the opening pages of *Poetics of Relation*. He does so precisely inside the Caribbean context, with all the qualifiers regarding history and memory in such an affirmation. This is to say, "nomadic" is not for Glissant the adverbial qualifier of subjectivity resulting from a critique of metaphysics, nor does it respond to various epistemological paradoxes as a radical reorientation of a tradition. It is not Deleuze's (or Guattari's) nomad. Glissant's nomad has another materiality, and therefore another genesis. Caribbean subjectivity is nomadic because of the very conditions in which Glissant finds Africans in the Americas, because of the work that needs to be done in the wake of *this* trauma, and so for reasons of where he begins as a thinker in the fullest, organic sense. In the abyssal beginning. Not in the break or breaks.

I want to get at this sense of the nomadic in Glissant by tracking his thought through three conceptual and figurative movements: birth, roots, and death. These three movements work across what Glissant calls, in his introduction to the "Riveted Blood" poems, a "tortured geography" (BS, 17). This tortured geography writes Glissant as much as he writes about the same; in conceiving births and roots, one writes as the living *without the place of the dead*, in the *geos* of whatever remains, or, in this case, cannot remain, of their bodies. One is written by one's birth, moved to word by one's roots, not just out of respect for the dead (though that is enough). Trauma is as much for the living as for the dead. Trauma is only trauma for those who *survive* and live from out of and within the disaster. In *Caribbean Discourse,* he writes:

> The spoken narrative is not concerned with the dead. We stand our mouths open under the sun like *bagasse*, silenced from elsewhere. We encumber our moons with ceremonies that lack fire. . . . Purify the breath until it reveals the harsh taste of the land: bring breath to the death of rocks and landscape. (CD, 237)

Under the sun like bagasse, *the fibrous remains of sugarcane drained of their juices, left in the sun without the resources of replenishment.* Again, this is a different kind of loss. This is the traumatic arrival of "us," Glissant's "us," the Caribbean context. To make space and identity and becoming in an archipelago—what Aliocha Lasowski calls, simply, Glissant's *conscience historique.*[21] To write trauma, then, is to be written by it—thus, we are "us," a collective in the accusative, trauma's direct object—and to return always to what remains after the draining and drowning, always with only a wholly gratuitous gesture of creation, silenced from elsewhere *first* by the harsh taste of the land. *Geos* that does not nourish roots, but underpins the *bagasse* and sets it in the sun without nourishment from the water, for water is first just as bitter as the land. Death without the body as wreckage and remainder. For Glissant, then, trauma is to be written beginning with this tortured a-geography of the ocean, from the absent rocks of departure and bitter sands of arrival, and with the salt in the earth, the water, the wound. Silenced from elsewhere. Breath brought to death.

The nomadic subject, this rhizome, writes as a response to tortured geography. From the rhizomatic subject we can begin to understand how futurity is created in a *post-topological* logic captured in the notions of the Imaginary and Relation. Here Glissant works in the confrontational space between Antonio Gramsci's organic intellectual—a central concern of the final chapter below—and the demands of writing after disaster. What is the abyss to beginning?

BirthAbyss

There can be no birth out of trauma without abyss. This is the pedagogy of oceanic experience, of passage, of bone soldered by coral to bone—the sea as history. What does it mean to be born a subject, to be born into a collective-which-is-not-one in the wake of the disaster of the Middle Passage? Glissant's account takes us back to the boat and the ocean, linked as they are to the conditions of this birth and saturated as they are with abyssal depths.[22] From this, in this, and always with this, birth is terrifying. In *Poetics of Relation*, Glissant writes:

> What is terrifying partakes of the abyss, three times linked to the unknown. First, the time you fell into the belly of the boat . . . the belly of the boat dissolves you, precipitates you into a nonworld from which you cry out. This boat is a womb, a womb abyss. . . . This boat is your womb, a matrix, and yet it expels you. This boat: pregnant with as many dead as living under sentence of death. (PR, 6)

This construction "womb abyss" is crucial for understanding the origins of the nomadic and rhizomatic subject in the Caribbean context, the formation on the shoreline, the mangrove rendered being and becoming. There is no sense of arrival in-world. Nonworld is not death. Therein lies both the trauma and the necessity. Terror marks this birth as traumatic with the vanishing of the intelligible—it is "linked to the unknown." The fact that birth comes with as many dead as living marks this birth with loss before the subject is capable of possession, so we cannot call it a birth as loss. We are already absent the terms necessary for loss to occur. A loss of the sense of loss. This is the temporal structure of trauma that, in the treatment of Carthage, was figured as the salt in the wound. Healing and reconciliation with the past vanishes as a teleology. Abyssal beginning begins with different structural principles.

The womb of the boat's belly gives way to the new time of birth in the new nonworld, which is what we call from the Afro-Caribbean perspective the New World, and so Glissant's conception of the Caribbean proper. This new time and birth is the end of the sea at the sand, an end of the terror and the beginning of the terrifying, the life of trauma for the living. The dead mark the time of this birth and give it a name—not the paternal name, for the dead are not fathers or a father. The dead mark the living and their sense of what it means to go on, but as a peculiar and utterly devastating absence: the balls and chains gone green. To repeat: water and fire leave different senses of nothingness. Genocidal violence that burns, the ash and the cinder of the Shoah, retains the proper name and the paternal figuration of identity even in loss; we know what to call the dead of the Shoah. For the Caribbean context, this is even *more loss* than loss, for the body does not remain as a haunting image, nor does it remain as a trace of itself in ashes. Proper name and paternal figuration drown in the Middle Passage. This is the abyss. This is the ball and chain gone green. The metal that decays—*this* sense of ruin, this sense of loss of loss at the bottom of the sea, this history—is only the remainder of what held bodies to the terrifying. Birth is marked with this time as an absence more absent than loss and its traces. We do not know what to call the dead after the Middle Passage, if calling them is always a reckoning with the paternal name. Yet, there is birth. So there is also the name: Antillanité.

RootsAbyss

Birth sets the human person. Birth "sets" in the sense of putting on a surface that, however shifty, however vulnerable to turns in tide and the thread of storm and wave, might sustain one's weight. But the abyssal conditions of birth in *this* trauma cannot sustain. Indeed, the very conditions that define survival in Shoah literatures split history into before and after disaster, devastating memory and rootedness in the black hole that is trauma. Glissant starts from another place. What remains is not a split in history, nor a black hole that stands between what was and what lives as ruins. The ruins of the Middle Passage are figured by Glissant as the deterioration of the ball and chain at the bottom of the ocean. But this is not a vessel, however fractured and ruined, of birth. Rather, and decisively, it is the ruined remains of what held a body—figuring, then, as millions of bodies—captive in the belly of the vessel and sank them into the sea's abyss. A birth-vessel that could never be one. The fate of the body and the character of trauma and traumatic memory are inseparable. And so too inseparable from the meaning of beginning again.

Bodies do not mark this traumatic Caribbean birth, as they do for Benjamin in "Theses on the Philosophy of History"; there are not bodies—decaying or ashen, bloated or decimated—in the shackles. Only the shackles—gone green, they too are fallen from the terror of origin—remain. Salt, as treated in such provocative detail in the *Black Salt* cycle, sits in the wound of those who survive, but it is also what destroys what cannot remain, what cannot even be conceived as loss: the body of the slave thrown overboard. Salt is everything. But it is everything in the sense that it makes what is into what is no longer and cannot be drawn to memory. Roots set and fail to take up in what is less than the remainder. There are not even the privileges of loss, namely, the object of mourning. Indeed, loss itself is stolen in the Middle Passage, so roots do not cling even to traces. In the poem "Gorée," an absolutely stunning reflection by Glissant on the island off the coast of Senegal where slaves awaited vessels to the new nonworld, Glissant attempts to think back to this origin, but finds this movement strangled by absence. The poet is stifled by what the past gives after the Middle Passage. This is a lesson about where traces fail language and language fails traces. Glissant writes:

He inhabited his cry treefull: his roots spilled into ravines shouting out.
He knotted into time's gorge rawness from the deeps, and stayed many
    a wind-bare sail with his gaze.
He had no room to call upon surpassing, once steered between coast
    and bluff shore, in the harbor island where yesterday's dreams
    garrotte dreams of tomorrow to their death. (BS, 117)

Strangulation of dreams, strangled by the iron clasp of transport, the garrotte—a terrifying recollection of terror that then generates a *specific* sense of absence for the Caribbean context. A companion piece from *Caribbean Discourse* extends memory's glitch, then failure, into passage itself:

> Off the coast of Senegal, Gorée, the island before the open sea, the first step towards madness.
>   Then the sea, never seen from the depths of the ship's hold, punctuated by drowned bodies that sowed in its depths explosive seeds of absence. (CD, 9)

"Seeds of absence"—the very phrase fails to make sense except as the failure of memory, not as a failure to recall, but a failure of any relation of recollection. It is an impossible phrase, something that can only be formulated after disaster. Disaster bequeaths absence, but also the seed? In this disassembled phrase, a peculiar sense of root is glimpsed. This sense: roots that emerge *toward* (not *from*) the absence of the depths of the sea, depths which, as we saw above, do not even bear the remainder but only the ball and chain gone green. So, the rhizomatic subject, the mangrove become person at the shoreline of history and memory, must be born unrooted in order to maintain any hope of creating on and in a tortured geography. A creating that is explosive. Remember that Césaire too warned of the volcanic, but his explosion-to-come drew its strength and force from the suppressed *élan vital* of Africa. Seeds of absence are explosive because they come from the abyss, this capacity to begin again, for the first time in fact, in the nonworld.

DeathAbyss

Trauma is as much for the living as for the dead, thinking both at once. But let us maintain our context: the living live by the seeds of their birth, an absence before loss, for the time of trauma is marked always by death. Death is here not the death of those who suffer, but of those whose voice is absented by both the terror of the unintelligible and the bodyless nonremainder of the ball and chain gone green. In a word, a voice absented by *abyss*. Abyss encases birth and replaces the soil roots might seek or from which they might spring forth. The abyss of this death, then, is at once birth and root. And in this death-abyss, that which makes futurity possible emerges. From *Black Salt*, Glissant writes:

Lands. Roots gone silent. Africa and far from its name, islands
Abandoned in death agony, banished from the world, naked
With blood clogged by nights' burden
Polynesia dying dark he sights you
And denies you come with burden and means you be fruitless
The way we see a rooster in the gold of old corn die
A bitter glittering death. (BS, 98)

This last line is crucial for understanding what, for Glissant, the trauma of the Middle Passage means to futurity. DeathAbyss is bitter death, yes. But also a glittering death. Again, paradox is archipelagic thinking.

What does it mean that death glitters? This is such a curious turn of phrase. Glissant, in a passage from *Caribbean Discourse* cited above, figured the subjectivity born of this trauma as the *bagasse*, the fibrous remains of sugarcane wrung dry—living in the nonworld wake of an abyssal death. But death is also glittering. Mouths open to the sun, wrung dry of all that might nourish, yet still capable of reflecting that sun, sparkling, decorating. This opens the time of catastrophic trauma back onto a possible future. DeathAbyss with a decorative sparkle. Historians falter; poets remain and have the future (this is also Glissant's nuanced reorientation of Aristotle's *Poetics*). Glissant writes, again from *Black Salt*:

It was the salt in time's bowl. Nothing was left but an obscure urn of words. Is there a morning? The darkness of course bodes well— when words are shining on the steps up to the house. In this realm of our hands. (BS, 107)

Salt in time's bowl is such a compelling characterization of trauma and beginning after the Middle Passage. Carthage as time itself. The peculiar temporality of this trauma lies in the figure of salt in time's bowl set alongside the salt in the wound. This is what makes time into *catastrophic time*. As well, we might see how this figure recalls Primo Levi's account of the temporality of the camps in *Survival in Auschwitz*. In that work, Levi describes the temporality of the camps as the loss of any fold in time, any sense of sequentiality; in death-camp time, each moment lies distinct without relation to past or future. This is in no small part what prompts Levi to ask in that work: "Is this a man?" Does the human remain without

this fold of time? But that is time in the camp; the time of survival is altogether different. Something comes after, in particular for a shoreline thinking. Sequentiality reemerges in survival, however fractured. This is what it
means for trauma to work for the living as much as the dead. What, then,
are the folds in time for Glissant? Survival born of and unrooted in Death-
Abyss folds differently, as it is without the distant shores of a burned history. There is instead this drowned history. Seeds of absence. There is no
fold into the past, then, except to arrive at the depths of the sea where only
slowly disintegrating and disintegrated shackles lie as absence of memory.
Beginning is where the ball and chain go green. So there is beginning,
and so time folded into a future, but without the same fold—however
ruptured—into the past. Glissant's survivor—the Caribbean itself, the
tortured *geos* of sand and sea, the death-arrival-birth—is not Levi's survivor for the very reason that the sequentiality of time does not suffer a sus-
pension and fracture. There is loss of loss, pure annihilation, death layered
on death. Did you know that you could lose loss? That death could die?
These impossibilities *are* abyssal beginning. They are Caribbeanness. And
so it begins there, where the ball and chain go green, the birthing to the
shores where DeathAbyss unroots, yet glitters still in its bitterness. That is
the Caribbean shoreline: at once the saddest place in the Americas *and* its
most beautiful place. Sublimnity. Cruel sublimnity.

The rhizome, whose elaborate structure as the condition of Caribbean
subjectivity is explored in chapter 3, is generated by these conditions: the
intersection and clinging of abyss to birth, root, and the death that brings
birth back to its glittering bitterness. The bitterness glitters; there is, in one
sense or another, light. A glitter to and after what is drowned? How can
this make sense? Simply put: *life goes on*, however marked it may be by the
abyssal absence of birth and root and death. Life goes on, so trauma is a
beginning as much as it is an end. For the Caribbean situation, this beginning is the unrooted subject, the rhizome, the nomad.
    What does it mean, then, to think as nomad working from the bitter
glittering death that is birth and root? Glissant's "answer" is simple: the
persistence of the Imaginary. By Imaginary, Glissant here means the ability to imagine, conceive, and know the world otherwise. This conception
of the Imaginary is organic in the sense of maintaining a profound and immovable connection to land and body. And yet, this is always also a sense

of organicity read against itself; there is always the tortured geography and the salt in the wound. The Caribbean context—Caribbeanness—is therefore *a method* for Glissant, not a state of being. The formation of the Imaginary, creativity and its actualization in creation, works with the founding elements of BirthAbyss, RootAbyss, and DeathAbyss (my terms), but not in order to overcome them. Rather, the cluster of founding elements provide the post-topological map—indeed, a "map" rendering topology impossible—deployed in response to that tortured geography which renders the world opaque. And always *rich* and *lush* in its opacity, giving a bitter-yet-nourishing salt to the rhizome. This is organic intellectual work without the privileges of loss. It is the intellectual work of repetition without resolution, sustained contradiction without neutralizing the right to obscurity. Glissant writes:

> An "intellectual" effort, with its repetitive thrusts (repetition has a rhythm), its contradictory moments, its necessary imperfections, its demands for formulation (even a schematic one), very often obscured by its very purpose. For the attempt to approach a reality so often hidden from view cannot be organized in terms of a series of clarifications. We demand the right to opacity. Through which our anxiety to have a full existence becomes part of the universal drama of cultural transformation: the creativity of marginalized peoples who today confront the ideal of transparent universality. (CD, 2; translation altered)

Transparency confronted. Thinking after trauma, toward the future, must confront transparency and universality, not because it is a remnant of an old world order, hopelessly square or even quaint, but because of the conditions of thinking in the Caribbean context. There is no history or memory lost. That would be a privilege enabling recollection with all of its regulative ideals—the way universality is so often smuggled in against things presenting as opaque. If there is rhizome, and the abysses which gave rise to it are method and so not a state of being to be clarified or overcome, then the future must be mapped and unmapped across a *geos* that puts salt in wounds. The future does not return to its losses to mourn. Rather, the future is created with gratuitous gestures affirming opacity, the impossibility of reckoning fully with the fact of abyssal beginning.

Glissant calls this affirmation of opacity Relation. The term is of course to be read against itself, for Relation traditionally signifies either correlation or dialectic, both of which clarify, resolve, and fix. But nomadic, rhizomatic subjectivity works relation against itself. So, Glissant will define Relation as detour, exile, and errantry. Relation, in other words, rejects filiation in the name of (however aporetic) a "chaotic network." What would filiation mean, filiation with a landscape initiated by genocide, then enslavement? Without filiation, there is only the moment of creation, a creation whose encroachments are not of a gasping light—unlike, say, Paul Celan—but of an abyss whose death-shadow glitters. Returns are always detours, for Glissant, and so too it is with the condition of the specific postcoloniality of the Caribbean, both as a state of arrival and a method. Glissant has here achieved his fullest and most fundamental distance from the Négritude movement.

A last word. Let us turn to the question of place. A tortured geography puts the nomad out of place with an act of violence to roots. So where is connection? How does place become something other than abandonment and a MemorialAbyss to impossible suffering? Post-natural, abyssally born, place is non-filial and nomadically traversed, which is not to say it ceases to or cannot *be*. Rather, there is for Glissant always a defining fragility to being and becoming in the Caribbean context. Thus, he moves the rhizome from noun to verb: "Is this some community *we* rhizomed into fragile connection to a place?" (PR, 206). The rhizome rhizomes—herein lies the elegant, melancholic simplicity of Glissant's work and the fiat, *ex nihilo* character of creativity after trauma, toward the future. The rhizome's rhizome is both an act of self-movement—an abyss cannot propel—and that moment wherein the collective is at stake. The organic intellectual rhizomes after trauma, and that intellectual's organicity always moves with abyssal shadows, unrooted.

It is worth noting here, in close, how profoundly significant intellectual work is for Glissant, as he rejects political action and/or violence as the decisive moment of identity formation (*pace* Fanon, of course). Indeed, this is why the political murder plotted by the eight Martinican protagonists in his novel *The Ripening* can barely be said to begin the formation of collective identity, and why *The Fourth Century* centers so much more on ritual and the vicissitudes of filiation in exploring identity work. Intellectual work, for Glissant, is this beginning, as it forges fragile connections—nomads in collectivity—that construct a "we" in poetry, architecture, painting—a *new* history in the nominative. And all of these (as well as other aesthetic adventures) are defined by their (at least possible) non-filial, rhizomatic character, as well as a finitude that is never a loss, but always only another detour. This is surely not without anxieties. How, as Allen Grossman asks, can we do things with tears? *Deliverance from the mist.* Deliverance as rhizomes. That is, rhizomes as nomads for Glissant, who *become* within death moved from a bitter glittering to an abyssal glow with its own ghosts, its own ambivalent salt, its own, in a word, *future.*

CHAPTER 2

Origins II

Memory, Future, Abyss

Here is allocated to praise a subterranean geography
whose breaches are never erased . . . Here is a remembrance
of seers and those who remain, may they recognize one another . . .

—Glissant, "Fastes"

*If the heroes of whom we dream (whom we dream up?) all meet at these
crossroads of poverty, storytelling, and enlightenment, it is because the
same song of light and shadow wells up from our Americas.*

—Glissant, Foreword to Chronicle of the Seven Sorrows

MEMORY IS FOR THE DEAD, but also for the living.

Whatever the pain of the past, whatever the obligations to the dead, there is also the obstinacy of the *future*. *Life goes on*: no matter the destruction of Being and beings, there is also—after—*becoming*. The notion of becoming-the-future, in the space of an imaginary saturated with the painful past, raises a cluster of epistemological and ethical questions. How does becoming engage the past in order to translate the future? Becoming irrupts in the interval. How is such translation, this enigmatic movement through the interval, brought back into contact with the past such that the creative work of making futurity is as much a memory project as a new horizon? Every reckoning is *poiesis*. How is that memory project ethical, both in relation to the past it renders and as a predelineation of a future it imagines or helps to imagine? We owe the dead something. They give to us. In a particularly complicated register: For the Caribbean context, what is the relation between memory and landscape? Place is space crossed with time. And, ultimately, how does the thought of the abyss dis- and refigure becoming and its translation(s) of past into future? Nothing is the same after the Middle Passage. It has no precedent. It only precedes.

In the previous chapter we saw how the experience of the Middle Passage overturns the figures, poetics, and theoretical language of trauma, moving discourse from concerns with remains, remainders, and ashes to an encounter with the abyssal beginning of the New World. The sea and its sub-marine entombment of atavistic origins produce an abyss without remains. This entombment and how it plays out across theorizing time and meaning marks an important break in the Caribbean tradition, a tradition of linking time, meaning, and subjectivity to a critical reconception of landscape—something begun in Ménil's surrealism, reoriented in Césaire's Négritude, and then wholly reconceived in Fanon's pan–Global South existentialism. Glissant's account of the past insists on irretrievable loss, and that sense of loss fundamentally alters the language of beginning. The abyss of the past is absolute. The island of Gorée figures this first beginning, a first passage that produces the past whose memory drowns. The drowning of memory is absolute: the sea is history, and what unifies is what is sub-marine. *Walcott, Braithwaite, then Glissant.* Glissant's recurring image of the ball and chain on the ocean floor, an image that repeats to such hypnotic effect in his work, conveys the loss of atavism in the irretrievability of drowned memory. With that loss, the language of traumatic memory conceived on the white European model—most emphatically in post-Shoah studies from Maurice Blanchot and Emmanuel Levinas in Europe through Cathy Caruth and Dominick LaCapra in the United States—is fundamentally altered. For Glissant, memory of the past weaves itself back *into* the abyss without seeking retrieval or reactivation, rather than, as with the European discourses on trauma, bearing witness to an origin reduced to cinders. The Middle Passage changes everything. The enigma of that weaving into the abyss without retrieval or reactivation is the fecund site of Glissant's work and the work of many of his contemporaries up through the *créolité* movement of the late 1980s.

And yet there is the question of the future; catastrophe is neither the end of history nor an appeal to messianic forces of thought, as it becomes for Benjamin and others.[1] Glissant, like Walcott and Braithwaite in his generation—creolizing thinkers through and through, no matter their differences—writes to the future. Obsessive return to the abyss, to what it gives and what it takes away, is not an obsession with the past. There is no future *without* the past, of course; this is a fundamental insight into human temporality and not on the face of it all that interesting. The past makes the future, whether through a retrieval of meaning that sets our anticipations—individual or collective—of what is to come or through a series of lessons that provoke revisions of how and why we want to live. At the same time, this fundamental insight is radically transformed by the interruption of memory and history in the Middle Passage, which calls into question certain presuppositions about the *contours* of time at work in both conventional accounts of temporality and key discourses on traumatic memory. Glissant works from an important and decisive claim: the relation of past to future needs to be liberated from the linear models of temporality that dominate white Western accounts of time. Whereas the linear model maintains a certain appropriateness and explanatory power in accounting for traumatic memory in the Middle Passage (the drowning of memory is the drowning of what begins as Africa's *pensée continentale*), the other passage, the passage that arrives at the shores of the Americas, disrupts any straight or folded model of time—the two models that dominate the white West. Indeed, the very sense of forgetting, remembering, and then rethinking futurity is, in Glissant's work, an introduction of the curvature and Chaos of time, replacing linearity with notions of the fractal, diffraction, and curve. The curving of time will be a central preoccupation of Glissant's conception of subjectivity, treated below in detail, but, in many ways, time's curve is already in the temporality of arrival, the Plantation, and traces among ruins. These sites—from shoreline to Plantation to the memorial City—prepare us to explore Glissant's conception of subjectivity. Thus, I focus here on the second site of beginning, the second sense of passage from arrival to futurity. This second passage into the New World and to the literal and figurative archipelago is a second sense of beginning. A beginning again *after* the drowning of memory that is always attentive to the ghosts and traces of the past. *Memory project, new horizon*. Ruins, melancholy, and traces therefore blend with creative work, with fragments in thinking through the formation of the New World's collective memory.[2]

In many ways, the reflections that follow below constitute a close and expansive reading of the opening section of *Poetics of Relation*. There are of course many texts to consult on the question of futurity in Glissant, but the first chapter, "The Open Boat," lays out all the crucial terms of abyssal beginning, gathering together motifs of loss, memory, and arrival in order to produce a shoreline thinking of beginning. It is, to my mind, the most profound cluster of meditations to be found in his theoretical work. As well, Glissant's thinking at the shoreline of the Americas enacts the first trace for memory, marking a three-part series of passages that moves the abyss into a second beginning—the future—and maintains a relation of beginning to abyss that ebbs and flows—like the shoreline itself. The first two of three metamorphoses or "partakings" of the abyss concern the drowning of memory in the Middle Passage. Falling into the belly of the boat (traumatic memory's first site of loss) and the depths of the sea (the sealing of the loss of intelligibility and irreparable loss of history) place beginning in the abyss of the past. A belly and womb, the first two metamorphoses cite and site the passage from origin to loss and traumatic memory. The third metamorphosis opens the text to the future, which places beginning in its second sense of abyss: the persistence of life after catastrophe. A second passage. This is the passage to another beginning, one that bears with it the impossible memory of the past but is *at the very same time* spread out without roots in the archipelagic New World. This begins beginning in a cluster of horizontally interlinked and fractured times, spaces, and places—the final break initiated by the end of linear temporality. Glissant writes:

> Paralleling this mass of water, the third metamorphosis of the abyss thus projects a reverse image of all that had been left behind, not to be regained for generations except—more and more threadbare—in the blue savannas of memory or imagination. (PR, 7)

The loss of rights to loss, that trauma attuned to the absoluteness of the Middle Passage, arrives in the archipelago without rooted memory; the sea is history. The atavistic imagination, a fantasy of redemptions and returns, retreats to the savannas of memory, a phrase Glissant comes back to in *Une nouvelle region du monde*, replacing the "blue savannas of memory" with "afflicted savannas of memory" (NRM, 189). On either rendering, nostalgia is rootless, a savanna in the sense of a treeless plain, and arrival at the shoreline loses the rights to the loss of atavistic roots, relation, and memory. *Arrival as the wake of the abyss*. What, then, are we to make of this arrival? What does it make possible at the very moment when possibility seems to disappear?

At the site of arrival, the problem of beginning moves from a largely temporal question of trauma and loss to a question of what happens in the intersection of time and space: the production of *place*. As we shall see, the other beginning, the beginning of futures, is the place of Plantation, where border crossings are not transgressions but rather everyday fecund mixtures that give birth to the fragments that form a collective sense of the human—something, perhaps, that would have satisfied Frantz Fanon's famous call for a new humanism. The first site of this place, this moment of translation from traumatic past to fecund future, is the shoreline. Glissant describes the shoreline, a literal and mythical event, as having three crucial phases:

> Experience of the abyss lies inside and outside the abyss. . . .
> But their ordeal did not die; it quickened into this continuous/
> discontinuous thing: the panic of the new land, the haunting of the
> former land, finally the alliance with the imposed land, suffered
> and redeemed. *The unconscious memory of the abyss served as the*
> *alluvium for these metamorphoses.* (PR, 7; my emphasis)

Glissant puts all the pain and significance of history on this shoreline. The alluvium ensures that the abyss remains *inside*, just as the suffering and redemption of the land takes account of the meaning of survival and all that it creates: the new, the unexpected, *Caribbeanness*. Experience is therefore outside the abyss insofar as beginning begins, but it is also always inside the abyss. Memory, however impossible, is part of the womb of individual and collective life. The question is therefore how Glissant accounts for the passage from sea to shoreline to landscape without oblivion, which is to say, how a haunted geography produces a people against the disjunct of despair or forgetting. "Thus, the absolute unknown," Glissant writes in *Poetics of Relation*, "projected by the abyss and bearing into eternity the womb abyss and the infinite abyss, in the end became knowledge" (PR, 8).

Let us begin, then, with the question of ruins.

On the Legibility of Ruins

In *The Origins of German Tragic Drama*, Walter Benjamin makes a famous analogy between allegory and ruins. Allegory's ability to stand outside the economy of, say, beauty, yet still instruct us about the beautiful is akin to how ruins hold a precarious relation to the life of things. When one couples this claim with the rendering of the angel of history in "Theses on the Philosophy of History," wherein the angel contemplates the meaning of the pile of wreckage and the slow, deliberate accumulation of death in cultural treasures, one catches sight of Benjamin's fundamental presupposition: the legibility of the ruin. The legibility of the ruin is as much the legibility of history and historical experience, insofar as the ruin takes on meaning in relation to what *has been,* even as history stands aside from the ruin. Indeed, Benjamin links allegory, ruin, and history in the full context of this passage where he writes:

> And in this guise history does not assume the form of the process of an eternal life so much as that of irresistible decays. Allegory thereby declares itself to be beyond beauty. *Allegories are, in the realm of thoughts, what ruins are in the realm of things.*[3]

The ruin invests the world of things, just as allegory does in relation to thoughts, with something other, perhaps something *more* than the literal meaning of history's objects. This investment is open. The cultural treasure, as Benjamin argues in "Theses on the Philosophy of History," might conceal the pain of history and invite empathy with the victors. Or the ruin, as we saw in the previous chapter regarding the destruction of Carthage, might bear the sadness of salted earth and the wreckage of "progress." In either end of the ruin's possibility, there is always legibility. The ruin allows us to read history with another kind of significance, which, in turn, allows us to read history back into the ruin. The ruin and history's objects inflate with meaning in this dynamic, even chiasmic, movement.

This inflation of meaning, the super-addition to what is only a trace-remainder of the past, links the meaning of ruins to storytelling. There is a twofold movement here: if the ruin allows us to read history, then that reading of history is itself structured by a companion, perhaps prior, reading of the ruin itself. Who tells the story of the ruin? How is that story told? And how is the story of the ruin related to the drama of morality and collective memory? In his 1936 essay "The Storyteller," Benjamin writes:

> A proverb, one might say, is a ruin which stands on the site of an old story and in which a moral twines about a happening like ivy around a wall.
>
> Seen in this way, the storyteller joins the ranks of the teachers

and sages. He has counsel—not for a few situations, as the proverb does, but for many, like the sage.[4]

It is such a striking turn of phrase: "like ivy around a wall." With this image, Benjamin simply confirms the decorative function and effect of telling stories, to be sure, but with the important depth dimension carried by the moral terms "proverb" and "sage." Although he writes this with the ruin as an occasion, we might, with a bit of an abuse of the text, reread it with the ruin as center and with story, proverb, and sage as characteristics that cling to the remainder of history. That is, the reading of the ruin is not a random assertion of meaning. Rather, the wisdom of history is culled from the ruin when it is read as a proverb, the word itself as a kind of sage; this is no doubt part of the meaning of calling a ruin a sacred site. Benjamin is skeptical of this sort of reading. We see that in his "Theses on the Philosophy of History," where the angel of history bears witness to the pain of history. The pile of wreckage is initially a kind of counter-ruin to the reading of history as a story about victors and discovery, a movement against how a certain secular theodicy is imposed upon historical events in order to make pain and suffering vanish. At the same time, Benjamin, in the figure of the angel of history, is the reader who finds the great wisdom in history's pain and generates a proverb of sorts: there is another history, another sense of human drama that is not subject to dialectical resolution. In this sense it is important to keep in view how the angel of history functions as a character in a story about the ruins beneath the ruins of history. Benjamin is a master storyteller in this regard, jolting the conscience of the historian and theorist of time. Adorno's work on negative dialectics can in many ways be read as a meditation on Benjamin's rendering of the moral lesson of history's other.

The moral lesson of the ruin draws out the narrative that both overlays the ruined site and opens the (counter-)meaning of history. There are of course many more nuances to Benjamin's account, but what is especially important for our purposes here is how the ruin remains legible. That is, the storyteller has the power to make something visible in the ruin, to draw out the proverb, wisdom, and moral drama in history's remainder. Benjamin's "Theses on the Philosophy of History" might call into question the stories told by historicism and forms of historical materialism, but in relation to the wreckage of history as a counter-reading of the ruin he remains a teller of moral stories. And that story is in both the storyteller *and* the ruin. The ruin is readable, even if it is subjected to, as though to allegory, the inflation of sense and significance. Therein lies the force of his insight and the jolt it has on conscience and consciousness. Legibility remains the measure—the measure, that is, even after history's catastrophe, oblivion, and subsequent epistemological retreat into the contraction of ruins.

The shift to the Caribbean context of course shares important structural features with Benjamin's world, in particular his sense of a world that is constituted by a series of disasters, rather than a sense of progress without a slaughter-bench that jolts conscience. As well, and perhaps this is a more general claim about what it means to be historical, ruins function as a sign that translates the elements of time; ruins bear a past into the present, but are also always at the interval to a future. Ruins, storyteller, *poiesis*. And yet there is also a critical chasm between Benjamin's Europe and Glissant's Caribbean in terms of the structure and meaning of historical experience, experience in which trauma signifies and fails to signify in so many importantly different ways. The ruin must therefore be submitted to the geography of reason, not just in terms of what a particular ruin might signify but also, and even foremost, in terms of how history gathers itself into the ruins of landscape and language—those ruinous sites that bear impossible memory.

What, then, is the New World ruin? This is no small question. Benjamin makes the stakes of such a question clear: there is no future without an individual and collective relation to the ruin. Being or becoming historical makes such a relation irreducible, and this ontological claim becomes ethical at the very moment in which the storyteller takes on the unresolved and unresolvable pain of history. The ruin is a site of pain in the very same measure that it is a relay of historical experience and memory. Indeed, after Benjamin it is difficult to make any distinction between pain, history, and memory. So, then, a few transitional questions: How does the storyteller in the Caribbean context—going by names of the *poet*, the *intellectual*, the *historian* and so on—address the ruins of the New World's myriad shorelines in land, language, and collective identity? How does that address attempt to reactivate the ruin's past? And how does reactivation fail such that the ruin might instead signify a shift (or relay) from atavistic inquiry and values to a Chaotics of composite culture(s)? In this relay, this signifying *otherwise*, the ruin *as such* becomes the ruin of *this geos* in and through which futurity is imagined.

Let us restart here with a short reflection on Derek Walcott's conception of history, fragmentation, and the poetic. In both "The Antilles: Fragments of Epic Memory" and "The Muse of History," Walcott explicitly links the problem of history's future with the relation of a collectivity to ruins. Ruins signify the past at the very same moment that they gather the past into an interval to the future, which implicates a material condition of individual and collective memory in the movement of becoming. To become is to be stretched across the expanse of time—perhaps even torn apart by time—and that stretch is occasioned, perhaps even sustained, by the materiality of what Pierre Nora calls *lieux de mémoire*. *Lieux de mémoire*, on Nora's account, function very much like the ruin in Benjamin's reflections on allegory and thought: without the full presence of the past, the ruin, for better or worse, is vulnerable to the present and future. Collective memory becomes a projection of meaning onto the screen of what is largely constituted by absence. Memory is about the future. Perhaps memory is *for* the future.

But it is crucial for us to consider here how the lack of full presence, the absence that makes a ruin a ruin, functions in different contexts. That is, ruins come to significance in the appropriation of them by historical experience, wherein a subject, a community, or the peculiar intertwining of the two (the storyteller) gives a remnant of life to the ruins in a gaze that beholds them. Or, in the double-movement of appropriation and creation, one finds in composite occasions—language, meaning, the world—shards of a past either forgotten or, too often in the New World context, destroyed. The shards are found to already be operative, which means that the reading of ruins requires just as much analytical work as storytelling—if in fact such a tenuous distinction obtains. Every ruin tells a story, but the storyteller embellishes. What is embellishment? And how is embellishment linked to the geography of reason? In "The Antilles," Walcott both bemoans the paucity of *physical* ruins in the Antilles (reflecting the sadness of history) and draws our attention to the *cultural* ruins scattered across the landscape. That is, he interrogates the conditions that condition reading and embellishment. The force of ruins, for Walcott, lies in their ability to overwhelm landscape and pull our poetic intentions away from nostalgic contemplations of place, back toward the register and registering of History. This requires a fundamental rethinking of the relation between History and ruin, one attuned to the geography of reason. Walcott writes in a famous passage:

The sigh of History rises over ruins, not over landscapes, and in the Antilles there are few ruins to sigh over, apart from the ruins of sugar estates and abandoned forts. Looking around slowly, as a camera would, taking in the low blue hills over Port of Spain, the village road and houses, the warrior-archers, the god-actors and their handlers, and music already on the sound track, I wanted to make a film that would be a long-drawn sigh over Felicity.[5]

This film, this sigh of History that would make the ruins speak not just to a painful past but also to some kind of future, leads Walcott to articulate a kind of *créolité*. But that gets us ahead in our reflection. It is worth noting here, though, how Walcott's lists all the *pleasures* of Felicity, ranging from India to the Muslim epic to the Chinese Dragon Dance to the synagogue. The pleasures of Felicity are amid the ruins; none of the sites in his musing on Trinidad are products of transfer or transition. The ruinous is pain, of course, but there are the pleasures of Felicity. All sites are transformed by the painful histories of detour and deterritorialization; atavism is the first concept to vanish in shoreline thinking. The ruins, then, are as visible as they are invisible, begging in both cases for the storyteller's intervention as actor, dancer, musician, and adoring poet. The intervention, however, first asks for a pause, one on the order of the slow contemplation of the opening pages of *Poetics of Relation*, where the pain of the past takes breath away but then bequeaths to the thinker-storyteller another breath to steady the body and word. An inhale fills the chest, ready with the word, but then breathes back out with the irrecusable melancholy that comes with abyssal beginning. The thinker-storyteller exhales a sigh of History, over ruins. This is what it means to carry melancholy in your breath. To sigh. Whatever the pain of ruins—remnants of the Middle Passage, the Kālā Pānī, and other stories of loss, of mass displacement, of death and survival— there is also the capacity of the ruin to bear the past into the future. In that bearing there are the conditions of unexpected and unprecedented creation. "I am only one-eighth the writer I might have been," Walcott writes, "had I contained all the fragmented languages of Trinidad."[6]

In evoking language, Walcott of course evokes so much more that words. Fanon famously remarks in *Black Skin, White Masks* that "to speak . . . means above all to assume a culture, to support the weight of a civilization."[7] But whereas Fanon intended to underscore the debilitating alienation of the colonizer's language-world, Walcott's sigh over Felicity gathers what *survives* in the ruin at the same moment that the ruin bears unconditional witness to loss. This sigh-that-gathers puts the Caribbean mixture of language and world—what becomes *créolité* in the hands of Jean Bernabé, Patrick Chamoiseau, and Raphaël Confiant—at the center of thinking about ruins, memory, and history. But Walcott puts it there as a *project* of the storyteller; it is a question for Walcott of *becoming* Caribbean *through* the reading of ruins, rather than an ontology of fully accomplished mixtures and obvious or extant meanings of landscape. The landscape is ruinous, but what is the poet? The poet makes the ruin speak futurity. And so Walcott's reflections on ruin, fragment, and the archipelago in "The Antilles" lead him to his perhaps best-known statement on the labor of identity-making. Identity-making begins with ruins, sensitive to the pain and possibility borne by the very same sites of memory and history. Walcott is careful to place the poet inside the interval of past and future—between abysses, really—and so the creation of a future becomes a *remaking* of "fragmented memory." Ruins are fragments, yes, but ruins and fragments are also always in need of the poetic work of bringing forth, forming and reforming, and so a kind of beauty-making memory project that loves the past as much as the future. Love reassembles fragments. The sigh becomes the poet's fidelity to possibility. Walcott is worth quoting in full here:

> Break a vase, and the love that reassembles the fragments is stronger than that love which took its symmetry for granted when it was whole. The glue that fits the pieces is the sealing of its original shape. It is such a love that reassembles our African and Asiatic fragments, the cracked heirlooms whose restoration shows its white scars. This gathering of broken pieces is the care and the pain of the Antilles, and if the pieces are disparate, ill-fitting, they contain more pain than their original sculpture, those icons and sacred vessels taken for granted in their ancestral places. Antillean art is this restoration of our shattered histories, our shards of vocabulary, our archipelago becoming a synonym for pieces broken off from the original continents.[8]

The pain of history, even as it erases origins and seals the abyss as the sea, gives something for thinking the future. *Reassembles. Shows. Becoming.* The temporality of Walcott's claim here is the temporality of Glissant's creolization: the present folding toward, into, and through the future, working with assemblage and reassemblage as bequeathals of trauma, but here rendered, in the reckoning with ruins, a trauma folded into the future. Post-melancholy, while still melancholic. Not paradox, but fold and glue and refitted pieces of memory and history. The scars of Walcott's imagined cracked heirloom is the life of fragments and the life of world-making. Life born from the abyss, born from mass death and unspeakable suffering, but still life. And beauty. *Life goes on.* This is an obstinate temporality. It is also the poet's temporality.

What does it mean to figure birth as the production of fragments? What is that memory? And how does that memory, that birth canal of culture, fold futurity back into the past and the past back into the obstinacy of the future? The future always comes. That is the nature of time. If we live, tomorrow comes. What, then, are the conditions of becoming the Caribbean future *as* Caribbean and *as* Caribbeanness?

Plantation, Relation, Future

Glissant's conception of futurity is largely elaborated through the notion of Relation. Relation is in a certain sense a name for the poietic work of reassemblage evoked in Walcott's Nobel lecture. But it is also the scars. The scars are the temporality inherent in any sense of Relation; the past wounds the present, and scars only become visible in the movement of becoming. Becoming is radical in Glissant's work. It uproots everything and re-territorializes in the movement of deterritorialization. Becoming is not teleological. It is nomadic, errant, and full of detours and returns. Chaos. But becoming, the movement-principle of Relation, is also temporality. Becoming is the effect of an obstinate future. A future that always comes.

If Relation is in some sense the *accomplishment* of futurity, a nomadic relation to time and possibility, then we must raise the question of the abyssal beginning of Relation. What is the abyss to Relation? Beginning's abyss is abyssal because traumatic memory drowns the questions of origin. If the sea is history, then the sea is History. We begin, with Glissant, at the ocean floor with the regulative ideal of the ball and chain gone green— the deterioration of an absence which, in that deterioration, becomes less than absence, an absence whose vanishing removes the idea of measuring absence as absence in a relation to presence. Radical trauma. The Middle Passage changes everything. Thinking after the Middle Passage, in transit and arrival, is abyssal and fecund. This beginning has two sites: the womb of the slave ship and the roots of the Plantation.[9] The slave ship is a two-fold site of beginning. There is the erasure of the past in the ship, where memory loses intelligibility. There is also the difficult matter of life, which persists even after the erasure. What does it mean to have survived drown memory and, after that drowning, after that trauma, to have met the obstinacy of the future? That is, what does it mean to have arrived at the shore-line, then said yes to life on the Plantation?

The opening section of *Poetics of Relation* explores the image of the slave ship as womb. The image of the slave ship as womb is as terrifying as it is instructive, blending death, melancholy, and unspeakable suffering with birth, possibility, and the obstinate future. That is the thing about preg-nancy: no matter what you think or want to think, the child comes and becomes herself—born from you, womb, but also born from the world, its negotiations, and its intersecting catastrophes, resistances, creativity, will, and spastic dialectic of world-making. Glissant writes:

> For though this experience made you, original victim floating
> toward the sea's abysses, an exception, it became something shared
> and made us, the descendants, one people among others. People
> do not live on exception. Relation is not made up of things that are
> foreign but of shared knowledge. This experience of the abyss can
> now be said to be the best element of exchange.
>
> For us, and without exception, and no matter how much dis-
> tance we may keep, the abyss is also a projection of and perspective
> into the unknown. . . . And for this Relation made of storms and
> profound moments of peace in which we may honor our boats.
> (PR, 8–9)

Glissant here locates beginning before arrival. There are no ruins visible in the sea, nothing to invest with a meaning exceeding what remains, for the drowning of memory and meaning is absolute. Absence in the sense made by the Middle Passage.

And yet there is arrival. At this moment of arrival, Glissant asks the first question of roots. Namely, what is the relation between uprooting, lost roots, and survival? The sea is history—this tells us, at the very least, a story about roots that cannot survive except as the shoreline botanical, the mangrove. Glissant's repetition of the figure of the ball and chain gone green, drowning memory in the depths of the sea, alters our conception of survival. There is no carriage of memory; this is what it means to say the unity is sub-marine. Still, life goes on. Whatever the pain and sadness of history, life goes on, and the question of meaning, of the future, is as *open* as it is obstinate. This is key: the open. What is meant by *survival* therefore proves crucial. In *Caribbean Discourse,* Glissant distinguishes his conception of survival from a conception subject to the logic of *mimesis.* The ball and chain gone green deeply structures this characterization:

> I feel that what makes this difference between a people that survives elsewhere, *that maintains Being* [*l'Être*], and a population that is transformed elsewhere *into another people* (without, however, succumbing to the reductions of the Other) and that thus enters the constantly shifting and variable beginning again of Relation [*recommencée de la Relation*] (of relationship, of relativity), is that the latter has not brought with it, not collectively continued, the methods of existence and survival, both material and spiritual, which it practiced before its transport [*transbord*]. (CD, 15; translation altered)

Glissant is careful in this passage to mark a sense of futurity in relation to the erasure of memory and history, which distinguishes the experience of the Caribbean from, say, that of European Jews. He notes this as the distinction between enslavement and the slave trade and persecution and diaspora—that surviving-elsewhere "that maintains Being." It also marks one of the most important distinctions between Glissant and the Négritude movement, articulated here as the problem of conceiving beginning.

What is arrival? And what is survival? Maintaining being? Or transformation into another people? These questions revolve around conceptions of how we relate to history's pain and how or to what extent the force of traumatic historical experience puts the very notion of roots in question. Glissant sees this in the "crossings of histories" (*histoires entre-croisées*) that produce being (*l'étant*)—being here understood as survival:

> We abandon the idea of Being [*l'Être*]. One of the most terrible implications of the ethnographic approach is the insistence on fixing the object of scrutiny in static time, thereby removing the tangled nature of lived experience and promoting the idea of uncontami-

nated survival. . . . The history of a transported population, but one which elsewhere becomes another people, allows us to resist generalization and the limitations it imposes. (CD, 14)

In this sense of arrival, Glissant overturns conventional meanings of survival. That is, the idea of Being and survival is subjected to the process of creolization, even as survival in the Caribbean context will come to *also* describe the conditions under which creolization and creoleness both arise and thrive. Mimesis, on this account, is a name for alienation, and mixture is a name for Relation and creation of the new and unprecedented. If survival of the slave trade and slavery drowns historical experience, then the African root becomes a matter of traces mixed into the lived-experience of the New World rather than the foundation of identity.[10] *Histoires entre-croisées*. All the languages of Felicity. The fragments of Trinidad. Imitation of the colonizer produces the worst kind of repetition, one in which the colonized are always fated to failure. If nothing else, Fanon's *Black Skin, White Masks* has taught us that. Glissant puts it in stark and uncompromising terms when he writes that "the mimetic impulse is a kind of insidious violence. A people who submits to it takes some time to realize its consequences collectively and critically, but is immediately afflicted by the resulting traumatism" (CD, 18; translation altered). Traumatism here expresses the experience of unbridgeable, painful distance between one who thinks and the search for origins. While this is most evident in the case of the language of the colonizer or *métropole*, it is also true, for Glissant, of the fantasies of Négritude. No matter the complexity of his relation to that movement, Glissant, under the term *reversion*, marks the return to origins with this traumatism. Négritude repeats the pain, sublimating the pain in pursuit of what Fanon, in "West Indians and Africans," famously called "the black mirage."[11] *Memory is gone. There are only traces, and so much mixture. Atavism is repetition of the sadness of history, restaging Carthage and failing the ruins.* This is why Glissant is careful to distinguish the Négritude of Marcus Garvey and Aimé Césaire, for example, from African variations on the same. "The most obvious difference between the African and Caribbean versions of negritude," Glissant writes, "is that the African one proceeds from the multiple reality of ancestral yet threatened cultures, while the Caribbean version precedes the free intervention of new cultures whose expression is subverted by the disorder of colonialism" (CD, 24). Negritude can thus be said to leap over the abyss, forgetting the original mixture of *becoming another people*. As J. Michael Dash notes, Glissant's Caribbean is not Naipaul's shipwrecked and bleak archipelago.[12] *Survival means becoming elsewhere. The future is obstinate. Poetry over ruins makes a world.*

Left to itself, reversion finds aesthetic expression in the problem of imitation. Imitation reflects not only anxiety about origins and the *métropole*, but just as much, and perhaps more, a sensibility disconnected from how the elsewhere *has already become* a here. At this moment, the geography of reason works as critique. Glissant writes:

> As we have seen, however, populations transplanted by the slave trade were not capable of maintaining for any length of time the impulse to revert [*la pulsion de Retour*]. This impulse will decline, therefore, as the memory of the ancestral country fades ... Where that coming to terms [with the new land] is not only difficult, but made obscure [*obscurcie*] (the population having become a people, but a powerless one) the obsession with imitation will appear.
> (CD, 18; translation altered)

The fading of the ancestral country, which was carried by a memory traumatized by the Middle Passage, is abyssal; it leaves "the population having become a people" with a memory-root, a womb that is an abyss, which, in turn, creates the philosophical difficulty of accounting for the kinds of knowing and being that emerge with such an impossible origin. The challenge of the abyss, the enigma of beginning again from the abyss, makes imitation of Africa or of the *métropole*—two illusions, two forms of alienation—seductive. Glissant is never surprised by the compulsion to imitate. Imitation is seductive because it solves all of the anxieties of the New World and its womb-abyss, and yet, in Glissant's terrifying turn of phrase, it is an insidious violence. So we return to place and begin there.

What, then, are we to make of ruins?

Benjamin is right. His articulation of the connection between the ruin and the future, especially insofar as that connection is negotiated through collective memory, is a foundational truth of the becoming of peoples and landscapes of memory. Except that his turn of phrase is normative and located in a certain geography. That is, ruins *ought* to say more about things by investing them with the myths of collective memory, building history's story into the fragments of a disassembled past. Glissant's reflections on the failure of reversion, however, locate that normative claim in Europe or, more broadly cast, in a *continental* history. The ancestral is carried, not by the ruins of place, but by the memory and historical experience invested in them by the historian's or citizen's nostalgic gaze. What is the ruin after the abyss?

In writing with such pain and insight about Martinican ruins, Glissant produces a poetics of place that haunts the ruin with the impossible memory of the past. And yet that past, especially because its pain is not legible in the sense that Benjamin finds in the ruin, is always precarious. The beauty and pain of arrival, the abyss of another beginning, unsettle the shoreline precisely because the shoreline is the site and citation of beginning. The shoreline *says* the New World. But the ruin fades its legibility in the echoes of Gorée and the underground slave prisons—the sub-marine and sub-*terre* that are Caribbeanness-as-history in its two sites of beginning. Let us quote Glissant in full from *Caribbean Discourse*:

> In the Center, the literal undulations of the cane fields. The mountains are subdued and become hills. Ruins of factories lurk there as a witness to the old order of the plantations. Where the setting sun yawns, marking the difference between the northern mountains and the central plains, the ruins of the Dubuc Great House (Château Dubuc) where the slaves disembarked (an echo of the island of Gorée they left behind) and where slave prisons still lie hidden underground. What we call the Plain, into which the Lézarde River emptied and from which the crabs have disappeared. . . . The agitation of the beaches, forgetful of all who climbed the coconut trees, once trying to reach out to Toussaint Louverture in the land of Haiti. The salt of the sea claimed them. The whites of their eyes are in the glare of our sun. We come to a halt, not certain what slows us down at that spot with a strange uneasiness. These beaches are up for grabs. The tourists say they own them. They are the ultimate frontier, visible evidence of our past wanderings and our present distress. (CD, 10–11)

As with all authentic reckoning with ruins, Glissant mixes political anxieties of the present (which we will here set aside) with a reading of the haunted present. This panoramic view of the Martinican landscape is populated by sites of disappearance, some of which recall histories of domination and some of which recall what cannot be recalled. *The salt of the sea claimed them*—in this remark, Glissant identifies the interval between immemorial past and creolized future(s) as open, even at times voracious. Château Dubuc is just this interval, for in it all the pain of history and creative gestures of identity-making are cited, gathered, then set in destabilizing contact. A claim in two senses: to pull away into oblivion *and* to put under obligations.

It is worth recalling here how Glissant describes shoreline in *Poetics of Relation*. The shoreline is a site of deposit, remainder, and mixture—an alluvium that links the abyss to the transformation of the Middle Passage into a sense of place. If the landscape begins with the shoreline, which is precisely the geography of arrival, then the future made in the landscape-place of the New World figures alluvium as constitutive. *Caribbean Discourse* also links landscape to history, even to the point of making them equivalent. And so Glissant arrives at an enormously potent statement— with the last bit put, perhaps ironically, in parentheses:

> So history is spread out beneath this surface, from the mountains
> to the sea, from north to south, from the forest to the beaches.
> Maroon resistance and denial, entrenchment and endurance, the
> world beyond and dream.
> 　　(Our landscape is its own monument: the trace it signifies is
> located on the underside. It is all history.) (CD, 11)

Landscape is ruin. Like every ruin, it is structured by the trace, which then invites the intervention of historical narrative. The Caribbean historical narrative sets out, not from Benjamin's analogy of allegory, but from the abyss in order to arrive at place and the peculiar mixture of times and spaces that comprise the nonlinear constitution of beginning.

Poetics of Relation returns this set of problematics to the question of ruins and the Plantation. Ruins, with their "uncertain evidence, their extremely fragile monuments, their frequently incomplete, obliterated, or ambiguous archives" (PR, 65), contain the structure of the problem of beginning again after the abyssal beginning. The ruin of the Plantation, Glissant argues, is "one of the focal points for the development of present modes of Relation," for the Plantation merges trauma, loss, and beginning in a way that *produces*, rather than merely annihilates, the human:

Within this universe of domination and oppression, of silent or
professed dehumanization, forms of humanity stubbornly persisted. In this outmoded spot, on the margins of every dynamic,
the tendencies of our modernity begin to be detectable. Our first
attempt must be to locate just such contradictions. (PR, 65)

The contradiction of domination and persistence continues the theme
of survival that emerges from the shoreline thinking of traumatic origins.
Memory's abyss becomes, in the Plantation, the formation of another
memory, a first utterance of history and identity. I say "in the Plantation"
here because Glissant's account of memory, history, and futurity emerges
from a rendering of the internal dynamics—constitutive contradictions,
really—of Plantation life, which is not simply life *on* the Plantation.
Rather, the internal dynamic of contradiction, which traffics in life and
death at one and the same time, produces a future. The contradictions
between boundary and mixture, autarky and external contact, slaveholder
and slave, colonizer and colonized—all of which receive a bit of reflection
in *Poetics of Relation* and elsewhere—can never hold. There is always what
Glissant calls the "unretractable breakdown [*coupure irrattrapable*]" (PR,
66) of distinction. Saint-John Perse and William Faulkner provide for
Glissant literary attestation to such a claim. What is limiting about *marronage,* for example, is its inability to think about the existential conditions
and effects of futurity on the formation of subjectivity, choosing instead
flight at expense of the beginning again *with* history's pain. Glissant is no
theorist of *marronage* and in fact is a profound critic. The Plantation is "dependent, by nature, on someplace elsewhere" (PR, 67), a claim that both
fragments the identities putatively set and kept apart in contradiction and
mixes the contradictory elements, however painfully and however curi-
ously, in the inevitable breaches of the system. *Une coupure irrattrapable.*

Now, this particular feature of the Plantation gives some important
contour to Glissant's anti-system rhetoric. It is not simply that systematic
thought privileges one constellation of ideas above another, or that it forgets what is other in the compulsion to articulate coherence against chaos,
but rather that the Caribbean geography of reason functions otherwise.
In the context of the Plantation, this functioning otherwise has two features. First, the problem of *marronage,* the fraught option of flight. It is important to say that Glissant does not simply dismiss *marronage,* no matter

its connection (at the figurative level) to Négritude, for *marronage* is in a certain sense a way of saying yes to opacity. Glissant underscores how the movement from "historical *marronage*" to "creative *marronage*" emerges as a doubled discourse, one that says yes to opacity and affirms that it is "no longer possible to consider these literatures as exotic appendages of a French, Spanish, or English literary corpus" (PR, 71). So, *marronage* is anticolonial and breaks with the problem of imitation. This is an important move. At the same time, creative *marronage* has as its "concern," "driving force," and "hidden design" in what Glissant calls "the derangement of the memory which determines, along with imagination, our only way to tame time" (PR, 71). In an important way, then, nostalgia permeates creative *marronage* insofar as it hearkens back to or yearns for a linear time—a time Glissant identifies as constitutive of the hegemony of the white West and, in the end, poorly fitted to the experience of the New World. Creative *marronage* is not an abyssal beginning. In the taming of time and the derangement of (traumatic) memory, there is only realignment against and suppression of the abyssal beginning of not just New World *poetics* but New World *existence* (individual and collective). It cannot account for the creolization that makes Caribbeanness both a force of cultural production and an identity.

To creative *marronage*, Glissant apposes the "*djobber* of the collective soul" (PR, 69). I say *apposes* here, rather than *posits* or *opposes*, in order to emphasize Glissant's commitment to Relation. That is, the apposition of creative *marronage* and the *djobber* of the collective soul mixes and transforms both terms, accomplishing the fundamental positivity of Relation. The commitment to opacity in creative *marronage* is taken on by the *djobber* of the collective soul in the storyteller's creation of oral literature. Oral literature makes language into language-as-world-creating, divine really, which, for Glissant, is nothing other than making identity on the shoreline. In so making identity, the *djobber* of the collective soul creolizes out of the fragments found *in* and *on* the Plantation, one of which is a sense of flight that is inseparable from survival and beginning. This is the appositive moment. Glissant writes:

> The oral literature of the Plantations is consequently akin to other
> subsistence—survival—techniques set in place by the slaves and
> their immediate descendants. Everywhere that the obligation to
> get around the rule of silence existed a literature was created that
> has no "natural" continuity, if one may put it that way, but, rather,

bursts forth in snatches and fragments. The storyteller is a handy-man, the *djobber* of the collective soul. (PR, 69)

The limit of creative *marronage*, then, lies in its commitment to a sense of natural continuity. The trauma of the Middle Passage, as we have seen, is understood by Glissant to have broken any sense of the natural and of continuity, which is why he describes the *geos* of the Caribbean as "tortured." But what is tortured is also beginning's engagement with the abyss. This produces the possibility of being *after*. This is how apposition and the pain of history create, in and on the Plantation, another beginning after beginning's abyss.

If the Plantation supplants *marronage* in Glissant's account of beginning, then the creolized and creolizing landscape of the New World comes to perform two roles. First, the Plantation names the space that, with the infusion of the fractured times of arrival, becomes the place of beginning again after abyssal beginning. The landscape and its language-identity formations, de-formations, and re-formations embodies the depth of shoreline thinking—the becoming of beings in the New World. Second, the Plantation is a source of resistance to the aftermath of Plantation life: colonialism and urbanization. *The Plantation labors against the métrople at every turn.* When paired, colonialism and urbanization seize upon memory and bury it like so many stories about origins, and thereby give what Glissant calls "impossible memory" a "dark side" of threatened oblivion (PR, 72). The Plantation passes into the literature of the City in language, but it is made all the more precarious by the vertigo produced by urbanity and modernization. Now, Glissant is not advocating a romanticized remembrance of or return to rural life; despite moments in his poetry, he is no pastoral thinker. Rather, it is a matter of fidelity to abyssal beginning. Glissant reads the traces of Plantation in language and identity in order to remember what it means to begin, to have begun, and therefore to build memory into theorizing the trajectory of becoming. A whole cluster of issues arise here concerning subjectivity, aesthetics, and the responsibilities of the intellectual, which we will here set aside for subsequent chapters. However, in thinking futurity and trauma together, it is important to see how the trajectory of becoming and the problem of beginning are intimate companions. The passage from beginning to becoming, and all the traces that structure both movements, prove crucial for the creation of language and world. In *La cohée du Lamentin*, Glissant writes:

Fractal unravelings of a kind of speech [*parole*], its rhetoric, its
broken sequences—forming a literature of the Plantation and a literature of the City [*Ville*]. It appears today as a literature of *passage*,
not of *transition*, but of a saying-between [*entre-dire*]—occupying
the distance that goes from the original plantation (countryside,
animals of the night, spirit-ghosts [*soucougnans*] of the morning, never ending mosquitoes) to urban diffraction, suddenly
so vertiginous and about which no one can speak ahead of time
[*pré-dire*]—a gaping literature, but one that . . . [follows] the path
from Plantation to Metropolis [*Metropolis*]. (CL, 103)

Glissant here draws a weave of relations between shoreline thinking,
opacity, creolization, and becoming. To begin, the *parole* of literature—
tantamount in this context to the beginning of identity—is fractal, composed of irregular and unforeseen shapes and their chance arrangements.
Let us recall, here, the relationship between fractal geometry and one
of its critical applications: the mapping and measure of coastlines and
mountain ranges, at once shoreline thinking and *marronage*. *Parole* is un-
raveled, not because of loss, but because of the irregular movement at
the shoreline, then in the Plantation, and finally in the movement to the
Metropolis. The movement to the City (*Ville*) is itself a diffraction, another
appeal to a figure from science that underscores how the fractal movement of *parole*—broken sequences from shoreline to mountain range to
Metropolis—modifies language and identity as it passes through opacities. Diffraction of light, which modifies light in contact with the borders
and surfaces (not interiors) of opaque bodies, nicely describes Glissant's
account of how creolization is a passage that works *against* conventional
models of transition. Diffraction distorts, bends, and chaotically reconfigures, whereas transition *promises* (even if it cannot realize) the preserva-
tion of what is prior in what is later. Sighs over history, love that bonds
fragments, the poet of all the languages—creolization is the logic of thinking the past and present, the ruin, really, in an interval to the future.

Traces and Melancholy

One of the questions that might arise from Glissant's account of the Plantation, mixture, contradiction, and beginning concerns the relation be-

tween the history of slavery and the colonial relation. The two cases are very different. The history of slavery is the lived experience of Plantation's mixture, the birth-space of creole language and cultural forms, and so the marrow of Caribbeanness, whereas colonialism threatens to dominate that mixture with the model of assimilation and what Fanon simply called "measure." The ruin is crucial at this moment. Colonialism reinvents the present. After colonialism, haunting and reassembly. Sincere ambivalence. How does the ruin resist? And how does the ruin's resistance summon the poet of Caribbeanness?

"Faulkner's landscapes," Glissant writes in *Faulkner, Mississippi*, "are suffused with a fragrance of mauve, with a power of melancholy" (FM, 106). The invocation of melancholy here suggests memory and trauma. Freud famously argues in "Mourning and Melancholia" for a distinction between the mournful subject and the melancholic subject on the basis of the object of loss. In traumatic experience, something is lost, which leaves the surviving subject broken in parts. What is our relation to that brokenness? How do we respond to loss? The mournful subject identifies the lost object, perhaps through the intervention of therapy, and begins the process of working through the difficulty of life after loss. Melancholia, however, is considerably more enigmatic and wholly intransigent. The process of working through loss requires considerable flexibility in the traumatized subject, something that begins (at least as a possibility) with the identification of the object lost. The melancholic subject cannot identify the lost object. The melancholic suffers without a narrative about *what* was lost and, without that narrative, the recovery from loss happens almost by fiat. Perhaps this is Freud's sense of abyssal beginning, writ small.

To melancholy, Glissant here couples the suffusion of fragrance. If Glissant's is a shoreline thinking and rooted (in a deterritorialized sense) in the geography of reason, a way of thinking that is not just attentive but structured by the memory and history of place, then we should not be surprised to see the sensuality of *geos* linked to the meaning of thought. Glissant writes:

> It is easy enough for me to differentiate this smell from that of *vezou*, the scent of fermenting sugarcane that bathed the country-side of my childhood which I can call up at will even now, when the distillery boilers no longer exist in the country.

> The two smells are similar enough to become superimposed,
> one in memory (*vezou*), the other in imagination, without their
> becoming confused. (FM, 106)

This bit of autobiography is revealing, for it identifies the sensuality of landscape with both memory and imagination. This double identification places landscape between past and future—between the origin of the poet and what poetry might make of what is to come, might say about what will (and can) be said. For, as he makes clear in *Poetics of Relation* and elsewhere, Glissant's sense of the imaginary is a primary site or even engine of creolization. It is where new registers and mixtures of meaning *become* out of the imagining of other possibilities. In the first prefatory note to *Poetics of Relation,* Glissant writes:

> Thinking thought usually amounts to withdrawing into a dimen-
> sionless place in which the idea of thought alone persists. But
> thought in reality spaces itself out into the world. It informs the
> imaginary of peoples, their varied poetics, which it then trans-
> forms, meaning, in them its risk becomes realized. (PR, 1)

Thinking and the word are spaced out across the world, making and re-making the people. He writes further:

> Thought draws the imaginary of the past: a knowledge becoming.
> One cannot stop it to assess it nor isolate it to transmit it. It is shar-
> ing one can never not retain, nor ever, in standing still, boast about.
> (PR, 1)

The imaginary, then, even when it reaches to the past for instruction—and here Glissant is rehearsing his critique of the Négritude movement—finds itself thrown back into a future. Césaire's version of Négritude wrestled with this problem, wondering how to affirm the unicity of particular cultures in the archipelago while also evoking and provoking the vital urges and possibilities in imagining Africanness. That is, Césaire wondered about the relationship between atavistic and composite models of culture.

Atavism is for Glissant drown memory, survived in the fragments and scars we find in reassembled cultural forms and expressions. That is one of the first lessons, as it were, of the Middle Passage. It is trauma's catastrophic teaching. But composite cultural practice, which is both an assessment of Caribbeanness and a normative claim about the emancipatory dimensions of cultural formation, is that moment in which trauma moves from a story about the dead to a story about the living. Traumatic memory as *histoire* in both senses: history and the story told and to be told. In *Faulkner, Mississippi*, for example, Glissant brings his distinction between atavistic and composite cultures to bear on Faulkner's long story about Yoknapatawpha County, and this story is instructive for conceiving the meaning of abyssal beginning:

> *Composite* cultures were created with western expansion and out of the mingling of many contradictory atavistic cultures. They do not generate their own creation story but content themselves with adopting myths from the atavistic cultures. For composite cultures, colonial expansion has no way of becoming naturally legitimate; it must find other "reasons." (FM, 115)

This search for "other reasons," which nicely blends both the necessity of landscape and *geos* with thinking and accounting for one's existence, is nothing other than Glissant's notion of Relation. Relation is both made by and makes the reasons of cultural formation, and in that making transforms atavistic myths into fragments and life.

Further, in the slow reflection that begins *Faulkner, Mississippi*, Glissant makes a curious and important association of memory with scent. He begins the work with a consideration of Faulkner's home, Rowan Oak, namely, what has become of it as it moves from a place of suffering history and writing to a place where "newlyweds spend their honeymoons" (FM, 12). Glissant is not making a mere racial or cynical quip here; there is actually a lot at stake. The manicured lawns and period furniture fundamentally transform space and time. "There is no trace of the slave shacks," he writes, "which would have been alongside the outbuildings and grounds. Everything has been cleaned, sanitized, pasteurized" (11). And just a bit later, Glissant revisits the sentiment when he writes: "Here, memory is selective, 'made objective,' rid of the whiff of slavery" (12; translation altered). On the one hand, this last remark is a figure of speech— the whiff of slavery—but it is one that nicely plays on both the crucial role of landscape in thinking about memory and the notion of trace. Scent gives contour to history and memory without making itself visible. Scent

capable of entering the body without announcing itself beforehand. We
are, after all, often surprised, even startled by scents. It appears in the body
as having already traveled from the exterior to the inner (olfactoric) life of
the subject. History's pain is in this sense pungent and haunting at one and
the same time. Rowan Oak makes memory precarious precisely because it
sanitizes and pasteurizes. As well, it is worth noting, scent concerns traces;
the passing of a person or a thing leaves a trace by leaving a scent. Indeed,
in French, *relents* (whiff) and *trace* (trace) are companion terms in an idiomatic register.

What, then, is the trace in Glissant's work? This is no simple question.
In his theoretical work Glissant often evokes the term, then collapses it
back into a cluster of related problematics rather than isolating it for de-
tailed treatment. And yet the thought of trace is crucial for understanding the problem of beginning and how it draws the past into the future.
As well, the trace provides an important site for understanding how profoundly the experience of the Middle Passage transforms the sense of
traces one finds in the European context. Emmanuel Levinas and Jacques
Derrida, for example, place the trace at the center of meaning. In their
treatment(s), the very idea of experience is dismantled and destabilized.
For Levinas, this leads to the transcendence of the ethical. For Derrida,
this splits any conception of meaning with deferral and delay. Now,
while both Levinas's and Derrida's notions of *la trace* resonate with Glissant's, the decisive difference lies, as always, in historical experience. The
ruin—or more generally the memorial object—sites and cites the trace,
which means that the trace must always for Glissant be thought in terms
of the geography of the Caribbean. Traces across the shoreline, but also
across the Plantation's boundaries—the trace is always linked to passage.
Passage, however, must be understood as informed by an opening onto
possibility, rather than, as with Europe's theoretical decadence, merely the
negation of possibility. In *Philosophie de la relation*, Glissant writes:

> The thought of the trace, on the edge of the desolate fields of the
> memorial object [*souvenir*], seeks the memories [*memoires*] linked
> in the components of the *tout-monde*. The thought of language
> and languages, that in which the play of the imaginary is decided
> for humanity. I write in the presence of all the world's languages.
> The echoes and obscurities and silences resound, one to the other.
> (PhR, 80)

Trace and ruin therefore share a critical intimacy. In much the same manner that the ruin exceeds its mere appearance and reveals something about the present and future in our articulation of its meaning, the trace inhabits the fringes of the memorial object. Like the ruin, the trace is fragile, precarious. The trace *seeks*, which is to say, the trace forges connections in order to find itself at home in *tout-monde*. Like Relation—or perhaps as the *dynamic source* of Relation—the trace operates by way of relay and deferral, mixing memory, knowing, and errancy between the known and unknown, forming Glissant's (largely) non-psychoanalytic sense of the unconscious.

At this moment, Glissant's conception of the trace gets quite close to the same in Levinas, as well as Derrida's conception of *différance*, both of which put time and space out of joint, not by way of critique, but by way of the time and space of life. Not unlike Levinas and Derrida, Glissant conceives the trace as an anti-systematic element in thinking, seeking to wrest the thought of the trace free of the language of origins; the trace is radical insofar as it is thought in an uprooted sense, never referring in any explicit or particularly helpful way back to an origin. Yet, and this is crucial, Glissant also insists on the productive character of the trace remains of *marronage* and the mixed experience in the Plantation. "Creole languages," Glissant writes, "are traces" (TTM, 19), which means not just that creole languages, dance, and music—so, cultural forms more generally—are composed of multiple linguistic strands, but more crucially that creole *becomes*, is creoli*zing*, because the trace structures according to an anti-systematic logic. (This is why Glissant hesitates before the term *créolité*. Fidelity to the anti-systematic thought of the trace.) And so Glissant will describe the trace as a *route* (TTM, 19), something that moves "into the land (*terre*)" without ever making that land into a territory. Land is never a matter of possession. In other words, the trace is what allows Glissant to see ruins and the past as sites and signs of knowing, but always without reading those ruins in order to possess secure, legible meaning. Impossible memory, the pain of history, builds an irreducible deferral and errancy into the ruin. The trace keeps the ruin precarious without eschewing the possibility of knowing (*savoir*). Trace is life is Caribbeanness. And so, in *Traité du tout-monde*, Glissant will write:

> Fragile knowing is not an imperious science. Let us see what happens when we follow a trace.
>
> Here is my second proposition:

That the thought of *the trace*, by opposition to the thought of the system, affixes itself like an errancy that focuses. We come to know that the trace is what puts us, all of us, from wherever we come, in Relation.

However, the trace was lived by some, over there, so far and near, here-there, on the hidden face of the earth, as one of the places of survival. For example, for the descendants of Africans deported in slavery, in what would soon be called the New World, the trace was the generally the only possible recourse. (TTM, 18–19)

The trace, at the shoreline site of beginning, is survival. Glissant reminds us here that Relation is inseparable from pain. An interval that makes time haunting, yes, but also one that transforms trauma for the sake of the life, not the death (social or otherwise), of the living.

The shift from continental thinking—with its presumption of a certain form of linear time, even when time is ruptured or fractured—to archipelagic thinking—which begins with fragmentation and dispersion—proves decisive for understanding the trace in relation to opacity. The simultaneity or crossing of relay and deferral—*errancy*, in a word—that defines the trace and Relation fundamentally transforms the general meaning of becoming in the Americas, and specifically *becoming Caribbean*. Beginning in the originary mixture of the Plantation, otherness and self are not opposed; identity—whether of self, of other, or of the space we share—is always a betrayal of opacity. Beginning and knowledge are akin to becoming and learning, and the thought of the trace works *with* and *through* the Plantation's fragments. In the Plantation, as we have seen, the trace is not *less than*, but the full and rich *condition for the possibility of*. "The trace," Glissant writes in *Traité du tout-monde*,

> does not represent an unfinished feeling in which, without recourse, one falters, nor is the trace an alley-way closed upon itself, bordering a territory. The trace goes into the land [*terre*], which will never be territory. The trace is the opaque manner of learning the branch and the wind: to be oneself, derived from the other. It is the sand in the true disorder of utopia.
>
> The thought of the trace allows us to go well beyond the entanglements of a system. (TTM, 20)

This passage irreversibly marks the problem of the trace with a Caribbean geography of reason. The sand of the shoreline is evoked in order to plot the *geos* of memory; at once discrete and whole, utopia—that not-a-site site—becomes a place disordered, yet still land. It is possible, as Glissant says of the maroon, to move across the land in a way that disputes and refutes the claims of territorialization. *The refusal to be enslaved is a refusal of territory's political, existential claim on the body.* As well, by dislocating the thought of the trace from territory, Glissant deepens our account of abyssal beginning by sealing the trace off from any relation to territory that would become a single root. Sealed off from territory, and thus never understood as a derivation or faded copy of it, land becomes a place in which traces can bear pain and beauty—survival—such that memory, history, and life become possible outside the regret and the sadness of nostalgia.

The relation of trace to the logic of imitation is critical for understanding the relationship between memory and beginning. Memory's fragrance, its tendency toward an ambivalent pungency that both repels with pain and draws in with the force of composite meanings, tempts us to understand or model the trace on a mimetic economy. But there is an important distinction to be made between the trace and the trail. The French term *la trace* runs both terms together, offering perhaps first and foremost a definition/translation that aligns *la trace* with the sorts of trails left by a fleeing creature. *La trace* as *trail* is wholly atavistic, supposing from the outset a transparent origin that, with a certain ingenious method, one could retrieve. This ingenious method, the dream of Négritude, is exactly what distinguishes a skilled tracker from a lost hiker: the ability to follow a trail to its origins. It is precisely this sense of *la trace* that Glissant—just like Levinas and Derrida—rejects, opting instead for the sense of *la trace* as *mark*. The trace leaves a mark, but never a mark that contains within it the possibility of reactivating origins. This is why it was important for us to theorize the ruin earlier, given the importance of traces in the ruin for understanding the relay and detour of historical experience. Glissant's notion of the trace as mark is defined by its movement across the sorts of creative and creating acts that comprise futurity, or what he calls in numerous places "accumulation." If the logic of accumulation helps Glissant gain distance from the logic of repetition, then the logic of the trace is what keeps memory and history entangled with accumulation. The trace, Glissant writes in *Une nouvelle region du monde,* resists researches concerned with transparency (and, can we say it, *analysis?*), but it still approaches magnetic connections. Its fragility is what makes its resistance and its fleeting nature [*fugacité*] guarantee its duration [*durée*]. The trace moves across our accumulations, our assonances, our repetitions, our circularities. The trace does not consent to the cunning economies of expression, in the sense that it does not authorize literal replication of our realities, those duplicates with neither opening nor invention. (NRM, 188)

The trace, then, is the very interval we have been seeking in this chapter: the site of the interlacing of past and future. That is, the trace labors against a conception of the recurrence of the past—so critical for thinking about intervals of time—that would root the past in a single, knowable origin. There is no pure repetition in a time structured by the trace. Every repeat is also a difference. *The repeating island.* Glissant argues that this eschewing of repetition does not, however, break the past off from the present and the future. To the contrary, the trace carries the past in unexpected and unforeseen ways, showing up in language, aesthetics, and various other cultural forms (Glissant will often take note of jazz or syntax in his discussion of the trace). And the trace, in this peculiar, non-atavistic interval, is also what opens the future as opening and makes invention a possibility. *Poiesis.* The trace, we could say, works according to a strange sense of passivity-as-superactivity in which it *moves across* the accumulations of composite culture—accumulations that make futurity—without commanding, directing, or *rooting* those accumulations. Glissant's trace is therefore ghostly, pungent, and compelling. One never grasps the origins of the trace. One rather registers how the trace makes an unexpected appearance. The creative act of making futurity is therefore concerned with traces, asking always what it would mean to welcome the ghost of the past, to say yes to its pain and pleasure both. The task, we might say, is a matter of conceiving what it means to say yes to the ghost without the atmosphere and resonance of colonial anxieties serving as the precondition of that coming-to-presence.

What, then, of melancholy? If the trace enables a certain relation to land that neither transports a prior world nor establishes a rooted identity in order to make earth into territory, and that sense of survival engages the trace in order to begin without nostalgia, then Glissant's evocation of the fragrant power of melancholy presents a bit of an enigma. Is it pos-

sible to think melancholy without nostalgia—that yearning for a continent or territory, and so for a beginning without abyss? In other words,
what is a melancholia structured around trace and archipelago? We can
here distinguish between two forms of melancholy, I think. First, there is
the melancholy of atavistic nostalgia, which presupposes the single origin
and then finds traumatic experience overwhelms memory of that origin.
On this account, which can be drawn from Freud's "Mourning and Melancholia," melancholia is produced by the inability of the traumatized
subject to identify the lost object. Even as melancholia is distinguished
from mourning in terms of the latter's ability to identify the lost object,
the economy of melancholic subjectivity proceeds from the logic of object
identification—melancholia is defined as the *failure* to do what the psyche
ought and *wants* to do. Glissant's nuance, which separates the trace from
the idea of territory, asks us, by implication, to think melancholia otherwise. And so we must imagine a second sense of melancholia, the melancholy of an abyssal beginning, a melancholy that operates in relation to
the abyssal beginning in the past but is affected always in the horizontality
of passage—from one composite element to another. The pain of history
passes in this sense.

Abyssal Beginning

We have seen above how the Plantation functions as a site of beginning.
The *djobber* of the collective soul makes identity in the creolized and creolizing space of the New World, keeping alive in and sustaining life with orality and its impossible memory. In our treatment of these matters above,
the primary focus was on the sense of return—on how, for Glissant, the
opacity of the original sources of beginning again renews anticolonial
struggle in saying yes to what confounds systematic thought and surpasses
any attempt to gather under a single story about History.

But there is also this problem of beginning again. The Plantation is not
just a historical factor or intervention in the movement of peoples. Rather,
and this is crucial, the Plantation is *cosmological*. It is the birth of an entire *cosmos* out of the pain of history and the vicissitudes of survival. Were
survival merely *marronage*, and so structured by retrieval and animated
by nostalgia and naturalness, then the Plantation would work *against* the
creation of a world. And yet Glissant is clear and makes a convincing case
that, as it is structured as an *idea,* the Plantation fails. It fantasizes a *here*

without relation to an *elsewhere*, but the elsewhere is persistent in its intervention in the here, and the here is drawn into the elsewhere by proximity and contact. The failure of the Plantation lies in its efforts to flatten time. But time is ecstatic, looping, and fractal when spaced across the world. Neither separation nor *marronage* is pure. This impurity is a matter of birth, origin, and so of the creation of a world—something characteristic of the very word *Americas*. Glissant writes:

> The Plantation is one of the bellies of the world, not the only one, one among so many others, but it has the advantage of being able to be studied with the utmost precision. Thus, the boundary, its structural weakness, becomes our advantage. And in the end its seclusion has been conquered. The place was closed, but the word derived from it remains open. This is one part, a limited part, of the lesson of the world. (PR, 75)

The belly of the world. This turn of phrase of course recalls the meditations on the slave ship with which Glissant begins *Poetics of Relation*, asking in those passages how beginning is possible in relation to traumatic experience. The Plantation asks the same question, here in the context of survival and the persistence of language and meaning in a place where boundaries fail and where closure, contrary to its deepest intentions, actually facilitates mixture of opacities.

In this context, then, we can begin to register the significance of Glissant's use of the term *digenesis* (*digenèse*) in *Traité du tout-monde*. The term nicely divides itself, self-dismantling in a manner both critical and fecund. The critical dimension lies in the contradiction of the very idea of genesis. Glissant's sustained critique of the notion of single origin, which he consistently identifies as both the foundation of European imperial violence (at times, even, any genocidal violence whatsoever) and the diversionary tactic of New World anticolonial work in Négritude, resists any easy sense of generating meaning, any linear conception of genesis. The division that *di* enacts upon its conjoined term *genesis* is thus important precisely because it forces us to think through the problem of beginning as mixed and split and chaotic, rather than pure, conceptual space. The experience of the Middle Passage, then the border crossing in and on the Plantation, requires such a shoreline thinking. The fecund dimension lies in how *digenesis* compels a rethinking of beginning as the persistence of possibility in survival; history's violence is borne by an impossible memory, and that memory makes a world. Even the slave ship is a womb. Destruction is never pure or absolute, nor is survival driven by nostalgia and reactivation. Loss arrives at the shore, then, in the Plantation. *Contact is cosmology*— this is everything. Glissant writes in *Traité du tout-monde*:

> The putting of atavistic cultures into contact in spaces of coloniza-tion has given birth, in those places, to composite cultures and societies, which are not generated by Genesis (adopting the Myths of Creation that come from elsewhere), and for that reason their origin does not lose itself in the night, which is obviously of the historical and non-mythic order. The Genesis of creole societies of the Americas melt themselves [*se fond*] on another obscurity [*obscurité*], that of the belly of the slave ship. This is what I call a digenesis.
>
> In coming to terms with the idea of digenesis, you grow accus-tomed to its example, you take leave of the impenetrable demand of the excluding unicity [*unicité excluante*]. (TTM, 36)

Glissant here takes stock of the manifold effects of digenesis in order to arrive at an entirely other intellectual sensibility. *Se fond* becomes *se fonde* in the cosmological moment, and this melting-become-founding is po-sitioned to make claims on our sensibility. Sensibility is overturned by the zigzag movement of a genesis that births a melting and a melting that births a genesis. Double movement, a certain creolized *différance* at or as the beginning. The cosmological function of the slave ship—which, as we have seen, then gives way to the Plantation as the second beginning— reformats the logic of beginning as a *composite* beginning. The abyss seals the composite off from atavistic myths of creation without characterizing abyssal beginning as lost or adrift. Composite culture is beginning as *be-coming*, a cosmos that is both unprecedented and incapable of setting the sort of precedent that typically ground myths of creation and beginning. Precisely because abyssal beginning forges a future without precedent, ever wedded to the emergent and new, beginning requires climate, habit, and habitation—all are constitutive of beginning again and making a home in an atmosphere that must be thought otherwise.

The meaning of a New World or Caribbean cosmology, then, con-sists of elaborating these conditions as figures of birth. The conditions are clear: traumatic loss in the Middle Passage, evacuation of collective memory, border crossing in the Plantation, and the sincere ambivalence of ruins. The figure for this cosmology is important, especially at the interval between the Middle Passage and the Plantation. This interval sites the relation of loss and birth. Both are at stake and co-implicated. In her *Orphan Narratives*, Valérie Loichot reads this moment of beginning in terms of the figure of the orphan. The word *orphan* is particularly helpful in this context, because it operates nicely as a noun, adjective, and verb. One can characterize Glissant's work as concerned with *an* orphan, an orphaned geography, or, in its various transformations, as orphaning those terms one might initially couple to single-origin thinking. The term *genesis*, for example, undergoes just such orphaning in the term *digenesis*—a term Loichot says "best encompasses [Glissant's] notion of beginning."[13] With the figure of the orphan, Loichot is able to construct a compelling and convincing story about Glissant's literary work. Glissant's novels are largely concerned—obsessively so, in the case of a text like *Le quatrième siècle* or *La case du commandeur* (Loichot's focal text)—with genealogy and fathers, asking how it is that identity is already creolized in the passage of generations, as well as how that creolization is variously effected and affected by colonialism, emergent conflicts inside the experience of modernity, and urgent political matters revolving around the question of departmentalization. Loichot writes the problem of familial relation large in order to show how Glissant's preoccupation with fragmentation is also a preoccupation with origins more generally. The orphan narrative trope, which Loichot describes as concerned with "modes of transmission," captures nicely how a futurity conceived without a single origin is still saturated with contact, connection, and multiple, rhizomatic roots; filiation and creolization operate in an orphaned space. The emerging narratives are always precarious, but, in that precariousness, also always open to the transformative effect of Relation and the critical function of opacity.

It is precisely this imperative of creation and its wholly human cosmological initiative that accounts for Glissant's persistent return to the figure of the *djob*. Is the *djob* an orphan? In the sense Loichot gives to the orphan, especially in the coupling of that term to the production of story and history, the *djob* is a kind of orphaned figure. At the same time, the *djob* plays a slightly different role. The orphan initiates narrative and sets out the labor and production of meaning in filiation, which accords to the orphan a certain authority in making relations between disparate and diverse parts. When Glissant describes the origins of *djobs* and the *djob-ber* in *Poetics of Relation*, he walks a (nuanced) line between the historical production *of* the *djob* and the production of the history of the same. To wit: in the post-Plantation moment (industrialization) there comes "the widespread development of small occupations, or what is referred to in the Antilles as *djobs*, a habitual economy of bits and scraps" (PR, 65). Glissant writes:

> The *djobber* has his secret, which is to invent life at every bend in
> the road. He crafts his rhetoric with a code reserved solely for its
> practitioners, but with an exuberance that splatters far and wide.
> His speech exalts an optimism that in its daily throbbing pulse
> almost becomes a kind of wizardry. The market, his natural habitat,
> is altogether the prodigious belly of the world. (WS, vii)

"Wizardry" and "market" offer important qualifiers to any notion of the orphan and his story. Whereas the orphan, by way of fiction and alternative modes of filiation, forges unexpected narratives, the *djobber* both *finds* himself and *makes* himself a home in the market; the bustle and exchange of difference *is* the meaning of the story, rather than the story that reconciles Chaos. Filiation and narrative, in the figure of the orphan, have to be understood as sustained by contradiction. The relay and deferral structure of Relation, underwritten as it is by the irreducible character of opacity, halts any pretension of narrative. The "kind of wizardry" of the *djobber* lies in the accomplishment of the impossible: to have survived, then continue to survive, on the basis of an impossible memory. The *djobber* is a fragment worker—in the sense of one who works both *on the basis of* and *with* fragmentation. Without parents, there is both nothing (traumatic memory) and the whole world (the market). An orphan who orphans himself in the very same moment that writing, speaking, and thinking might pretend to set up roots. A *djobber*, in other words, is the one whose secret is the invention of life *at every bend in the road*. Without cessation, the *tout-monde*.

In *The Fourth Century*, Glissant tells the story of origins in fragment and contradiction. There is no rooted home, but rather only a *lieu commun* that, as Glissant puts it in *Poetics of Relation*, disperses and gathers, gathers and disperses along the anti-logic of the nomad. Glissant's thinking in *The Fourth Century* is at the shoreline, split between two opacities, two impossible memories, and two sites of beginning. The shoreline thinking is thus twofold. First, it is a story about the Caribbean *geos*, told across centuries. This is a story that begins in the between of Africa and the Americas without leaving the landscape of the New World. Second, the two primary characters in *The Fourth Century*—Longué the maroon, Béluse the slave—mark for the Plantation the contradiction of origin as womb that includes, as its contrary force, *marronage* in history and of creativity.

And so here we have to recall the recurrence of the abyss in beginning. The orphaned narrative of Relation is an orphan in the sense that parentage, the single origin, and History cannot address what it means to begin in the Plantation, yet the trope of orphan narrative suggests a bit too strongly—Loichot's nuances notwithstanding—that futurity is pure. The future, for Glissant, is always unprecedented and unexpected. Without a doubt. At the same time, the abyss haunts every beginning, making itself a companion to fiction's interventions in the problem of collective memory. Again, it is worth reading closely a passage from *Faulkner, Mississippi* in which Glissant writes himself back into Faulkner's landscapes:

> Let us draw closer in time. The most solitary tree beckons us, there, here, connecting us to the ancient time when its tender root first bore into the earth. Even the densest undergrowth lets the light of former years shine down from on high, and it accumulates, and there we plunge deeper each day. The most tortured city holds this cemetery in its depths, and someday it will be found. Place is the seam of time. (FM, 233)

Glissant works in two directions in this passage. On the one hand, the tree and root evoke the very figure he comes to reject, pursuing instead the rhizome's life without a fixed root. On the other hand, Glissant employs this image in order to think about the fold or interval in time that structures the relation between traumatic memory, impossible memory, and the *djobber*'s narration of a new memory of the collective soul. The city is tortured—a phrase that ought to recall Glissant's evocation of the tortured geography of the Caribbean—precisely because the past carried across the interval is saturated with pain and death, even as it also carries traces and fragments. And the *cri*, as Romuald Fonkoua's reading of Glissant shows us, is written first as the ruinous memory of the enslaved, then as the *cri* set out in Relation to *tout-monde*.[14] Fragments travel, but memory has location and citation. That is, there are always ruins. Ruins signal both more and less; Benjamin is right and limited. The *djobber* of the collective soul *can say* more about the ruin than the ruin speaks of itself, yet the ruin also brings the abyss of the dead to bear on the living. Benjamin meets the limits of *his* geography of reason.

Place is the seam of time. In this turn of phrase, Glissant gathers together the meaning of an abyssal beginning as futurity. A seam is such a peculiar between, pulling together separate parts and holding together tightly, but also because of all the contingencies due to design. This is design by historical cruelty. In imagining place, the geography of thinking the black Americas, Glissant's evocation of seam ought to remind us of Walcott's close to the 1974 essay "The Muse of History":

> I, like the honest of my race, give a strange thanks. I give strange
> and bitter and yet ennobling thanks for the monumental groaning
> and soldering of two great worlds, like the halves of a fruit seamed
> by its own bitter juice, that exiled from your own Edens you have
> placed me in the wonder of another, and that was my inheritance
> and your gift.[15]

The bitter juice that Walcott evokes in characterizing the interval between worlds is precisely Glissant's abyssal beginning toward the future. Bitterness is the perfect affect and taste in the mouth. It is no simple pleasure. It seams two halves of fruit—the verbal sense is important here, too, giving movement and process to the thought of the interval—with what is bitter. Melancholy is not absent the moment of beginning. But it seams fruit. Pleasure, excess. This is Walcott's inheritance. This is Glissant's interval between traumatic memory and the future, the seamed world of the Plantation, the bitter juice of creolization. Shoreline thinking is never pure. It makes impurity into world-making force.[16] *Creolization, creole,* and certain senses and resonances of *créolité.*

In all, this long meditation on trauma, loss, arrival, and shoreline thinking places the abyss at the center of the problem of beginning without drawing from the abyss two kinds of conclusions about making meaning and connection. First, the prominence of survival and the fecundity of fragmentation in his analysis allow Glissant to avoid conceiving collective meaning and identity as derived from shared pain. Identity is not forged *as* abjection. To be sure, as we have seen, the centrality of the trace means that the pain of the past is both sacred and persistent in any sense of

futurity, but it is not pain itself that makes identity. Trauma is not cosmology. Rather, the shoreline thinking that begins with pain and its fragments
makes a world possible, though only possible through the creative work of
Relation. The *djobber* of the collective soul is more than a trope. The *djobber* of the collective soul is a kind of divine force in making the cosmos of
the New World, and so trauma and its painful wake condition fragmentation without determining the kind of meanings that come out of fragment
work. Antillanité is not derived from suffering alone. Second, Glissant's
attention to the painful yet productive significance of the Plantation keeps
his discourse and thinking about beginning inside the Caribbean itself.
Such delimitation renders *marronage* a contribution to the composite cultural forms of creolizing life, rather than the last hope of atavistic thinking.
As well, by folding *marronage* back into the becoming of beginning, *marronage* labors as a critical force against the anxious effects of colonialism,
bearing a creative trace of the other experience of arrival, then survival.
Perhaps *marronage,* when placed in the fractal logic of broken sequences
(the *morne* as the other shoreline), is the ruin come back to life, animated
with traces and impossible memory, and always in the process of translation, de-translation, and re-translation—*creolizing.*

Trauma makes the shoreline. The Plantation makes another beginning.
The collective soul is commenced in the *djobber*'s work with fragments.

And so Glissant's question of the accomplished future: Who is the subject of this beginning?

CHAPTER 3

Ontology of an Abyssal Subject

He fell into the other side of his own truth, across a bridge, and the
  bridge
In flames, ran into the abyss
From careless height to itinerant lowland.

—Glissant, "The Great Chaoses"

IN *ABSOLUTELY POSTCOLONIAL*, Peter Hallward advances the provocative claim that Glissant is "perhaps the most thoroughly Deleuzean writer
in the francophone world," and that recent works (Hallward writing in
2001) "provide, in fiction and in theory, an extraordinary tribute to Deleuze's smoothly nomadological philosophy."[1] *Thoroughly Deleuzean* and
tribute—what is happening in Glissant's engagement with nomadology
and its companion concept of rhizome that makes his work simultaneously Deleuzean *and* Caribbean? That is, what does it mean to put Glissant in that peculiar form of contact called Relation with Deleuze and
Guattari? What happens to Deleuze and Guattari when read, by Glissant,
with the frame and method of Antillanité? And how does that method
translate the sense of Hallward's claim, especially the important theoretical claim that Glissant is committed to a Deleuzean plane of immanence?
Is Glissant a Deleuzean? Or is his nomadology a fundamentally different
science of subjectivity?

There can be no doubt that Glissant's work authorizes such a characterization, even as it transforms what it means to think about *influence*;
Antillanité does not transmit concepts and forms of knowing and being
without complex rewriting. As a matter of personal and intellectual biog-
raphy, we can think here of how Glissant dedicates his novel *Tout-monde*
(1993) *"en mémoire de Félix Guattari."* As well, one cannot underestimate
the importance of notions of rhizome and nomad—ideas borrowed directly from Deleuze and Guattari's *A Thousand Plateaus*—in Glissant's

theoretical work, especially *Poetics of Relation* and after. In his poetry and fiction Glissant was obsessed with the question of root and roots from the beginning, but the poetics he developed in the last decade and a half of his life work closely with Deleuzean concepts transformed by the Caribbean context. Mostly, though, there is between Glissant, Deleuze, and Guattari the intrigue of shared philosophical space as such. That is, Deleuze and Guattari are no mere instruments for Glissant, nor are they simply philosophical friends. More broadly, and certainly at greater theoretical depth, Glissant's interest in fragmentation as a fecund concept and lived historical experience, rather than as nihilistic and destructive, significantly predates his appropriation of Deleuze and Guattari, as does his preoccupation with the critique of roots and rootedness.[2] But his encounter with *A Thousand Plateaus* clearly opens up a new theoretical vocabulary that, as with all theory, brings finer grains of analysis into view. In particular, I am thinking of how Glissant's work is reframed, by way of Deleuze and Guattari, as a discourse about singular and collective *identity* in the Caribbean context. The question of subjectivity and its roots, the mangrove as subject, is drawn and redrawn from out of this new set of motifs. The language of rhizome and nomad informs Glissant's ontology of subjectivity and, crucially, guides his description of subjectivity as both interwoven with geography and liberated from the subordination of questions of subjectivity to questions of Being as such. Glissant's inquiry into how the subject *is* and *becomes* in space, time, language, and history links subjectivity to abyssal beginning—and therein lies the importance of theorizing futurity. Glissant's ontology of the subject emerges out of, rather than intervenes upon, space, time, language, and history. In fact, siting that emergence is essential for moving from generalized Deleuzean geophilosophy to the specific geography of Glissant's subject.

In the exploration of this problematic of Caribbean subjectivity, I want to turn first to a reading of *Poetics of Relation* on the problem of Being, beings, and earth. This reading establishes the intimacy of Relation to subjectivity, which prepares us to appreciate both the particular fecundity of Deleuze and Guattari's work for Glissant *and* how the process of creolization marks the limits of that work. Glissant's creolization, I will argue, demonstrates the (intentional or not) parasitic relation of Deleuze and Guattari's work to what Glissant calls "compact national entities" (PR, 18). For Glissant, as we shall see, this parasitic character offers a new language against colonialism and its wake, but it also finds a limit when the archipelago, in what Glissant calls a "circular nomadism," turns to creoleness/creolization as a principle and process of identity—that condition in which the very idea of compact national entities is absent. What does Glissant's creolization of rhizome and nomad say about Caribbean subjectivity? And, further, what is the normative and descriptive purchase of Glissant's rewriting of Deleuze and Guattari in his articulation of the thought of errantry and the poetics of Diversity?

Relation, *En Route*

In the fifth section of *Poetics of Relation,* Glissant offers a series of interwoven, aphoristic proclamations concerning the meaning and significance of the text's focus: Relation. The stakes of his claims concerning Relation, in particular how the problematic of Relation puts archipelagic thought into motion, are raised in this short set of proclamations, moving from programmatic inquiry to assertions about ultimate reality. From suggestive to metaphysics, really. This is no small elevation of discourse. Relation, of course, had been at issue in Glissant's work from the outset, but what is particularly compelling about the fifth section is how he distinguishes the thought of Relation from the problem of Being as such. In this distinction we find a common Glissantian theme revisited in an ontological register, namely, the rejection of universality. As well, in addressing the question of the meaning of Being—including the very relevance of asking such a question—Glissant brings the method of Caribbeanness to bear on the ontology of subjectivity, stretching what initially *wants to be* a self-sufficient sense of being back across the fecund absences of the Atlantic and the Caribbean archipelago. Subjectivity is remade in this stretch.

The shift toward the question of ontology allows us to explore the structure of subjectivity more directly precisely because Glissant is careful to discern the difference between Being and beings. In marking his departure from Being as such, Glissant places the movement of Relation *inside* the subject or even *as* subjectivity itself. This account of ontological difference brings abyssal beginning to bear on the conditions that condition the meaning of subjectivity: language, history, space, and time. An ontology of the subject. Relation begins in archipelagic thought. Beginning in archipelagic thought, subjectivity manifests and negotiates a very specific connection to fragmentation—in particular, a connection in which the movement *between* fragments defines subjectivity, rather than, as with traditional European models, the fragments themselves, along with the measure that binds them in a preexisting origin, defining the subject. A post- or pre-atavistic ontology of the subject. Indeed, when Glissant writes that "Relation is the knowledge in motion of beings" (PR, 187), he underscores three crucial conditions and guides for the articulation of Caribbean subjectivity *after* the abyssal beginning.

What are the conditions for articulating Glissant's subject? First, Relation is an *epistemological* event, inseparable from knowledge in the widest sense—particularly, that is, in the sense of thought (*pensée*) and knowing (*savoir*), as opposed to comprehension or understanding as *comprendre* and its dependency upon those figures of "grasping" and "seizing upon" that have such a "dreadful, repressive sense" (PR, 26; see also PR, 191). Relation is thus a movement of knowing and a way of transforming, through the labor and spontaneity of creolization, both subjectivity and the world. This transformation depends upon Glissant's account of the positivity of chaotic cross-cultural contact for its legitimacy, and that account is intimately entwined with questions of collective and singular subjectivity. Second, and from inside the epistemological moment, Glissant puts *beings* at the center of the notion of Relation. There is no Relation without beings; the idea of Relation "does not preexist." The distinction between Being and beings, which cedes priority to the movement of beings, helps clarify Glissant's claim that Relation does not preexist. Indeed, were Glissant to posit Relation as another name for Being or assert it as an imperative foundation for knowing (the standard strategies of ontology), then one would be justified in complaining that he has simply replaced one absolute with another—mimicking, for example, the very logic criticized in his departure from Césaire's Négritude, which notes how one root is swapped out for another, no matter how noble or instructive the motivation. Relation therefore becomes a paradoxical name, one that can only be understood on the basis of a rhizomatic and nomadic subjectivity. And so Glissant will write that "the idea of relation does not limit Relation, nor does it fit outside of it" (PR, 185). Third, and last, beings are understood as motion. Movement is central to subjectivity, which clears the conceptual space for Glissant's argument that subjectivity resists localization, substance, and calcification. On the one hand, this joins Glissant with an often and well-traveled path of thinking a non-teleological becoming against Being. Such a characterization captures something essential about the nomadic sense of Glissant's notion of subjectivity, insofar as he will argue that movement between fragments makes Caribbean subjectivity Caribbean and couples that subject to abyssal beginnings. On the other hand, the insistence on the poly-rooted rhizome, the first component part of subjectivity we will examine below, drags becoming across the *earthly* character of subjectivity. Movement, by itself, remains much too abstract of a characterization; the rooting, even if always precarious in its multiplicity and commitment to opacity, adds a substantiality to beings. Motion and roots must be thought simultaneously in order to sufficiently think beings against Being. This is a subtle but crucial shift in thinking.

The turn to subjectivity in *Poetics of Relation*, which of course draws on so much of the work preceding it, allows Glissant to rethink space and time through the kind of being enacted in spatial-temporal horizons (language, memory, history). Subjectivity is both enactments at once. The abyssal beginning of Caribbean subjectivity reminds us that Glissant is laboring against not just Being as the absolute but also the shadow of nothingness, of Non-Being that is cast by the sea that is history. Our previous considerations of birth, survival, and the cosmological function of the Plantation brought an important feature of subjectivity into focus: the question of territory. The trauma and loss of the Middle Passage change everything, unrooting beginning in the depths of the sea, but Non-Being does not replace a lost Being. This is a foundational insight. Without the absoluteness of the terms of loss, *with* saying yes to impurities, the abyss of beginning is more than Nothing. Perhaps there is, from the abyss, *everything*. That *perhaps* is of course the question of beginning, which is firstly a question of geography. So, the issue of subjectivity is, at some level, an issue of geo-subjectivity. *To be* is to be in relation to territory, in relation to the earth. Glissant writes:

> Beings, which subsist and present themselves, are not merely
>   substance, which would be sufficient unto itself.
> Beings risk the being of the world, or being-earth....
> It depends upon Relation that the knowledge in motion of the being
>   of the universe be granted through osmosis, not through violence.
>   (PR, 187–88)

In this assertion of the connection of subjectivity to Relation, Glissant comes back to a particularly material figure of the geography of reason: the earth. And from that coupling we can also see why the work of Deleuze

and Guattari becomes so important for Glissant in his work on subjectivity. The earth is a literal and figurative evocation of place, where a people
stand, the where and how, as well as what and when, an identity can be
established (and dis-established, in the strange, spastic dialectic of Relation). The earth is territory, which, in the movement of Relation, is deterritorialized. Yet, being *are* as earth, a certain kind of reterritorialization
that does not grasp, seize, or control. It is entry into Chaos, the life of beings. Earth, then, sustains the subject; to be in the Caribbean landscape,
this earth, is to be in the motion of being and knowing: becoming. What
is this subject?

Tree, Rhizome, Root

"Our landscape," Glissant writes in one of the introductions to *Caribbean Discourse,* "is its own monument" (CD, 11). We had occasion in the
previous chapter to reflect on how this passage engages the problem of
ruins and beginning, but it is worth revisiting for a moment in order to
emphasize Glissant's repeated returns to the language of nature and earth.
If memory is at least partly, if not nearly wholly, captured in the descriptions of nature and earth, then how might the same sorts of descriptions
figure Caribbean subjectivity? Who is the sensual subject, entwined with
the history and memory of place, to be sure, but also with the ontology of
earth and roots? How is ontology properly understood as the language of
a fecund anti- and ante-system of natural life and how it figures subjectivity? With this turn to the language of natural life, Glissant places himself
in important proximity to the work of Deleuze and Guattari. Let us begin
with this proximity.

A *Thousand Plateaus* stands as the singularly important work in Glissant's later constellation of influences, and that later work joins Antonio
Benítez-Rojo's *The Repeating Island* as a crucial rewriting of radical French
theory in the context of the archipelago. And, like Benítez-Rojo, Glissant's
primary concern is with the blend of geography—landscape, earth, soil,
roots, archipelago—and the visceral, creative life of the subject *thought in
place.* That place is at once rooted and unrooted. Landscape and earth in
shifting, irregular relation. In the introductory remarks to *A Thousand Plateaus,* Deleuze and Guattari begin with what they describe as the two critical figures of the book. The first is the figure of the tree, a (problematic,

totalitarian) conception of writing and describing that identifies a single root as the foundation of difference:

> A first type of book is the root-book. The tree is already the image of the world, or the root the image of the world-tree. . . . The law of the book is the law of reflection, the One that becomes two.[3]

The reduction of the two to the One, of the multiplicity of being and beings to Being, is root-thinking, a thinking from the root, which renders difference as only variation, never unicity or originary, irreducible fragmentation. The book: a figuration of diaspora as always already unified, in which scattering is always only a loss of unity, held in atavistic imagination and the measure of all that is scattered. The root is juridical. It rules and judges. Deleuze and Guattari write further that

> the book as a spiritual reality, the Tree or Root as an image, endlessly develops the law of the One that becomes two, then of the two that become four. . . . Binary logic is the spiritual reality of the root-tree.[4]

Deleuze and Guattari are here theorizing authoritarianism and fascism as such, in the broadest term, by underscoring the movement from the One to the book to the law, which is juridical and therefore irreducibly a logic and figure of domination. It is also a description of colonialism. Binary logic, what Fanon more dramatically called Manichaean though in *The Wretched of the Earth*, sets out not just division—there are two, it is either/or all the way down—but also measure. The split and the dualism are not a shortchanged notion of difference. Rather, the one generates the other. The other is only meaningful insofar as it is a variation of the same. *The law of the One that becomes two, then of the two that become four.* There is always a measure. There is always colonialism. Thus, the single-root model and mode of thinking is inherently vulnerable to (if not an outright expression of) totalitarianism.

Against this figure of the tree, Deleuze and Guattari propose the fascicular root. This term "fascicular" is peculiar and exceptionally suggestive. On the one hand, it describes a book that is written in divisions, published in parts. Writing as fascicular does not simply uproot itself, contesting the single root from the fragmentation of its derivative parts. Rather, it operates with a wholly other logic, beginning with difference with only a partial allusion to a whole, which prompts a reference to William S. Burroughs's cut-up method of writing—"the folding of one text onto another, which constitutes multiple and even adventitious roots."[5] The multiple and adventitious roots of the fascicular root put the term "root" under a certain kind of erasure. An anti-authoritarian, antifascist, and therefore *anticolonial* kind of erasure. The best kind of erasure, for once. There is for Deleuze and Guattari no "root" in any conventional sense of the term, except, perhaps, in the sense that there is something set down and into the earth which gives life to Life. But the root does not hold life to it; there is no One that becomes two, which would only, in the end, really be the One that measures, as its origin and sense, every last other. Deleuze and Guattari's fascicle instead gives way to the organic case of the rhizome, which they claim is not a figure or metaphor, but a direct description of a decentered and deterritorialized subjectivity. Heterogeneity does not *resist* homogeneity, but rather exposes the fraud and authoritarian impulse of even an interest in the One and the single root. But heterogeneity, paradoxically, is also connection. Roots give life. Thinking origin in the plural does not cancel out conceptions of Life, but instead enhance and intensify it. We can already see how it is that archipelagic thinking will turn to, then creolize, Deleuze and Guattari. In their enumeration of the features of rhizome, Deleuze and Guattari keep the aporetic character in full view:

> Principles of connection and heterogeneity: any point of a rhizome can be connected to anything other, and must be. This is very different from the tree or root, which plots a point, fixes and orders.[6]

The rhizome is fundamentally unplotted. Without eschewing connection, the rhizome does not draw life from a particular connection or set of connections. Unplotted *and* connected, the rhizome is mapped on the model of chaos, fractals, and indeterminacy precisely because it is never fixed and ordered while simultaneously producing shape and possibility. Rhizomatic life is not regimented and in fact draws its intensity from errantry, to deploy one of Glissant's terms.

Rhizomatic life, the life of roots unplotted, is contrasted to the "tree root" in plain terms when Deleuze and Guattari bring insight into the rhizome to bear on language. What is language, so conventionally tied to a whole range of singular roots from grammar to nationalism, in the rhizomatic context? It is a decentered language, unplotted by engagement with and dismantling by dimensionality and the plurality of registers. And so they write:

> There is always something genealogical about a tree. It is not a method for the people. A method of the rhizome type, on the contrary, can analyze language only by decentering it onto other dimensions and other registers. A language is never closed upon itself, except as a function of impotence.[7]

The open boat, the mangrove. The rhizome therefore opens the system and disrupts any pretensions to genealogy, signifying instead a multiplicity whose life is not dependent upon a unity or single root, but rather fascicled outside the logic of fragmentation as loss of unity. A book written in parts, not adhering to a pre- or post-established unity. *Becoming without Being or beings.* And so Deleuze and Guattari write in a passage that will prove crucial for Glissant's later work:

> A rhizome may be broken, shattered at a given spot, but it will start up again on one of its old lines, or on new lines. . . . Every rhizome contains lines of segmentarity according to which it is stratified, territorialized, organized, signified, attributed, etc., as well as lines of deterritorialization down which it constantly flees. There is a rupture in the rhizome whenever segmentary lines explode into a line of flight, but the line of flight is part of the rhizome.[8]

In this passage, a number of features of the rhizome come into focus. First, the general form of the claims concerning rhizomes is largely ontological. That is, the rhizome describes the complex interactions that comprise the intersections of body, action, and life. Being is thought as Being, but also in terms of a multiplicity before, outside, and/or after the Oneness of Being and beings. This last bit is crucial. Being is rhizomatic, which means, in some sense, it is not in any fundamental way Being as traditionally or conventionally conceived. Being as fragments. Being unplotted. Being regenerated in every death, which is death as root-life, identity-life. The life of the One is death. Beings, too. Beings are fragments unplotted, unreconciled *as a matter of beginning and origin.* Before fragments, perhaps, only abyss. Beings draw life from the abyss because the abyss plots no points and sucks the compulsion to set segmentary lines and to plot territory back into itself, not as death, but as explosion of life.

A second feature of the rhizome, then, following directly from this series of claims about Being and beings: life and multiplicity are primordial. Multiplicity does not put life at risk. Dimensionality and diversity of registers give life to language, which gives or reflects the life of the subject. One can already see the fecundity of this configuration for thinking through Creole and creoleness as creolization. *Difference in movement, fragments as fractal and in Chaos.* Third, for Deleuze and Guattari, territorialization and deterritorialization are not contraries, nor is deterritorialization a privative form of territorialization. Land, earth, landscape—these too are subject to the logic of the rhizome. Deleuze and Guattari write:

> How could movements of deterritorialization and processes of reterritorialization not be relative, always connected, caught up in one another? The orchid deterritorializes by forming an image, a tracing of a wasp; but the wasp reterritorializes on that image. The wasp is nevertheless deterritorialized, becoming a piece in the orchid's reproductive apparatus. But it reterritorializes the orchid by transporting its pollen. Wasp and orchid, as heterogeneous elements, form a rhizome.[9]

Wasp and orchid? There is also the Caribbean shoreline. Difference is not surmounted by identity. Multiplicity is, rather, sustained by the simultaneous movement of territorialization, deterritorialization, and reterritorialization. The constancy of movement in this description provides a particular challenge for an ontology of the subject, for the sedentary character of ontological description would seem, *prima facie*, to be incapable of sustaining such obstinate and inordinate motion. And yet, the claim: heterogeneity is subjectivity. The subject is not a rhizome. The subject *rhizomes*.

This shift from rhizome as a kind of being—something a taxonomy of plants could establish, which could then form the basis for an analogy to subjectivity—to the rhizome as the verbal sense of the subject—the subject in motion that is made by and made in rhizomatic swerves, nothing like an analogy—already begins to describe the archipelagic figure of thought, the abyssal time of Caribbeanness, and various composite cultural forms that comprise Caribbean life. But it is also a thought experiment, an antifascist *strategy* for Deleuze and Guattari. And that is of no small importance in the Caribbean context; anticolonial struggle and decolonization are always forms of antifascist thinking. How far can we take Deleuze and Guattari into the Caribbean? What happens to Deleuze and Guattari's conception of rhizome set in Glissant's conception of Relation? To put it plainly: What is the creolized rhizome?

In the concluding pages of *Poetics of Relation,* passages that muse on the possibilities of the future drawn from the abyssal beginning, Glissant raises the question of the rhizome at the shoreline. At the shoreline, Glissant is again provoked by the memory of the dead. The memory of the dead functions as a moral call, a call to "honor our boats." Honoring our boats—this is a solemn and complex utterance. The traumatic past might give life to the future, but it also demands respect for opacity, words for silence, and cosmologies sprung from loss. This memory, which is of course *also* an interval to a future, mixes the sea as history with the cosmological function of the Plantation—that "tie between beach and island" (PR, 206). This tie is the transcendental condition of Caribbean subjectivity, the abyssal subject. Glissant muses in *Poetics of Relation*:

> I have always imagined that these depths navigate a path beneath the sea in the west and the ocean in the east and that, though we are separated, each in our own Plantation, the now green balls and chains have rolled beneath from one island to the next, weaving shared rivers that we shall take our boats. (PR, 206)

Glissant here moves seamlessly between "our own" and "our," a move that signifies multiplicity as its own kind of deterritorialized, which is simultaneously reterritorialized, identity. A repeating island. Identity as repetition, in repetition, and for the sake of repetition—but always with chaotic difference across that repetition. In *Caribbean Discourse,* Glissant establishes the relationship between the sea as history and a rhizomed sense of place. Nearly a decade before writing it as the epigraph to *Poetics of Relation,* Glissant recalls Brathwaite's turn of phrase "the unity is submarine." *Unity.* The formation of singular and collective subjectivity is already in that very term, and in it *prominently,* which shifts the register of Brathwaite's words from the question of birth and origin in *Poetics of Relation* back to the structure of subjectivity more broadly in *Caribbean Discourse.* In Braithwaite, Glissant sees a conceptually, as well as existentially, subversive utterance in the term *unity*. Located beneath the sea, beneath H/history itself, and emerging out of the drowning of sense and meaning, there is the life of a difference neither derived from nor measured by the single root or singular inspiration. Rhizome. Glissant writes:

> And so transversality, and not the universal transcendence of the sublime, has come to light. It took us a long time to learn this. We are the roots of a cross-cultural relationship.
>
> Submarine roots: that is floating free, not fixed in one position in some primordial spot, but extending in all directions in our world through its network of branches.
>
> We, thereby, live, we have the good fortune of living, this shared process of cultural mutation, this convergence that frees us from uniformity. (CD, 67)

Convergence—one of Glissant's names for the site of unity—is not only difference, but *mutation*. As mutation, difference becomes the new and the possible, what he calls, in a fascinating turn of phrase, a "new contradiction" (CD, 92).

The archipelago opens up at this moment. Glissant evokes contradiction as passage, which is not the Middle Passage but, as both memory and honor of the dead, the passage *between* territories, *between* earth and landscape, the possibility of connection and roots in territory *between* peoples, *between* islands. Motion, movement, passage, repetition. This second, *shorelined* sense of passage is crucial. Geography is meaning, reason, imagination of space as rhizoming the subject and the people. Glissant writes that Relation "is passage, not primarily spatial, that passes itself off as passage and confronts the imaginary" (PR, 188). Passages navigated across the literal *and* figurative archipelago of thought engage multiplicity, not *in light of* a prior unity, but as formations of an imagined connection to place whose light is the right to opacity—the opacity of origin, the opacity of memory, the opacity of language, the opacity of the new, and therefore the opacity of contact and encounter—with all the transformative work done in that contact and encounter. Fragile and always precarious movements move (this is the subject or Subject in motion) between imagined worlds, spaces, places, or sites common in their irreducible differentiation. That movement, this weaving, is the Caribbean sense of *intermezzo*. Glissant writes:

I am doing the same thing in the way I say *we*—organizing this
work around it. Is this some community *we* rhizomed into fragile
connection to a place? Or a total *we* involved in the activity of the
planet? Or an idea *we* drawn in the swirls of a poetics? (PR, 206)

Glissant's use of the first-person plural here makes it clear that the intertwining of personal and collective identity is at stake in any articulation of
subjectivity. Unity is submarine, yes, but also the trans-marine that gives
life out of death; the sea is history becoming the unity of what takes root.
Glissant continues:

Who is this intervening *they*? *They* that is Other? Or *they* the neigh-
bors? Or *they* whom I imagine when I try to speak?
   These *we*s and *they*s are an evolving. They find their full sense,
here, in my excessive use of the words *totality* and *Relation*. This
excess is a repetition that signifies. (PR, 206)

Totality and Relation. In the repetition of these terms, what Glissant here
says is to the point of excess, Relation becomes the multiple root or rhizome (the movement of subjectivity) and Totality becomes the ground
that nourishes and sustains poly-rooted, opaque assertions.

   What are we to make of the invocation of repetition? With repetition,
Glissant of course wants to labor deconstructively in Jacques Derrida's
sense of disassembling through reiteration against the Western fantasy of
mimesis, but what precisely happens to subjectivity in repetition? What
does it mean for the subject of the Caribbean to say yes to itself, naming
and repeating the name? Does it set a root? Or does it rhizome connection
to place? The motif of repetition recalls Glissant's remarks on Négritude
and Europe in *Caribbean Discourse*, where he articulates the simultaneous
pain and ecstasy of saying *yes* to Africa and France (CD, 8). The pain is of
course in the sense of loss (Africa) and the long shadow of colonialism
in language and culture (France), but the ecstasy of creolization makes a
world out of the pain of history. *Abyssal beginning*: subjectivity is defined,
in the consciousness produced by this repetition, by the diachronic "flood
of convergences" in which repetition "is an acknowledged form of consciousness both here and elsewhere" (PR, 45). The simultaneity of here
and elsewhere, of pain and ecstasy, changes the notion of root for Glissant. Repetition, on the model of the Western fantasy of *mimesis*, *ought* to

illuminate the condition of every variation, the Being at the root of every being, but the dislocation of history splits the time of being and knowing. Indeed, Glissant is declarative on this point when he writes in *Caribbean Discourse* that "this notion of a single History, and therefore of power" is "one of the most disturbing consequences of colonization." Repetition of a single History is alienation and the repetition of dispossession, whereas the creolizing project of Relation, this

> struggle against a single History for the cross-fertilization of histories, means repossessing both a true sense of one's time and identity: proposing in an unprecedented way a revaluation of power. (CD, 93)

Cross-fertilization returns history to nature, against the single root, perhaps against the book as tree, but always without a teleology of calcifying filiation.

Who is this subject?

It is here that Glissant's rereading of Deleuze and Guattari's rhizome offers a crucial figure for a singular and collective subjectivity of abyssal beginnings. We can already see this poly-rooted, de- and reterritorializing work of the rhizome in *Caribbean Discourse* when Glissant writes that the "intention" of the work of creolization is

> to accumulate [*d'accumuler*] all levels of experience. This accumulation is the most suitable technique for exposing a reality that is itself being scattered. Its evolution is like a repetition of a few obsessions that *take root*, tied to realities that *keep slipping away*. . . . Repetition of these ideas does not clarify their expression; on the contrary, it perhaps leads to obscurity. We need those stubborn shadows where repetition leads to perpetual concealment, which is our form of resistance. (CD, 4)

Repetition therefore enacts destabilization in the very same moment that it affirms something crucial about life: mixture and opacity. Because repetition is identified with life, and accumulation trumps distinction and exclusion, Glissant's phenomenological description of Caribbean subjectivity risks the language of roots. The rhizomatic consequence of repetition is linked to the simultaneity of an imperative to speak against the disappearance of realities, to save what has persisted and persists after the sea as history, *and* the insistent character of obscurity. And so there is also an ethical dimension to Glissant's early articulation of the rhizome, an ethics of the inscrutable, which is evident when he writes:

> He makes contact, beyond every lived humiliation, a collective meaning, a universal poetics, in which each voice is important, in which each lived moment *finds an explanation*.
> (Thus, Caribbean discourse cannot be readily seized. But does not the world, in its exploded oneness, demand that each person be drawn to the recognized inscrutability of the other? This is one aspect of our inscrutability.) (CD, 8)

On the one hand, one might read this passage as an ethics of transcendence in which the excess of discourse forbids *seizing it* in a unified conceptual schema. This reading would suggest that exceeding totality is the very meaning and significance of the *our* or the *we* that one finds in both *Caribbean Discourse* and *Poetics of Relation*. On the other hand, with the explicit reflections on Deleuze and Guattari's work in *Poetics of Relation* in view, the use of "root" in *Caribbean Discourse* directly suggests a language of difference as the dispersion of rootedness, the diversity of "explanations" of the lived moments of creolized life. The rhizome, then, infuses difference with the risk and force of identity without putting life at risk in the single root. Subjectivity thereby lives from its very inscrutability, obscurity, and opacity precisely because the roots do not make life precarious. Rather, like the mangrove, the poly-rooted mixture elevates life above what most puts it under threat: the pain and violence of history.

If Relation transforms the elements and items of Caribbean life, creolizing in what Natalie Melas nicely calls "an intrinsically incommensurable relationality,"[10] then the very term "subjectivity" is a paradox. To put it precisely, there is the assemblage into a subject, sited in place, full of history and memory and the traces they bear in language, gesture, and all of the expressions of composite culture. But, when seen in the frame of the verbal sense of rhizome, that assemblage disassembles and reassembles. So is the productive chaos of archipelagic thinking. And so, we can here see again the importance of the mangrove for Glissant's account of subjectivity. The *rhizophoric* sense of roots works from the (non-)logic of the accident and chaos, bending time, folding it back into itself, full of errantry and detour and return. That is, Glissant's is an adventitious subject: not native, not grown singly from the soil, yet on the earth, in the landscape, at the shoreline, structured by the outside.

In raising the question of history, memory, and roots, Glissant returns the question of subjectivity to time. And here we get a first glimpse into Glissant's creolization of Deleuze and Guattari. Historical experience transforms not only the very context within which one enacts a rhizomed sense of root, but also the prompt to such a search. In the 1961 preface to the edition of *Monsieur Toussaint: A Play,* Glissant writes:

> For those whose history has been reduced by others to darkness and despair, the recovery of the near or distant past is imperative. To renew acquaintance with one's history, obscured or obliterated by others, is to relish fully the present, for the experience of the present, stripped of its roots in time, yields only hollow delights. This is a poetic endeavor.
>
> Of course this attempt seems incomprehensible, indeed useless, if not harmful, to those who, far from feeling an absence of history, may on the contrary feel that they are laboring under the tyrannical burden of their past. Struggling with, and in, history is our common lot. (MT, 15–16)

There is so much in this passage, recalling as it does the shoreline thinking of Caribbean history's interval between past and future. History is, for Glissant, a struggle. The womb-abyss is no easy birth. History is painful, and the transformation of history into memory, that doubled movement that deepens the submarine unity, is a loud, crashing wave, as decimating as it is beautiful. Struggle with history is "our common lot," Glissant here writes, and that is the crucial shift from the decimation of history's pain to a pain lived in the repetition(s) of colonialism. But there is also the repetition that creates the new.[11] This is what Glissant means by struggle. Struggle that overcomes colonial repetition, but also struggle that remakes the world in creolized and creolizing cultural forms—those forms built on the shoreline, at the sea that is history, and also the land and place that *is* the Caribbean. Thinking at the shoreline, this struggle to nourish from land and sea, this mangrove-thinking and *poiesis,* births subjectivity as rhizomatic. Thinking at the shoreline is a philosophical method.

Nomad, Deterritorialization, Reterritorialization

Rhizome functions for Deleuze, Guattari, and Glissant as a noun, adjective, and verb. Subjectivity is a rhizome, a formulation that already calls for its own disassembly of the copula (rhizome dismantles Being), and we can also say that certain forms of subjectivity—elements and concepts thought in terms of space, time, and language—are rhizomatic. The rhizome rhizomes; the elements of rhizome are themselves rhizomes. This is why Glissant pushes back against the creolist formulation of *créolité*, which suggests a state of being or fixed point in cultural history. If the elements of the rhizome are themselves rhizomes, or *might* at the very least split roots and reterritorialize outside the lines of growth and its time, then creoleness is always creolizing. *Creolization,* not *créolité,* as Glissant always insists after the *Éloge de la créolité* manifesto. And so rhizome also functions as a verb. We can say that subjectivity rhizomes insofar as it incessantly and chaotically enacts the zigzag movement of speaking and acting against sedentary forms of territorialization. The differences between Deleuze and Guattari's and Glissant's account of the rhizome are critical, situated in different landscapes and histories and memories, but they share this rejection of the single root and territorial location.

Rhizome, then, performs the conceptual labor of ontology. That is, rhizome describes the *being* of subjectivity; what it means to *be* a subject is inseparable from the repudiation of roots and territory. Subjectivity as rhizome is therefore a kind of aporia or a deconstructive and deconstructed word: every naming of the Caribbean subject, this archipelagic rhizome, is deferred and deferring, composed as much by excesses of presence as by delays and their attendant absences. The deferral structure is no game or conceptual play, but rather the repeating island, the dynamics of creole languages and the various histories and memories that arrive on the shoreline in order to make a world. There is not one Africa in the Caribbean. Africa is not a country. And the Caribbean was created, the new of the New World, as the crossroads of the world. *Tout-monde* from the (abyssal) beginning.

A shift: the rhizome who defers and delays is also a nomad.

The central chapter from *A Thousand Plateaus,* "Treatise on Nomadology: The War Machine," treats the nomad and the nomadic in juxtaposition to—if not outright war against—what Deleuze and Guattari call "the despot." The despot claims territory and resists deterritorialization and reterritorialization, which, of course, is precisely the play of the colonizer in the colonial relation. The nomad wanders yet is not placeless or outside contact with territory. Nomads wander *somewhere*. In fact, for Deleuze and Guattari the nomad is fundamentally connected to territory, even as the nomad-ness of the nomad hinges on the economy of constant motion:

> The nomad has a territory; he follows customary paths; he goes from one point to another; he is not ignorant of points. . . . But the question is what in nomad life is a principle and what is only a consequence. To begin with, although the points determine paths, they are strictly subordinated to the paths they determine, the reverse of what happens with the sedentary. The water point is reached only in order to be left behind; every point is a relay and exists only as a relay.[12]

The relay between points, then, is not an interval between distinct modalities of being. Rather, and this is crucial the point, movement is itself the interval and cannot be accounted for outside of the ontological category of "relay." This is how Deleuze and Guattari describe the centrality of motion in the nomadic, which, like the rhizome, is an anti- and ante-foundational claim. The nomad's location in the relay, and so in an irreducible motion, alters the language of ontology by displacing the idea of root and despotic relation to place. At the same time, motion is connected to territorialization. The being of the nomad is located, so to speak, in the relay between what Deleuze and Guattari call the life of "*intermezzo*," but that relay always "has a territory." The nomad moves in order to arrive at the very same time that arrival is always already coupled to departure and leaving behind. This is what distinguishes the nomad from the migrant, for the migrant, even when she has given up the atavistic imagination, always holds the possibility of settlement and a single rooting like the figure of the tree. One can see, then, why the nomad is such a compelling notion for Glissant, especially in thinking through the logic of orality and creolization. The *intermezzo* character of the nomad repudiates the sedentary just as the rhizome repudiates the single root of the tree figure. Deleuze and Guattari write:

> A path is always between two points, but the in-between has taken on all the consistency and enjoys both an autonomy and a direction of its own. The life of the nomad is the *intermezzo*.[13]

The nomad's life suggests an ontology—so enigmatic, so without conventional language—of the in-between. The life of the nomad is a pause,
an interval, a break—territorialization ("I am here"), deterritorialization
(motion), and reterritorialization (arrival at the new). The nomad is therefore always already an in-between. Deferral and delay, while also full of
sense and meaning. Deconstruction's transcendental moment, perhaps.
Certainly an ontology of the subject against Being.

But this between-ness of the nomad does not simply call for an ontology
of motion and movement. Rather, because the nomad moves across and
toward territory as a matter of *consequence* (and not *principle*), an ontology
of the nomadic subject must also account for motion as the movement of
territorialization. "The nomad distributes himself in a smooth space," Deleuze and Guattari write; "he occupies, inhabits, holds that space; that is
his territorial principle. It is therefore false to define the nomad by movement."[14] The nomad is not adrift. Like the rhizome, there are roots, but the
root is not life. Life is not put at risk by losing a root, for another grows
in its place. The nomad re-locates at the very moment he de-locates. The
territorial principle, however, must be thought *against* the sedentary. This
generates the language of deterritorialization, where the sedentary stands
in for the problematic, calcifying sense of setting roots and locating life
without movement. Deleuze and Guattari offer a careful distinction here
when they write:

> If the nomad can be called the Deterritorialized, par excellence,
> it is precisely because there is no reterritorialization *afterward* as
> with the migrant, or upon *something else* as with the sedentary. . . .
> With the nomad, on the contrary, it is deterritorialization that
> constitutes the relation to the earth, to such a degree that the
> nomad reterritorializes on deterritorialization itself. It is the earth
> that deterritorializes itself, in a way that provides the nomad with
> a territory.[15]

Deterritorialization, then, needs the migrant and the sedentary as points
of juxtaposition. The migrant clings to the logic of the tree root, seeking
what *was* in the homeland in what *could be* in the arrival-land of the future.
Nostalgia is recast in the present as a rootedness in the arrival-land that is
measured—for better or worse—according to the model of the original
homeland. The single root remains the measure. In that way, the migrant

is not much different from the sedentary, whose intimacy with questions of ideology, notions of proprietary right, and other state apparatuses gives a certain mobility to the single root. Sedentary territorialization is not threatened by change and alteration, but can always absorb it precisely because of such intimacies.

This question of territoriality is precisely the condition of the Americas, and the Caribbean in particular. That is, the black Americas are always already nomadic in name. The archipelago is no single place or space, but always a scattering that repeats with a difference. To the extent that the Americas bear, even just in name, the memory and historical experience of conquest and the slave trade, the origins of the geography and borders of the continent and archipelago are themselves nomadic. There is the nomadism of the explorer-cum-conqueror, of course, and also of the dispossessed nomad produced by the Middle Passage. These are two very different subjectivities, both constitutive of the Americas as such and of the Caribbean in particular.

If we understand subjectivity as constituted by historical experience, emerging out of space, time, and language, then nomadic subjectivity locates its being in a transformative creolization of the notion of movement. Glissant's first distinction in conceiving the nomad is between the circular and the arrow-like, which, as we shall see, is the site of an essential distinction between the anticolonial and the creole. While the arrow-like nomad engages Relation as a *possibility*, it ultimately gives way to circular nomadism's movement-without-center-or-end.

To begin, arrow-like nomadism has three key movements. In these three movements we can see Glissant making a critical conceptual move from domination to dialectic to the beginning of Relation. Deleuze and Guattari posit the nomad against the authoritarianism of the sedentary administrative system, yet Glissant is quick to point out that the movement *outward* resonates differently when registered by a dominated people. In *Poetics of Relation*, Glissant accounts for the first movement of the arrow-like nomad in terms of a poetics which—and this is crucial—"culminate in the thought of an empire." Empire, Glissant argues, is totality manifest as the absolute or Being, whose indifference to difference is the (attempted) defeat of Relation. The development of a poetics of place, then, becomes something very much like the gaze bearing violence. The first movement of arrow-like nomadism is exactly this violence because it enacts the Absolute—here called Center—as measure. Glissant writes:

It projected toward. As if it set out all over again on the trajectory of an earlier arrow-like nomadism. Moreover, the movements of these poetics can be located in space as trajectories, their poetic import being aimed at completing these trajectories in order to abolish them. These trajectories link the places of the world into a whole made up of peripheries, which are listed in function of a Center. (PR, 28)

Already, we have come upon an interesting creolizing translation of the nomad. Thought from the margins—the Caribbean as a place without center, but also produced as not-center under centuries of colonial rule— the arrow-like nomad is bound to the colonial logic of domination. The arrow-like nomad *begins* this process by coupling itself to lines of flight and keeping them straight, ordered, linear. A fixed, plotted line.

The second sense of nomad emerges in what we might call a first itera- tion of the creole: exilic experience that undergoes radical transformation. Remember, the tropics change you. Perhaps your nomadic movement, your wandering into the tropical sun and heat and landscape, has made you a different person. The margins have a way of taking the center away from you. An errant nomad who repudiates the center, fleeing it—this is a first iteration of the creole. Glissant writes:

A second itinerary then began to form, this time from peripheries toward the Center. Poets who were born or lived in the elsewhere dream of the source of their imaginary constructs and, consciously or not, "make the trip in the opposite direction," struggling to do so. (PR, 29)

Saint-John Perse, on Glissant's rendering in *Poetics of Relation*, is exem- plary of this movement, expressing and elaborating an exilic sense of sub- jectivity and creation. Still, what is so curious about the first and second movements of arrow-like nomadism is the reversal-yet-persistence-of dialectic. A paradoxical double movement. Even as the Center-periphery relation is reversed, there is a dialectical relation, whether that is the com- plete absorption of difference in the first nomadism or sublation of that difference in the second nomadism.

In the third movement of arrow-like nomadism, Glissant detects a move against or even just outside of dialectic. Why the move away from dialectic? The arrival at Relation opens at least the *possibility* (for Relation is always a process, nomadic, never settled) of surmounting the problem of comparison and the Absolute—a problem made existential when posed as a question of subjectivity. The third movement of nomadism breaks with dialectic in two senses. First, it eschews the problem of comparison and the Absolute, which breaks movement from the center-periphery dynamic—in a certain sense, this deterritorializes the nomad for the first time. This deterritorialization of the nomad breaks with dialectic in a second sense, not by abolishing geography but through a *curvature* of space and time. The space of relation begins to surmount lines of contact from and through which centers and peripheries can be documented through inquiry into origins. Second, the temporality of relation is disrupted in the refusal to order modalities of presence, reclaiming the trace as constitutive of the present, rather than asking for complete presence or sedimentation. Of this curvature and break with dialectic, Glissant writes:

> In a third stage the trajectory is abolished; the arrow-like projection becomes curved. The poet's word leads from periphery to periphery, and, yes, it reproduces the track of a circular nomadism; that is, it makes every periphery into a center; furthermore, it abolishes the very notion of center and periphery. (PR, 29)

The advance of the third movement is that it begins to think difference without measure, especially in the abolition of center-periphery language. *The anticolonial word.* In the curvature of projection, we surely ought to register the echo of another term here, one passed along, no doubt, through an association with Albert Einstein: *the relative.* Indeed, Glissant begins the fourth section of *Poetics of Relation* with a short meditation on Einstein's work, seeing the kindred motif of a relative without measure; *after* the absolute, which is really just *before* its pretensions and violence, the relations between things disorient any sense of linear movement and one-way traffic of meaning.

Still, Glissant will claim that the third movement of the arrow-like nomadism *reproduces* the circular nomad in the effort of the repetition of difference without root identity. And so, with an important shade of difference, Glissant outlines the structure of a "circular nomadism." Circular nomadism is "experienced as a search for the Other" in which uprooting and exile produce the "work toward identity" (PR, 18). *Toward.* The circular nomad is therefore the movement of the archipelagic rhizome, setting multiple roots without declaration or expansion. If the single root is monolingual, as Glissant says in numerous passages, and the rhizome is at least the possibility of the polylingual, then we might say that the circular nomad is the thinking of the polylingual. The circular nomad moves so that no root is identified as life itself. Nomadology, then, expresses the "consciousness of consciousness" in its full accomplishment, something that Glissant identifies of the "end of the world" (PR, 26); there is no exploration left, only dispersion and the possibility of creolized thought. Rhizome *put to work* as nomad. An open and errant *pensée,* the circular nomad, this work across language and geography, which places subjectivity not *in,* but *as* the relationship with the Other. Put another way: if, as Celia Britton has convincingly argued, the trajectory of Glissant's work is guided by his engagement with the language-identity equation, even to the point of rendering the hyphen of that relation unstable,[16] then the poly-lingualism of the circular nomad cannot be said to *spread* identity out into the world, but rather *realizes itself* in these moments, sites, and rifts of difference. "We write," Glissant notes in *Traité du tout-monde,* "in the presence of all the languages of the world" (TTM, 85), a note that now resonates as subjectivity put into word, however precariously, by the circular nomad's fidelity to rhizoming thought and language through the curvature of space and time.[17]

Space and time, curved through the creolizing labors of the circular nomad, at once conceives and dismantles any sense of place. Territory, the singular concern of the figure of the nomad, can now be seen as the space of subjectivity intertwined or crossed with *toutes les langues.* "Relation identity," Glissant writes in *Poetics of Relation,* "does not think of a land as a territory from which to project toward other territories, but as a place where one 'gives with' [*donne-avec*] in place of 'com-prehend' [*comprendre*]" (PR, 144). Giving-with- and searching-for-the-Other stand opposed to the predatory and sedentary character of comprehension, where the latter, at least as an aspiration, seeks possession of the Other. In *Caribbean Discourse,* for example, Glissant sees this kind of "*avec*" in Roberto Matta's paintings, which are described in that text as "a visible continuity, the contact [*rapport*] of the inside and outside, the dazzling experience of here and elsewhere" (CD, 118; translation altered). *Poetics of Relation* thematizes contact and the dazzling experience of mixture in terms of the *trame chaotique,* the chaotic fabric of Relation (PR, 144), which breaks the nomad free of any arrow-like relation to place(s) of origin or destination. There is no departure or arrival. There is productive chaos. But this chaos is productive for two critical reasons. First, it is always a search for the Other, especially the Other of multilingualism; "no language should be chosen or promoted at the expense of another," Glissant writes, "once the other one is *spoken* by a people" (CD, 117). Second, and this gives a certain depth to the search for the Other, the *trame chaotique* is at the same time nomadic and rhizomatic. There is the *chaotique* of circular nomadism across the curvature of space and time—eliminating expectation and anticipation, moving language-identity from *métissage* to *creolization*—at the same time as the *trame* of the rhizome's poly-rooted life. Nomadism is not a game or adventure or a pre-scribed destiny. This nomad is not Odysseus or Abraham, the foundations of the West as a project. The Other of thought, which Glissant opposes to the *thought of the Other* (PR, 224n3), is what gives life without offering soil or a root source. How are we to think this peculiar cluster of possible characterizations of circular nomadic life—"giving with," "search for the Other," "contact of inside and outside," "experience of here and elsewhere"—in the *trame chaotique*?

It is instructive to consider for a moment Glissant's conceptual relation to Benítez-Rojo's *The Repeating Island*, that other Caribbean text so concerned with Deleuze, Guattari, chaos, and rhizomatic identity.[18] For Glissant and Benítez-Rojo both, the distinction between order and chaos, especially when the latter is conceived as destructive to the former, is too clean; when mapped on to the Caribbean archipelago, chaos takes on a fecundity that cannot be anticipated in the fantasies of continental thinking, where the measure intervenes to control excess. Systematic thought is not only imperial and colonial in its epistemology and metaphysics—which is plenty sufficient for critique—but also insufficient to the chaotic excesses of the Caribbean. Deleuze and Guattari's work is important for Benítez-Rojo, as for Glissant, precisely because the anti-systematic *imperative* of rhizomatic and nomadic thought offers crucial critical models for *both* diagnosis and resistance. And though *The Repeating Island* is largely a theory of history and culture, it is also, like any historical-cultural study, concerned with the zigzag movement of a subjectivity who constitutes and is constituted by those forms of meaning. Benítez-Rojo writes:

> The rhizome state . . . is a labyrinth in process. It can be understood also as a burrow, or as the system of tunnels in an anthill. It is a

world of connections and of trips without limits or proportions. In a rhizome *one is always in the middle, between Self and Other*. But, above all, it should be seen as a nonsystematic system of lines of flight and alliance that propagate themselves ad infinitum.[19]

Benítez-Rojo's rendering of rhizome, which he sees as constituting "the Caribbean psyche,"[20] situates subjectivity between Self and Other. This *between* unsettles the single root, of course, but it also employs—consciously or not—the language of measurable space. To that extent, Benítez-Rojo stays very close to Deleuze and Guattari and, from Glissant's perspective, surely within the aligned yet fragmented spatiality of the arrow-like nomad's third movement. It is surely noteworthy that *The Repeating Island*, for all of its concern with chaos and lines of flight, moves away from the poly-lingualism of the archipelago—which he says "seems to divide irreparably the letters of the Caribbean"—and toward what he calls the "common dynamics that express themselves in a more or less regular way within chaos."[21]

Perhaps, then, Glissant's conception of the circular nomadic subject's search for the Other is akin to Emmanuel Levinas's claims about the Other, particularly the central chapter of *Otherwise Than Being,* in which Levinas argues that alterity is constitutive of the identity of the subject. Indeed, there is much to suggest this connection. To begin, there is between Glissant and Levinas the metaphysical common space of a theory that puts irreducible difference *outside* the logic of comparison and measure, in which the liberation of difference from the fantasy of the single root generates an anarchical sense of the Other. The epistemological effect, for both Glissant and Levinas, leads to a critique of knowledge as *comprehension,* the grasping and possession of the Other that is so characteristic of Western models of knowing. To wit: one can surely hear the resonance of Levinas's critique of "the Same" when Glissant writes:

> It is not necessary to try to become the other (to become other) nor to "make" him in my image. These projects of transmutation—without metempsychosis—have resulted from the worst pretensions and the greatest of magnanimities on the part of the West. (PR, 193)

Indeed, Glissant's imperative when it comes to the problem of the Other is just that of Levinas: resist representation. In fact, it is not just an imperative to resist representation, for representation is already contested—Levinas will say *ruined*, in a well-known essay titled "The Ruin of Representation"—by the opacity (Glissant) and transcendence (Levinas) of the Other. It is not simply that we are obligated to respect the alterity of the Other. That respect, we could say, is itself premised upon the Other's already exceeding the grasp of the knowing subject *before* the act of knowing. Epistemology is entwined with ethics, and both draw on a metaphysics of distanciation, deferral, delay, and irreducible difference.

However, there are important distinctions to be made, distinctions that bring Glissant's ontology of the subject into focus.[22] In particular, if we attend to how the problem of identity—that ontological moment in Glissant's analysis—is entwined with the notion of the Other, then we see how the curvature of space and time fundamental breaks Glissant from the Levinasian problematic. This shared concern with identity and otherness is nicely gathered in the fact that both Levinas and Glissant engage Rimbaud's enigmatic phrase, found in a letter to Paul Demeny from 1871, which overturns the primacy of self-sufficient subjectivity in a single abuse of grammar: *Je est une autre,* "I is an other." Why are Levinas and Glissant drawn to Rimbaud's phrase? What does the abuse of grammar tell each about the meaning of subjectivity? For Levinas, and this is true of both *Totality and Infinity* (1961) and *Otherwise Than Being* (1974), the Other troubles subjectivity, but in that troubling there is never the closing of distance. And so *Totality and Infinity* will speak of the meaning and structure of "separation" and *Otherwise Than Being* describes the subject as "de-nucleated" or "carved out" at its very core. Such is the Other's effect as the transcendence-being who puts the subject in question. Diachronic time describes the rift between subjectivity and the Other, a rift in which the Other's time is itself wholly other than my time and thus cannot be reconciled in a synchronic time. Rather, there is always, irreducibly, separation and distance. The priority of the Other, captured in the famous Levinasian claim that ethics is first philosophy, makes sense of Rimbaud's "I is an other." The Other makes me an object, sets me in the accusative such that I am first *moi* before I am *je*. I am held under the accusation of the Other (the origin of the ethical), and this accusation, this subjectivity-in-the-accusative-case, is what first makes subjectivity. Hence Levinas's claim that subjectivity is for-the-Other. I *am* only insofar as I am put under the accusing, constituting gaze of the Other. Whatever his resistance to the language of ontology, this is a kind of ontology of the subject, describing, indeed, what it means to *be*.

For Glissant, Rimbaud's abuse of grammar bears a very different lesson, and I think this lesson illuminates some of Glissant's hesitations about the language of transcendence. The linkage of rhizome to life and the insistence upon the motion of the circular nomad run contrary to Levinasian transcendence in a couple of ways. First, the rhizomatic conception of roots and life goes beyond separation by conceiving the relation to the Other as a *donner-avec*, one that does not contradict opacity (Levinas's concern about dialogical conceptions of otherness), but instead underscores the positivity of an identity formed in contact. Second, the motion of the circular nomad describes a dynamism of identity that surely labors against the rather static description of subjectivity as de-nucleated. The result, then, is a surpassing of the synchronic-diachronic distinction that lies at the heart of the Levinasian account of the Self-Other relation. For Levinas, the encounter with the Other is always a confrontation, where the Other devastates the subject in making the subject a subject. But for Glissant, the Self-Other relation is a moment of creation *and* opacity. Consider a remark from *Poetics of Relation*, where Glissant writes that creolization

> is not merely an encounter, a shock (in Segalen's sense), a *métissage*, but a new and original dimension allowing each person to be there and elsewhere, rooted and open, lost in the mountains and free beneath the sea in harmony and in errantry. (PR, 34)

The Levinasian project keeps the Self-Other frozen in the moment of shock; no response is possible after the Other puts me in the accusative. But Glissant emphasizes how the shock of encounter, the violence of opacity to authoritarian gazes and knowledge regimes, is fundamentally productive *because* it fragments and decenters. This is precisely one of the points on which Glissant has great praise for Segalen, writing that "Segalen's decisive thought (*pensée decisive*) was that encountering the Other over-stimulates (*suractive*) the poetic imaginary and poetic understanding" (PR, 29; translation altered). Over-stimulation creates both the conditions *and* the necessity of nomadic movement; opacity exceeds and initiates another imaginary. That is, opacity stalls one form of knowledge—the grasping and possessing characteristic of comprehension—in order to reinscribe the work of understanding in the poetic. This reinscription forms and distorts subjectivity from within the circular nomadic move-ment of the rhizomatic de- and reterritorializing of the imaginary. The en-counter with the Other, then, produces a curvature of space and time in the sense that a "correspondence" or an "addition" of Self-Other is no lon-ger possible. The nomadic subject is born at the very moment it surpasses directional senses of relation. *Curving identity.* In that transformation, rootedness and openness are no longer opposed, but somehow related.

We are still seeking the precise character of this relation.

Let us, then, return to Rimbaud's enigmatic phrase. Glissant's distance from the Levinasian Self-Other relationship requires us to reread the abuse of grammar in *je est une autre.* For Glissant, Rimbaud is not putting subjec-tivity in the accusative. While Rimbaud signals the closure of a certain kind of imperial subject, that subject assured of its first position and set in arrow-like fashion on the course of adventure, the archipelagic reception of that signal re-renders fragmentation. Levinas's notion of subjectivity is thereby exposed as a kind of continental thinking, where a center is carved out by what is marginal; at best, from Glissant's perspective, the second phase of nomadism. At the same time, though, the intimacy of the Other to identity in the Levinasian problematic marks an advance on the model provided by Benítez-Rojo and the *between.* The Other is my identity. This is a first prem-ise of Relation. So, Rimbaud's shift in verb tense, and the aporetic relation it sets between Self and Other, implicates, for Glissant, the one in the Other, but not one *for* the Other. In *Poetics of Relation,* at the close of a sustained reflection on poetry's varied responses to otherness, Glissant argues for Re-lation as the culmination of the encounter with difference:

> The consciousness of Relation became generalized, including the collective and the individual. We "know" [*savons*] that the Other is in us and affects our becoming, as well as the bulk of our concep-tions and the development of our sensibility. Rimbaud's "I is an other" is literal in terms of history. In spite of ourselves, a sort of "consciousness of consciousness" opens up and makes each of us into a disrupted [*troublé*] actor in the poetics of Relation. (PR, 27; translation altered)

Consciousness of Relation is subjectivity, which Glissant here captures in the self-fragmenting phrase "consciousness of consciousness." The phrase self-fragments because Glissant locates coming to consciousness at the "end of the world" (*l'accomplissement du monde*), where understanding begins to replace discovery and the Diversity of *tout-monde* is not just a curiosity, but the very structure and meaning of subjectivity. "Starting from the moment that cultures, lands, men, and women were no longer there to discover but to know," Glissant writes, "Relation has figured an absolute . . . that, paradoxically, set us free from the absolute's intolerances" (PR, 27). Without the absolute, there is no here to be subjected to the Other, no continent of the subject that stands to lose its center or core in its encounter with the Other. Glissant's subject *is* an Other. Not between or put in the accusative. Whatever the opacity, there is also an absolute intimacy in the encounter, this strange, peculiar, yet always productive of another imaginary. The subject is rhizomed. The subject moves, nomadic, in curved space and time. The *donner-avec* is therefore never an exchange or meeting or devastating collision. Subjectivity is configured in this *avec,* and the rhizomatic and nomadic qualifiers on that site of configuration curve the space of Relation.

The enigma of Glissant's conception of the Other, and the resultant conception of subjectivity, therefore lies in conceiving the problem of re-lation in a language-identity woven through multiplicity, as well as how all of these notions bear descriptive and prescriptive registers. I want to postpone the matter of description and prescription for a moment and consider how language-identity functions in multiplicity. The key here is maintaining the sense of rootedness captured in the figure of rhizome-identity and the incessant, unforeseen, and unforeseeable motion of the circular nomad. That is, maintaining the *trame* and its character as *chao-tique* is the entire story here, for *web* names the logic or economy of the rhizophoric contact of Relation and *chaos* captures the ceaseless motion of the unrooted. The *between* of Benítez-Rojo's rhizome-identity and the dis-tance and separation of Levinas's denucleated subjectivity for-the-Other capture the sense of unrootedness and the principle of motion, but, as we have seen, neither is sufficient to the curvature of space and time that for Glissant (de-)maps the nomad's movement. What is the structure of the *trame* such that it is ceaselessly *chaotique*?

My suggestion here would be that *trame* is best accounted for in Glis-sant's (albeit only occasional) evocation of *chiasm*. Chiasm names a cross-ing that is at once contact and distance. There is interweaving, to be sure, so the rhizomatic sense of root is possible—the crossing blends and marks

a moment of identity formation—and yet each term of chiasmic relation arrives at, and then departs from, the site of contact without losing
difference—there is no closure to the *trame*. As well, and this is every bit as
important as the crossing of lines, chiastic structures are reversible. While
there are lines of movement, there is also reversibility. The crossing of one
across the other is therefore not occasional contact, nor is the contact an
exhaustive meeting. Rather, the reversibility of chiastic relationality affirms and takes place in the ethics/paradox of contact and opacity. In this
sense, then, the chiasm can be said to keep the *search* of the search for the
Other in motion. There is no exhaustion. For Glissant, we might say, this
inexhaustible relationality gathers, without canceling out any of the items,
the features of the subjectivity of *tout-monde*: opacity, Relation, rhizome,
and nomad. In *Introduction à une poétique du divers,* following a compelling
reflection on what he calls the "excess of excess," Glissant makes a suggestive remark, which I am here taking as a sign of the structure of subjectivity. By the excess of excess, he makes clear, Glissant does not mean
the anarchic or pretensions to profundity, universality, or diversity—all
of which he attributes to mere or contingent excess—but rather the *tout-
monde* (IPD, 94). "If I want to be rigorous about it," Glissant writes

> I can say that I have passed from the measure of the measure to
> the excess of the measure to the measure of excess to the excess of
> excess, and I have made a chiasm. MM, EM, ME, EE. I have made
> a chiasm. *Tout le monde* cannot make a chiasm. But one can make a
> chiasm with the literature of *tout-monde*! (IPD, 95)

Glissant critically nuances chiasm by elevating the poetic technique to a
figure of cultural contact. The movement back and forth is not trivial or
a play of words or internal to a certain poetic logic. Rather, the chiasm of
nomadic movement moves continually away from measure until it arrives
at an excess that is measured only by its exceeding the idea of excess. In
a word: *opacity*. This is why the world cannot make a chiasm: the visibility and legibility of component parts in (non-Glissantian) relation would
circulate any excess back into the object of that relation. Perhaps a universal history. Or cosmopolitanism as a universal right. And so on. And yet
Glissant preserves the reversibility of the chiasm for the excessiveness and
opacity of literary contact—that movement of subjectivity, collective and
singular, in the poetic.

The subject is implicated in this chiastic motion. The reversibility of chiastic relation in *tout-monde* is neither between nor separated, but rather co-implicated in Self and Other *without losing the character of "subjectivity."* This co-implication that is still subjectivity links chiastic relation and movement to the intransitivity of Relation. Relation is *like* an intransitive verb, a provocative claim that we can here read as Glissant's attempt to say two things. First, Relation is a form of knowing that does not take the object to which it is addressed; the address is always about subjectivity. Second, and this is where nomad and chiasm are crucial, the subject *is* the engagement with a non-possessed, non-seized-upon or grasped (*comprendre*) Other.[23] Glissant affirms the analogy in order to name a knowing and being that relates without seizing, but his hesitation, I think, has to be read in terms of the incessant movement of the circular nomad. *Subjectivity as the movement of poetics.* Glissant writes in *Poetics of Relation* that

> when we speak of a poetics of Relation, we no longer need to add: relation between what and what? This is why the French word *Relation*, which functions somewhat like an intransitive verb, could not correspond, for example, to the English word *relationship*.
>
> We have already said that Relation informs not simply what is relayed, but also the relative and the related. . . . But because what it relates, in reality, proceeds from no absolute, it proves to be the totality of relatives, *put in touch and told*. (PR, 27–28, my emphasis)

The chiastic relation can be read over this passage to describe circular nomadic movement that crosses across difference, while always remaining different, relative, Other. Relation maintains that opacity and difference without eschewing the promise of contact. The nomad's Relation-lines, drawn out as chiastic movements and contacts, are neither lines of flight nor bloodlines. The nomad is not the maroon. Relation is not *marronage*.

Glissant's commitment against the single root is borne out, then, as the refusal to articulate the subject's origin by either negation (defiance, flight) or affirmation (nostalgia, rooted memory). Rimbaud's *je est une autre*, read with a chiastic dynamic, reverses direction, repeatedly, in order to both maintain and disorder the subject: the I is the other, but the I is also I in contact with the other. Chiastic movement is too dynamic and too entwined for Benítez-Rojo's *between* (Self and Other are cross-pollinated) and still too rooted for a Levinasian separation and denucleation (creolization crosses the gap, even while maintaining it). In this chiastic, intransitive movement, Glissant has accounted for a circular nomadic subjectivity that is, as Celia Britton says by way of Jean-Luc Nancy, "singular-plural."[24] Individual, collective, and *the search for the Other*. As Glissant puts it:

> Thought of self and thought of other here become obsolete in their duality. . . . What is here is open, as much as this there. I would be incapable of projecting from one to the other. This-here is the *trame*, which weaves (*trame*) no boundaries. The right to opacity would not establish autism; it would be the real foundation of Relation, in freedoms. (PR, 190)

What is particularly Caribbean about this account of the circular nomad? To be sure, the anti-totalitarian pulse of Deleuze and Guattari's nomadology draws Glissant's attention, especially in its capacity to dismantle the pretension of the colonial gaze and cultural imperialism. However, one might, with Glissant, wonder if there is not still a trace of arrow-like nomadism in Deleuze and Guattari's nomadology. This trace functions just like that: a trail of the arrow-like character. Rather than an end or purpose that is still conquering—for they are plainly and unqualifiedly anti-authoritarian—I would suggest that the characteristics of the nomad in Deleuze and Guattari's work retain the territoriality of what Glissant, in *Introduction à une poétique du divers* and elsewhere, calls "continental thinking" (IPD, 43) at the point of origin. That is, the nomad bears traces of a certain power and privilege that comes with single-root thinking, even as the nomad outlines, then acts upon, lines of flight. Consider a passage from a 1973 essay on Nietzsche, where Deleuze writes:

> Entire groups take off on a nomadic adventure: archeologists have taught us to consider nomadism not as an originary state, but as an adventure that erupts in sedentary groups; it is the call of the outside, it is movement. The nomad and his war-machine stand opposite the despot and his administrative machine, and the extrinsic nomadic unity opposite the intrinsic despotic unity.[25]

The nomad leaves. In that departure, a rooted beginning, nomadology is already split between Deleuze and Guattari and Glissant on the motif of originary movement. Now, following this passage, Deleuze will nuance his nomadology by arguing against the adventurous nomad's repetition of the imperial notion of identity—"the nomad attempts to invent an administration"—and surely his notion of multiplicity keeps motion in motion, but the point remains the same. The nomad departs and labors *against* the sedentary, even when Deleuze and Guattari retrieve an original nomadism that is not only derived from or erupting in sedentary, administrative state apparatuses.[26] This sense of departure recalls the remark Glissant, in noting the poets' protest over the "colonization of the world" (IPD, 76), makes on the distinction between the phrasings of Rimbaud and Césaire: the Europeans *arrive* (Rimbaud) or the Europeans *disembark* (Césaire). To this, of course, Glissant offers the arrival and disembark of Africans in the Americas, which never adventures and never awaits arrival. Who is this nomad outside the exchanges of arrival and disembark?

The difference between the phrasing of Rimbaud and Césaire reminds us again of the centrality of the geography of reason. This geographic character distinguishes elements even at the shoreline: arrival and disembark. In an important distinction, Glissant underscores the fundamental difference between nomadologies in terms of birth. Glissant writes in *Poetics of Relation*:

> We will agree that this thinking of errantry, this errant thought, silently emerges from the destructuring of compact national entities that yesterday were still triumphant and, at the same time, from difficult, uncertain births of new forms of identity that call to us. (PR, 18)

At the same time. With this qualifier, Glissant sets out a critical distinction. Nomadology is creolized in the Caribbean context as an anticolonial intervention against the authoritarianism of language, culture, and politics. This means a critique *from abroad*, rather than, as with Deleuze and Guattari, within the *continent*, from within the system of territorial borders. Glissant's coupling of the *from abroad* to the *continental*, however, pushes the margin back into the center with the effect of deconstructing the center with what it seeks to exclude. This arrow-like nomadism has its possibility in this moment, no matter the limits Glissant ascribes, and the Caribbean context thereby supplements—in a transformative and dangerous fashion—a continental nomadology. *At the same time*, there is the circular nomadology closest to the Caribbean, one that labors without the recurrence to and against the center. The Caribbean, that is, as an archipelago without *métropole*. The *creole* Caribbean. This circular nomadism underscores the "uncertain births" as wholly other than the anti-authoritarianism that contests the center from the margins, births that, in turn, think identity without the antechamber task of destructuring national identities. In other words, Glissant's Caribbean nomadology as circular *begins* with the positivity of the abyssal space of the archipelago. He writes:

> In contrast to arrow-like nomadism (discovery or conquest), in contrast to the situation of exile, errantry gives-on-and-with the negation of every pole and every metropolis, whether connected or not to a conqueror's voyaging act. (PR, 19)

Without the systemic item of center, nomadology is circular without closure. Without a territory to be *firstly* deterritorialized, circular nomadology begins with something other than, as with Deleuze and Guattari, the compulsion to ward off the state apparatus. Glissant's circular nomad, we might say, is not a war-machine. Instead, Glissant's nomad, with all caveats and paradoxical characteristics in mind, is an identity-machine. Indeed, one need only look to *Introduction à une poétique du divers*, where, upon reflection on his relation to the concept of rhizome in *A Thousand Plateaus*, Glissant writes that he has "applied this image to the principle of identity" (IPD, 59). Rather than liberate life from the death-culture of totalitarianism and the re-calcification of compact nation-states, circular nomadism, in Glissant's hands, forges Relation as an *already* creole and creoliz*ing* life. This life, which is already in Relation's open and unexpected field of mixture and difference, is constituted as abyssal beginning. That is, it is at the moment of beginning, not of accomplishment, that Glissant has already marked his distance from Deleuze and Guattari. Beginning otherwise, Glissant's nomad *is* otherwise.

The birthplace of the nomad therefore signifies the conditions of territorialization in all of its modalities, which, in turn, marks an important site of creolization in Glissant's reading of Deleuze and Guattari. Caribbeanness transforms the nomad into the thought of errantry. Circular nomadism attends to two features of the archipelago: the positivity of exile and creoleness as a condition and a consequence of survival. The nomad puts the condition and consequence into motion. Or, perhaps, describes the motion that is already the character of nomadism. Glissant writes, linking nomadology to the rhizome:

> In this context uprooting can work toward identity, and exile can be seen as beneficial, when these are experienced as a search for the Other (through circular nomadism) rather than as an expansion of territory (an arrow-like nomadism). Totality's imaginary allows the detours that lead away from anything totalitarian. (PR, 18)

Glissant's aesthetic sensibility begins in this precise place, the circular nomad who works from the fragments of exile. This is Glissant's conception of creative *marronage* as well, which he distinguishes from the atavistic notions of a *marronage* that would flee the composite culture of the Caribbean imaginary. Creative *marronage*, the *poiesis* of the abyssal subject, moves against the totalitarian impulse by both producing and reproducing the imaginary—with roots in the shoreline—of Caribbeanness. Exile is fecund at the shoreline. A war against the despot.

In his evocative poem in praise of chaos, "Pays rêvé, pays réel," blending the language of wound, earth, and the rhizome, Glissant writes:

> *I take my earth to wash the old wounds*
> *From a hollow of brine entangled with avowals*
> *But so heavy to carry, O mangroves, so heavy.* (CP, 200)

Glissant's recovery and transformation of Deleuze and Guattari's notions of rhizome and nomad subjects subjectivity to the method of Caribbeanness. The method, like any philosophical method or modality of reading, translates the given and its possibilities. Geography proves decisive, as the figures of landscape, earth, and the historical experience that inform the given and its possibilities condition subjectivity's content and structure. While the specificity of geography functions only nascently in Deleuze and Guattari's work, signifying a generalized territoriality contested by rhizome and nomad, Glissant's method gives a name to the space of subjectivity. This name, "Caribbean," reshapes the drama of rhizomatic and nomadic movement by infusing motion with an alternative historical

experience of modernity, and so an alternative story to be told about identity. Thus, lines of flight come to be replaced by fragile connections and
cultural contact.

At the same time, the problem of geography's specificity is surmounted
by the sense of the global. Territory is dismantled in part by the diversity
of subjectivity's relation—between diachrony and synchrony, in curved
time—to here and elsewhere, but also by the *possibility* of what Glissant
calls the *tout-monde*. *Tout-monde* is already a curved space (the physical
form of the globe) and a curved time (composed of divergent, incompatible historical narratives that nonetheless touch), and so that term itself
bears many of the characteristics of the circular nomad and its rhizome-
identity. Glissant's exploration of *tout-monde* is varied and spread across
decades of theory, poetry, and literature, and all of those explorations raise
an important issue: To what extent is Glissant's notion of *tout-monde* descriptive, and to what extent is it prescriptive? The question is critical to
understanding the philosophical lesson to be drawn from Glissant's work,
especially when that work informs or even constitutes subjectivity in the
twenty-first century. For example, when Glissant considers the terrifying plight of the Roma in Europe or reflects on the genocidal violence in
Rwanda (see IPD, 90ff.), a whole cluster of *alternative paths* for social orga-
nization and conceptions of collective subjectivity emerge. And yet he will
often repeat, in one form or another, the claim from *Traité du tout-monde*
that we write in the presence of the world's languages, which suggests that
we are all always already creolized. So, the question: Is Glissant *describing* how we are *already* nomadic, rhizomatic subjects? Or is he *prescribing*
such (anti-)forms of subjectivity? Further, if he is prescribing a notion of
subjectivity, against what forces is that normative account directed, and
for what purpose?

In the end, Glissant's sense of Caribbeanness and how Caribbeanness
remakes the rhizome and nomad is a descriptive account of the history
and memory of the archipelago. Taking the archipelago seriously means
taking on the pain of history, theorizing how that painful exile transforms
thinking, and thereby or therein decolonizing the subject. *Against the despot.* At times, Glissant will describe this moment, which is conceptually
articulated in his work but as an existential condition dates back to the
moment of disembarking, a shoreline thinking, as the Caribbean's irruption into modernity. But I would say it differently: Glissant is here naming the Caribbean as the first moment of postmodernity, ironically (or

deconstructively) present at the very moment of modernity's inception. Postmodernity's fraught relationship with fragmentation and the death of the metanarrative, and the notions of delay and deferral at the heart of the strategies that comprise deconstruction, is already the Caribbean experience of the shoreline and after. However, Glissant's vision of this postmodernity—the Afro-postmodern—does not fuss with so much am-bivalence. Instead, the nomad and rhizome produce; this is a theory of life, not the entwinement of life and death, while at the same time always being a theory of haunted life. Trauma is for the dead, yes, but also for the living. And the living live. What is that life? What does the abyssal sub-ject produce? What comes in the wake of, or as the effect of, the rhizome and nomad?

In other words, what is the aesthetics of the abyssal subject?

CHAPTER 4

Aesthetics of an Abyssal Subject

Purify the breath until it reveals the harsh taste of the land: bring
breath to the death of rocks and landscape.

—Glissant, *Caribbean Discourse*

MEMORY, HISTORY, FUTURITY, AND SUBJECTIVITY are displaced by
the abyss, and yet this displacement remains open to the movement of creation. Traces of the painful past, then made fecund, move across space
and time, creating a place in which rhizomatic, nomadic subjectivity finds
a home amid the wakes of trauma, Plantation life, and the cosmological
effect of movement, mixture, and transformation. In tracking this sense
of becoming, we have seen how a circularity that opens and a curvature
that sustains opacity lie at the center of Glissant's shoreline thinking. How
are we to understand the element of that becoming, of that movement?
How is affect transmitted across space and time? How does, or how ought,
representation work in this transmission? Such questions are immanent
to the problematics developed in previous chapters and push us into the
sphere of aesthetics.

In the following reflections, then, I want to explore the structure of
what Glissant calls the life of "contradiction," here in the context of aesthetic modes of creation, representation, and affective transmission. In
particular, I want to situate Glissant's aesthetics of an abyssal subject in two
contexts. First, I want to examine how the aesthetics of an abyssal subject
modifies two of the dominant accounts of aesthetics and Caribbean subjectivity: Aimé Césaire's conception of the relation between culture and
civilization, and George Lamming's existential account of the writer. For
both Césaire and Lamming, alienation is critical for Caribbean aesthetics. The problem of literature and the black writer brings the problem of
alienation into questions of aesthetics, drawing heavily on various conceptions of memory, history, and subjectivity. And it is precisely in relation to

that alienation, coupled to the forms of diversion, reversion, and detour it inspires, that Glissant's archipelagic thinking takes up important new themes. Second, and out of this archipelagic thinking *cum* aesthetics of an abyssal subject, I want to offer as an exemplary case a short reading of Raoul Peck's quirky documentary *Lumumba, la mort du prophète*—a film similarly concerned with the structure of transmission without a single root or fixed place—in order to show how cinematic language might work as precisely this sort of aesthetics.

Glissant's long meditation on subjectivity, which traces out its multiple and always mobile roots, is at once a description of what it means to arrive, then begin in the New World and a normative account of non-alienated subjectivity. That is, the anxieties that provoked the returns to Africa in the Négritude movement, and also motivated the existentialist rebuke and re-formulation of Négritude's valorization of blackness in writers like Fanon, turned on the problem of alienation. What does it mean to call Caribbean subjectivity alienated? In what sense is a form of authenticity at work in such an assessment? And what is the legitimacy of that authenticity?

Glissant's articulation of the abyssal subject revisits the problem of alienation in order to contest the specter of authenticity. We can already see this at work in previous chapters, where the repudiation of atavistic thinking about memory and history and the critique of the single-rooted subject call mimetic or duplicative models of alienation into question. To wit: if there is no single origin or territory in which to ground thinking, then there is no measure (*mesure*) to which one can hold individual or collective subjectivity. There is instead excess (*démesure*). The excess, here, is of course that which exceeds the very idea of measure itself in what Glissant calls the excess of the excess of measure (IPD, 94–95). But this excessiveness is a complicated matter. We cannot simply begin with what lies ahead; futurity is set, inextricably, in contact with the past, however abyssal, however passed on in traces. The question of Africa and the African presence in the New World is constitutive of the traces, the abysses, and therefore the excesses that comprise composite Caribbean culture. Césaire's retrieval of the past is therefore inseparable from any discussion of alienation and excess, no matter the distance Glissant wants to gain from him and the Négritude movement. As well, this sense of excess is precisely what Glissant means by his simple yet potent phrase *tout-monde*. The entirety of the globe is implicated in the project of thinking, not just localized traditions and conceptual schemes. Although such traditions and conceptual schemes are necessary conditions of the thought of opacity (Glissant will always insist on the *inconnu* of specificity and place), they are not sufficient to thinking excess as abundance, curvature, nomad, and rhizome. There must be Relation. It is interesting to note, then, how Lamming's reflections on the meaning and significance of the black writer might be staged as what draws Glissant's *tout-monde* sensibility back into contact with Césaire, the persistence of *pensée continentale*, and the existential problem of the imagination. Between Césaire and Lamming, as we shall see, Glissant instigates an important transformation of alienation and authenticity through the production of an aesthetics of an abyssal subject.

So, as I will argue, the abyssal subject—Glissant's ontological claim on the human—is also the subject of aesthetics. The abyssal subject is the *subject* of aesthetics in two senses. First, and perhaps most importantly, the abyssal subject fundamentally changes the conditions of representation precisely because, when thematized, it breaks narration and unification at its root. This is the foundational innovation of Glissant's conception of beginning as a *shoreline thinking*. Saturated with the abyss of the sea *as* history, beginning begins with a radical break. The abyssal subject is therefore a subject of aesthetics insofar as the articulation of subjectivity requires a transformed modality of the aesthetic. Second, and related to this problem of thematizing representation after the abyss, the transmission of affect settles both the creator and the atmosphere of reception into a different register. If we reckon with Glissant's commitment to opacity and creolization, then the transmission of affect cannot be guided by a regulative idea of transparency. *Pensée archipélique* is not just transformed and fragmented conceptual space. It is also an affective fragmentation, with all the complex modes of representation and transmission that (must) accompany.

An aesthetics begins *somewhere*. An aesthetics, in other words, is never dislodged from the site of its articulation, transmission, and reception, and so the geography of reason begins our sense of beginning. Time and space—which is to say, place and its history and memory—give birth, as it were, to an aesthetic sensibility and to certain principles that attend to the ethical questions of abyssal beginning and the transmission of affect. Near the close of *Caribbean Discourse*, Glissant marks the beginning of an aesthetics with all the motifs of a generalized notion of an abyssal beginning:

On disembarking, elusive utterance. The secret resin of our words, cut short in our mouths, uprooted from their night. A kind of hope for those who prey on the people. A whole desolate Creole, twisted in the murky depths of mangrove.

Then, this other language, in which we keep quiet. (It is the timid owl frightened by the speech of Domination.) Nip it in the bud. Weave it, not into the greenness that does not suit it, but in the stripped truth of our contradictions. (CD, 237)

Glissant writes these lines "from the perspective of shackles [*Boises*]," a perspective that locates his reflections in trauma and its aftermath. From the loss manifest in disembarking to the rhizomatic ante- and anti-roots of the mangrove, a subject and its intimate aesthetics are generated. *The abyssal subject*, a subject of aesthetics whose affective life—as both representation and creative force—begins with the abyss. For Glissant, the aesthetics of an abyssal subject is tantamount to a defense of the elusive utterance, its opacity and murky depth, and thus a return to the life of contradiction.

The life of contradiction describes the sites of contact and dynamics of magnetic connection between opacities that sustain the life of Relation. "Relation exists in being realized," Glissant writes in *Poetics of Relation*, "that is, in being completed in a common place." And further:

This movement allows giving-on-and-with the dialectic among aesthetics. If the imaginary carries us from thinking about this world to thinking about the universe, we can conceive that aesthetics, by means of which we make our imaginary concrete, with the opposite intention, always bring us back from the infinities of the universe to the definable poetics of our world. . . . Thus, we go into the open circle of our relayed aesthetics, our unflagging politics. We leave the matrix abyss and the immeasurable abyss for this other one in which we wander without becoming lost. (PR, 203)

Much of what follows in the present chapter will revolve around this passage, for in it Glissant evokes so many of the pressing issues in articulating an aesthetics. With his deployment of the term *common place*, Glissant opens up the space of aesthetic production. An aesthetic object is a common place in which contradiction does not dissolve the notion of *commun*, but rather constitutes it as *lieu*. As well, this siting and citation of

Relation in the aesthetic makes the imaginary "concrete"; the imagined and open world engages in the transmission of affect and therefore begins in a different register. Ontology is not aesthetics. It is noteworthy here, as well, that the nomadic structure of subjectivity, which receives such nuanced treatment throughout *Poetics of Relation*, is introduced as a way of describing the location of the work of art in the world *and* the location of subjectivity in that work of art. This double movement of relay, zigzagging from artwork to subject to world and back, suggests that the structure of an aesthetics is indispensable for the life of Relation. Indeed, this is the central claim of the present chapter. And so we begin.

Whence Glissant's aesthetics? And why?

Land and Alienation

What do we want from an aesthetics?

This is quite a question. Indeed, if we emphasize the *from*, then the very orientation of the question could be read as drawing from a long tradition in Western philosophy of rendering aesthetics a secondary, if not altogether problematic, theoretical task. Not accidentally does aesthetic theory continue to be that place in which philosophers simultaneously become relevant to other disciplines and slowly slip from prominence in philosophical circles. This is especially the case in a given thinker's *œuvre*, as, for example, with Kant's aesthetics in relation to his epistemology or ethics. The problem, if I can venture a massive generalization, is that aesthetic objects and the theorizing that clusters to them are (or feel) compelled to be about something beyond the artwork. Even Kant's aesthetics can be interpreted as an extension of his critique of metaphysics or his concern with philosophy of nature and so on, which leads one to read his aesthetics and the objects he might study as *about* something altogether other than the structure and content of affective transmission. This "something," then, becomes what is primary and most significant for serious philosophical reflection and analysis. Aesthetics becomes a secondary or even instrumental concern. To wit: if we demand that an aesthetics produce *something*—whether an ethics or a politics or that it solve some sort of epistemological enigma, and so on—then aesthetic theorizing and object production is merely the handmaiden of another project. While helpful, the decisive and fundamentally more incisive analysis is to be found in another mode of philosophizing. If only the handmaiden, then the transmission of affect, the production of beauty, and other questions of aesthetics fail to obtain the autonomy expected of serious philosophical labor. So goes the story.

At the very same time that aesthetics plays a handmaiden role in philosophy, it could also be said that everything in a philosophy of history and culture hinges on aesthetic sensibility. This reversal of priorities has its own (albeit more muted) intellectual history. Hegel's aesthetic theory, for example, famously entwines with philosophy of history in order to produce claims about the development of Spirit, hegemony, and so the realization of absolute knowledge (or at least aspiration toward). In his *Lectures on Fine Art*, for example, Hegel makes the argument that "art belongs to the same province as religion and philosophy," and so, in art, "Spirit liberates itself from the cramping barriers of its existence in externality, by opening for itself a way out of the contingent affairs of its worldly existence . . . into the consideration and completion of its being in and for itself."[1] This being in and for itself, for Hegel, is the becoming of Spirit in history's movement across the globe. No longer a handmaiden, and now an engine of historical expression and experience, aesthetics suddenly emerges as perhaps *the* site of historical becoming. Aesthetic meaning and experience marks the movement of civilizations through time in the long march of Spirit, rather than, as so often before Hegel's work, being the mere conduit of other, more serious forms of discourse and concerns of theory.

And one cannot merely attribute this understanding of history and aesthetics to the decadence of European philosophy (which it certainly does reflect, but to which it cannot be reduced). For example, we find that when stripped of a few of its loftier and more speculative (and therefore most exclusivist) pretensions, the Hegelian motif generally, and the aesthetics-history link in particular, animates much of W. E. B. Du Bois's "Conservation of Races." In this essay, Du Bois's defense of the "Negro race," undertaken in a largely Hegelian register, turns on a claim from philosophy of history regarding the advance of humanity. Without the Negro race, Du Bois contends, *universal* humanity lacks the fullness of possibility and will thus always be under-realized. This contention prompts him to write in the first item of the Academy Creed that "we believe that the Negro people, as a race, have a contribution to make to civilization and humanity, which no other race can make."[2] It is noteworthy that in this essay Du Bois turns to aesthetic examples—spiritual strivings borne by music, literature, poetry, and so on—in making his case for setting "a Negro school of literature and art, and an intellectual clearing house, for all these products of the Negro mind, which we may call a Negro Academy" among other practical matters of economy and governance.[3] Perhaps even placed above, for the spiritual strivings that serve as the entryway to history, that grandest site for the contribution of black peoples, manifest most profoundly in the arts.

Hegel and Du Bois, to take only two (and very different) examples, reverse the traditional role of aesthetics and aesthetic objects. In that reversal, aesthetics becomes the study of how a culture understands and reveals itself, thereby becoming the study of how a story of *this place* and *these people* enters the larger story of History: what it means for humanity *to be* and *to become*. The intimacy of the aesthetic to such questions of place and identity breaks aesthetics free of metaphysics, epistemology, and ethics in order to carry *and* create meanings of ultimate significance. In this sense, we can raise the issue again without reversion to the elsewhere of the question: What do we want from an aesthetics? Or perhaps better, what does an aesthetics want, even demand, of *us*?

This momentary excursus helps us stage the important debate between Césaire and Lamming concerning the meaning and significance of the black writer. Both thinkers take on the forms of alienation specific to Afro-Caribbean history and life in the context of developing an aesthetics, and while they share this concern and distinct focus, how such an aesthetics is to be written into a global philosophy of history is importantly different. In particular, and in order to contain the discussion, it is interesting to see how this debate is carried out in the context of the 1956 First International Congress of Black Writers and Artists in Paris, which a young Glissant attended as a representative from the francophone Caribbean.[4] In this parting of ways, Césaire and Lamming map two senses of writing the question of Caribbean aesthetics global—for the former, toward Africa, and for the latter, toward a larger theory of the human condition. As well, Césaire and Lamming nicely frame Glissant's aesthetics; all three share a commitment to collapsing the distinction between art and theory, whether that be in evocative, lyrical essays or in creative work saturated with ontology, epistemological questions, ethical and political drama, and so forth. And so the questions raised between Césaire and Lamming are of the highest theoretical concern generally, while also rooted in the specificity of the aesthetic for historical, cultural transformation in the Caribbean context. Césaire's essay "Culture and Colonisation" brings many of the insights and claims of Négritude to bear on metaphysical and aesthetic questions, merging a philosophy of history with provocative, quasi-essentialist claims about transnational blackness. Lamming's essay "The Negro Writer and His World," which reads as a profound, searching critical response to Négritude's scope and ambition, is largely anti-metaphysical and full of *ennui*, bringing so many of the insights and claims of existentialism to bear on the very same issues raised by Césaire and Négritude more generally. This is not just a scholarly disagreement. Nor is it a matter of thinking through a moment in intellectual history. Césaire and Lamming put geography into thinking, land into the aesthetic of alienation, which creates a split vision with which to return to questions of Caribbean memory, history, identity, and, ultimately, aesthetics. With such split vision, both Césaire and Lamming think Caribbeanness in two sites simultaneously: the here of the fractured Caribbean, and the elsewhere of the wider, more significant problematic that repairs that fracture with an alternative future.

Glissant's elaboration of the notion of Relation and thinking as *tout-monde* is helpfully framed by this schism. The debate between Césaire and Lamming, of course, takes place in the very same year that Glissant publishes his massive memorial poem "The Indies." As well, and perhaps more important, insofar as Glissant understands the globalization of thinking—which marks particular forms of alienation and despair for both Césaire and Lamming, while at the same time secretly mapping the liberation of the imagination—to be critical for any address to alienation, the terms of thinking as *tout-monde* demand precision. To where does the globalization of thinking lead us? This question is a matter for philosophy of history and, perhaps, a bit of metaphysics. For Césaire, Lamming, and Glissant it is largely, or even primarily, a question of aesthetics—always an aesthetics derived from a specific geography of thinking, being, and creating. What sort of aesthetics is generated (in a descriptive and/or normative sense) by the black writer in this movement toward, then fully into, the global? This is partly an ethical question for all three thinkers. In particular, it is a question of the responsibility of a specific group of writers and their aesthetic productions. But it is also a deeper question regarding the sorts of structures necessary for the transmission of the Afro-Caribbean experience. How is such experience transmitted *authentically* to both that community and the world with which it is engaged? Authenticity, of course, will prove to be a key concept. From what sort of *here*, and so also from what sort of *there* or *elsewhere*, does the writer write? And toward what place? This is the intellectual space of Césaire's and Lamming's contributions to the 1956 Congress, and it is also the space within which Glissant's aesthetics is transformed by Relation.

In this schism regarding the geography of reason, between Césaire and Lamming, Glissant undertakes an aesthetics of the abyssal subject.

Césaire's essay "Culture and Colonisation" brings into theoretical focus much of what he had articulated a decade and a half earlier in his *Notebook of a Return to My Native Land*. *Notebook* dramatizes double sense of "return" by locating blackness in both Africa and the New World. This double location begins with testimony to the pain of history. The pain of history in *Notebook* is treated with a complexity and sensitivity absent in the understandably more polemical *Discourse on Colonialism*, where Césaire's evocation of the suffering of black people in Africa and the Americas served as the motivating outrage for a larger, wider-ranging statement about the future of colonized peoples. In *Notebook* the tone is at once introspective and collective. Europe's indefensible character in *Discourse*, which prompts Césaire to suggest locating the future of humanity (a new humanism) in emergent postcolonial nations, becomes (if we read backward) in *Notebook* an incarnation of the experience of history's long, painful shadow. In *Discourse*, Césaire measures Europe according to the ideas put forth by Europe itself in the most rational of moral categories—*humanism*. When "it most often mouths the word," Césaire writes, "the West has never been further from being able to live a true humanism—a humanism made to the measure of the world."[5] Saying and living are two very distinct humanisms, and the failure to live what one says indicts not just the idea but the entire culture in which the idea was incubated, then thrust upon the world. At this point in *Discourse*, closing its penultimate chapter, Césaire has provided plenty grounds for his opening claim in the text that "*Europe is indefensible*."[6] The rhetoric-cum-grounds for this opening claim appeals simultaneously to reason as Europe's self-assigned measure *and* the "trickery and deceit," the closing of the eyes, and the decadence of European civilization. This contradiction, in the end, renders Europe "unable to justify itself before the bar of 'reason' or before the bar of 'conscience,'" taking instead "refuge in a hypocrisy which is all the more odious because it is less and less likely to deceive."[7] Césaire's great postcolonial insight lies in this indictment of Europe on its own terms, which in turn generates an important ethic of suspicion in relation to European ideas, values, and general historical claims.

Notebook shifts tone from polemic to introspection. Indeed, *Notebook* is a story about the author's own movement across a multiplicity of senses of alienated home and homes, and then, after that alienation, the retrieval of the New World's saving power. Written in Césaire's voice, it is also the voice of Afro-Caribbean experience as such. One of the consequences of this shift is that the reason or rationality of Europe shifts from an object of ridicule or condition of the inferiority complex to a comprehensive instrument of harm. That is, it is not just that Europe is insufficient to its own measure, but also (and perhaps firstly) that the idolatry of rationality serves as a first site of conquest, subjugation, and alienation. *A brutal and violent alienation inside the psyche.* Césaire writes:

> Reason, I crown you wind of the evening.
> Mouth of order your name?
> To me it is the whip's corolla.
> Beauty I call you petition of stone.
> But ah! The raucous smuggling
> of my laughter
> Ah! My treasure of saltpetre!
> Because we hate you, you and your reason, we invoke dementia
> praecox flamboyant madness tenacious cannibalism.[8]

Reason appears here as an affliction that afflicts its pain from the interior, yet, in its interiority, functions at the same time as an external force. Discipline of psyche and body orbit around the same figure: the whip's corolla. Césaire's imagery links reason to the whip, and so to slavery's cruelest discipline, which has now become a psychic device. Reason therefore cannot be reduced to an instrument among instruments, for, like beauty, reason sets a measure for not an aspect or accidental quality, but *the very being of the human*. The whip's corolla, reason as a cultural and political practice, provokes Césaire's counter-poetics, which, on grounds that are both strategically adopted and quasi-essentialist, opposes Europe's idea of madness and dementia with an African(-ized) poetics of the same.

The place of reason in the psyche of Africans in the New World begins Césaire's long examination of the sufferings and anxieties of beginning.

The resonance of reason as whip and the long shadow it casts in the history of the Americas builds remembrance into aesthetics. One must remember history's pain in order to put the figure and image to work, which means, at the very same time, that the figures and images of violence and abjection make remembrance happen. An aesthetics *makes* the event of remembering, just as it is *made by* remembrance. Like Glissant after him, Césaire's poetics is also a memory project. Césaire makes this clear near the middle of *Notebook* when he writes:

> So much blood in my memory! In my memory are lagoons. They are covered with death's heads. They are not covered with water lilies. In my memory are lagoons. On their banks no women's loincloths are spread out.

> My memory is circled with blood. My memory has its belt of corpses.

> A bombardment of rum barrels genially lacing our ignoble revolts, eyes swooning sweet from the gulp of ferocious liberty.[9]

Remembrance does not bring knowledge to the surface, nor does it adorn the past with redemptive or reproductive figures. Here, as we shall see, we catch sight of no small part of Glissant's distance from Césaire. For Césaire, memory *is* the blood of suffering. History in the New World *is* abjection. Still, as memory comes and unfolds its pain, remembrance also becomes the radical trace of blood-as-bloodline, the thread of the past that lives *before* memory's belt of corpses. To put it simply, out of the blood, lagoons, and corpses, *Notebook* becomes a book about an aesthetics of the future that is folded into two senses of the past: abjection and the trace of what will redeem the diaspora.

In the transformation of memory as the blood of suffering into memory as the blood(line) of the previous past, Césaire, in a trope surely open to many psychoanalytic interpretations, characterizes loss as a shrunken and retracted spear. Retraction spatializes the temporal stretch of memory and the effect of pain on that memory in history. History's pain shrinks or pulls back the virility of life, of culture, and so the memory of that past remains squarely within the logic of retrieval and reactivation. He writes:

I have now deciphered the meaning of the ordeal: my country [Martinique] is the "spear of night" of my Bambara ancestors. It shrinks and its blade desperately retracts toward the handle if it is dabbed with chicken-blood and it says that its temper requires a man's blood, his fat, his liver, a man's heart and not chicken-blood.[10]

Césaire follows this with the exhortation to seek "for my country" the "hearts of men which . . . beat with virile blood" and have eyes for the paternal land (*terre paternelle*).[11] This begins Césaire's sense of beginning as its own kind of orphan narrative, where the *terre paternelle* marks both the lost father and the fatherlessness of the New World landscape. But the New World is not yet capable of sustaining life; Césaire's figure is paternal, an important contrast to Glissant's invocation of the Plantation-womb. The spear is retracted. Césaire offers an exhortation, which indicates, if nothing else, that this is a relation to a paternity-to-come. Having eyes for the paternal land comes as a response to alienation from land: seeking return to a home-land, whether that be here or elsewhere or in a between-place or in a wholly new place. Most importantly, for me, the motif of *terre paternelle* commences Césaire's account of Négritude, an account in which, he notes in *Discourse*, "the problem is not to make a utopian and sterile attempt to repeat the past, but to go beyond. . . . It is a new society we must create . . . warm with all the fraternity of olden days."[12] This "new society" animates the loftier aspirations of *Discourse,* and that aspiration cannot be reduced to mere and naive nostalgia. And yet, those aspirations are always oriented toward the Africanness of Caribbean, then Martinican, life. Négritude thereby doubles the sense of the new: a new space *and* a new sense of Africanness through the work of retrieval. Aesthetics lies at the heart of this newness. In particular, the Négritude aesthetic addresses the problem of how memory and history are (and *ought* to be) transmitted in the affective structure of language and expression. "I have always striven to create a new language," Césaire says in a 1967 interview with René Depestre, "one capable of communicating the African heritage. . . . I wanted to create an Antillean French, a black French that, while still being French, had a black character."[13] Still, were this to remain a matter for literary or poetic language one would miss the metaphysical sense of Césaire's claim; Césaire's intervention in the meaning and possibilities of language transforms the very geography of thinking, and so, as a metaphysical and epistemological consequence of the aesthetic, transforms *in toto* the relation between alienation, land, and home. In *Notebook*, Césaire writes:

> my negritude is not an opaque spot of dead water of the dead
> eye of the earth
> my negritude is neither a tower nor a cathedral
>
> it reaches deep down into the red flesh of the soil
> it reaches deep into the blazing flesh of the sky
> it pierces opaque prostration with its straight patience [*droite
>   patience*][14]

The problem of language is the problem of roots, place, and knowledge. With the image of the soil, coupled to flesh, Césaire situates Négritude as a matter of identity in both body and place. With the image of the sky, coupled to flesh, Césaire places Négritude in the logic of knowledge production—both knowledge of self (the preeminent preoccupation of *Notebook*) and knowledge of the nature of one's place (the cultural and political reach of the poem). An aesthetics of language, then, functions as the hinge of knowledge, identity, and the transformation of history.

Césaire's turn inward, then outward in the contemplation of place prepares the grounds for an interpretation of "Culture and Colonisation." In many ways, Césaire's essay from the 1956 Congress repeats the central concern of *Discourse* (published one year prior) by posing the same motivating question: What is meant by "civilization," and what does that meaning have to say to black people in a south Atlantic context? However, *Discourse* is largely guided by the political concerns of the moment, exhorting the reader to join the cultural, economic, and widely political efforts of anticolonial, then postcolonial struggle. "Culture and Colonisation," on the other hand, is considerably more metaphysical in its concern with philosophy of history, guided as it is by the biggest question at stake in the Négritude movement: What does it mean to say that an essential Africanness survives across the forced migration of African peoples across the Atlantic, then subjugation of the intellect under enslavement, the plantation, and colonial domination? The question of transmission and re-transmission is central, and this question couples political identity to aesthetic production and possibility. Politically, this means for Césaire that black people have "a *solidarity in time*, due to the fact that we started in an original unity, the unity of African civilization."[15] The aesthetic problem is intertwined with the politics of solidarity in time, for, as Césaire famously notes by way of his citation of Lenin's citation of Hegel, a dominated people cannot produce a poetics of life. "A political and social system that suppresses the self-determination of a people," Césaire writes, "thereby kills the creative power of that people."[16] Creative power is not just expression or outlet. *An aesthetics produces life.*

As the site of the production of life *against* alienation, aesthetics, for Césaire, is situated at the interval of beginning. "In the culture that is yet to be born," he writes, "there will be without any doubt both old and new. Which new elements? Which old? Here alone our ignorance begins."[17] In exactly this moment, Césaire's aesthetics of the Négritude subject proves crucial. Freed from domination, the power of transformative reactivation—that intertwined space of the past and a pure future—is in the hands of the poet. Césaire's word is the word of the transmission of historical experience in its strange temporality. That is, the word transmits both memory of blood and the creative reading, then rereading of the traces of African civilization. In that moment, a given culture becomes a variant of a governing civilization. And so Césaire concludes "Culture and Colonisation" with an exhortation to write Afro-Caribbeanness out of its "cultural chaos":

> "Free the demiurge that alone can organise this chaos into a new synthesis, a synthesis that will deserve the name of culture, a synthesis that will be a reconciliation and an overstepping of both old and new." We are here to ask, nay to demand: "Let the peoples speak! Let the blak [*sic*] peoples take their place upon the great stage of history!"[18]

Négritude, not unlike Du Bois's conserved race, is thus an aesthetics of a subject-to-come, a subject who is, in a certain sense, waiting in traces and fragments of civilization, and so waiting to become world-historical in the fullest sense. And, to say it again, Césaire's aesthetics is not just an expression of the subject upon and after arrival in the culture to come. Rather, aesthetics is located at the site of beginning subjectivity (reckoning with history's pain and traces), and then, on the other side of transmission, emerging as the effective cause of the becoming of the yet-to-be-born culture now come to fruition. Or, to put it rather more loftily, Césaire's poetic word carries the vicissitudes of memory and hope. A double time manifest in retrieval: the fullness of the past and the openness of the future. Only the present is repudiated.

In the problem of culture, then, Césaire is able to generate an aesthetic of Africanness without naive nostalgia. That is, Africanness—for which space must be created *in* French—is at once something new and something ancient. The newness locates Africanness in a globalized context, always in some measure site-specific, and yet this newness, as a *diasporic thought,* is possible on the basis of an atavistic reading of traces. The temporality of this reading could be described as a kind of future anterior— the reading *will have been* African—in which the creative intervention of the writer makes a hidden something apparent *and* creates a new object of aesthetic contemplation. We can see a good bit of this at work in *Notebook,* where it is difficult to locate the temporality of a claim in Césaire's rhetoric; he often seems to be simultaneously remembering the past and imagining the future. *The chiasmic racial time of hope.* In this sense, Césaire's aesthetics are imaginary in the fullest sense of the word: free of simple mimetic qualities, but also engaged in the difficult, painful work of memory. Césaire imagines *through* the blood of memory to the pre-memorial traces *and then* imagines a new Africanness in the Caribbean *in order to envision* the pre-memorial trace. A double-movement. Négritude as a kind of future anterior. The writerly ethics that emerges from Césaire's double movement—a political aesthetics in the grandest sense of *polis,* addressing how a "we" is to live together—places important obligations on the black writer. The writer *must* and *ought to* write in this temporal register. Négritude's aesthetic is both justified and guided by these obligations.

To such lofty language and conceptual space, Lamming's contribution to the 1956 Congress, "The Negro Writer and His World," offers an existential reflection on alienation and aesthetics in black literature. With its anti-systematic intervention in the particular problem of the black writer, who *ought* to concern himself with "the world of men," Lamming's essay provides an important and fascinating aesthetic counterpoint to Césaire's globalization of the black aesthetic. Like Césaire, Lamming is concerned with the meaning of aesthetic experience from a largely normative perspective. What *ought* the black writer write? And in what manner? But Lamming's existentialism, which inheres in both his attention to alienation as the human condition as such and his suspicion that "blackness" is

as much a product of the Other's gaze as an essential Africanness,[19] draws
these questions down from the ether of a philosophy of history and back
into contact with the *pathos* of reflection and composition. An aesthetic
follows suit. The *pathos* of Lamming's writer is inseparable from the problem of race and racism, and his existential suspicions about the veracity
of the category "race" give immediately over to the lived reality of what
he calls "colour prejudice." Color prejudice is firstly an external problem,
generated by white racism, hatred, and denigration. And then, as the external problem begins to form the life of human reality—the racist world
and its gaze as constitutive of experience and identity—color prejudice
becomes an internal problem. The existential identity of the writer, which
becomes aesthetic sensibility and obligation, is constituted in this zigzag
movement:

> The Negro writer is a writer who, through a process of social and
> historical accidents, encounters himself, so to speak, in a category
> of men called Negro. He carries this definition like a limb. It travels
> with him as a necessary guide for the Other's regard. It has settled
> upon him with an almost natural finality, until he has become it.
> He is a reluctant part of conspiracy, which identifies him with that
> condition which the Other has created for them both.[20]

Whatever the anti-metaphysical skepticism of an existentialism that eschews essentialism in the name of the open possibilities of subjectivity,
Lamming settles here on the characterization of race as something "like a
limb." This is a decisive hesitation before the term, reminiscent of Fanon's
and Sartre's theorizing of the same, which registers the deeply constitutive
power of race without opting for essentialist economies. Like a limb, race
is a part of what it means to be a body that moves in the world. As such,
the *pathos* of race creates a twofold sense of alienation: alienation from the
world (the Other's gaze rejects) and alienation from one's self (the Other's
gaze is internalized by way of social and historical experience).

For Lamming, the crucial question for an aesthetics emerges from the
careful negotiation of the relation between the inner life of the writer and
the writer's world. The two are not wholly separate or separable, of course.
Race is lived *like a limb*, and thus race is constitutive of the very movement
from the writer to his world. And yet writing cannot simply be reduced
to reportage or testimony; the body must be both described and *elevated*

by aesthetic intervention. With just this dynamic in view, Lamming offers a three-part schema for thinking about the writer-world relation. First, there is the relation the writer has with himself. Self-relation is that "priceless possession" which "contains the range of his ambitions, his deceits, his perplexity, his pride, his shame, his guilt, his honour, his need"; in this "world," this first site of pathos, "all these qualities are there, hidden in the castle of his skin."[21] The inner life of the writer remains the origin of Lamming's aesthetic, the touchstone of the greatness of expression and the transmission of affect.

Still, the inner life is not an island. If race is lived like a limb and self-relation is a priceless possession, a relation then linked to the existential (not essential) status of race, then the origin must have its supplement: the *relation* to the world. The relation is a supplement because it intervenes in and changes the priceless possession. This supplement to the original inner life of the writer, functioning as a para-origin of sorts, is one without which aesthetics and the poetic life is impossible. In the para-origin of race-as-worldly-relation (the external made internal), the first world of self-relation gives way to Lamming's *second* sense of world: that "world in which he moves among other men." Tracking the movement of origin and para-origin, and therefore the often cruel economy of racial identity formation, Lamming writes:

> An identical suffering holds them together in attack or defence with those who are part of his misfortune; and since this misfortune of difference enters his private world, one expects his work as a writer to be, in part, a witness to that misfortune. Not because there is a moral law which demands that he address himself to his social world, but rather because there is a fundamental need to present his private world in all its facts and one of its vivid experiences will of necessity be the impact of that social world, with all its reservations and distinctions, has made on his consciousness. This is the sense in which it is true to say that a writer has a real and primary responsibility to himself.[22]

The writerly self is for Lamming composed of the origin and its supplement. The supplement of race is not a mere accident of life. Lamming's topic, after all, is the *Negro* writer, not the writer as such. Rather, race is constitutive of the inner life of subjectivity *conceived as existential*; the lived experience of race and color prejudice, no matter the fact that they emerge as historical accidents and name nothing essential about the body or intellect, forms a self. The writer's responsibility to himself—a responsibility to the origin of aesthetic sensibility in inner life—is therefore inseparable from race and its history. Race does not happen to or against the inner life of the writer, coming as it does as part of the body that "moves among other men," and yet the priceless possession of the self's relation to self is its own world. Thus, we can say that for Lamming, race and racism function as *para-origins*, decisive supplements without which the origin is inconceivable. The writer becomes in two different places. For the black writer, these two sites of identity and identification are simultaneous and maintain a paradoxical relation: race is and is not the condition of the writer and his responsibility.

Lamming's account of the writerly subject as origin and para-origin outlines an ontology of aesthetic space. The being of this space is the being of black existential subjectivity, a subjectivity whose meaning and fundamental orientation mixes the singularity of inner life with the internalization and transformation of the social experience of race. The aesthetic dimension of this subjective space is clear. If the authentic artist writes of what is most critical in experience, nature, and the world as such, then the black writer cannot but write from origin and para-origin, transmitting that peculiar and in many ways unprecedented affect which emerges from the mixture of Lamming's first two senses of world. But, there is also Lamming's globalizing moment. From (and thus not after or above) the mixture of the two worlds of the artist, the writer then moves to the consideration of humanity as such. *A third sense of world.* Near the close of his essay, Lamming writes that if

> a writer's senses have been consistently assaulted by the vast pressure of a single issue, it is not difficult for him to lose sight, for a time, of the connection between the disaster which threatens to reduce him, and the wider context and condition of which that disaster is but the clearest example. The Negro in the United States, for example, symbolises an essential condition of Man, not only in his urgent need to correct a social injustice through powers of law, but also in his need to embark upon a definition of himself in the world of men.[23]

Lamming here locates the writer in a strange globalized aesthetic space. A *second* space, which is generated by the contact of the origin/para-origin with the writer's third sense of world. The first aesthetic space of origin and para-origin is written *about*, but that writing-about is also a writing-toward. This writing-toward is the third sense of world in Lamming's essay, the "world" or "community" of men to men *outside-yet-informed-by* the mixture of inner and social life. So, just as Césaire's aesthetic was split between times—the ancestral and the to-come—Lamming's aesthetic moves from the concretion of black subjectivity to the intersubjectivity to-come. When Lamming writes that "for the third of his worlds, the world to which he is condemned by the fact of his spirit, is the world of men," I would suggest that we read this as an oppositional posit of a literary space not yet possible, while at the same time constitutive of the act of writing in which "every utterance he makes in this direction is an utterance made on behalf of all men."[24] The doubling of aesthetic space in many ways deepens Lamming's claim in "The Occasion for Speaking" and other essays that the specific sense of exile for the Carribbean writer is defined by his empty yet purposive intentional relation to a not-yet, still to-come audience.[25]

What, then, is the dispute between Césaire and Lamming in terms of the aesthetics of black subjectivity? To begin, there is the matter of a common space of discussion. For both, there is an inextricable link between blackness and aesthetics. This link places irrevocable obligations (Lamming's remark on moral law notwithstanding) on the black writer-artist. The experience of race, racism, and colonialism is crucial for the transmission of myriad affects. So, when Lamming writes that an aesthetic is measured "not only by the authenticity and power with which his own private world is presented, but also by the honesty with which he interprets the world of his social relations, his country,"[26] we ought to also hear the resonance of Césaire's closing exhortation in "Culture and Colonisation" to "let the black peoples take their place upon the great stage of history."[27] To be sure, Lamming's claim is particularist and existential, while Césaire's remark operates in the ether of a metaphysics of history and race. Yet, and this is the shared postcolonial root, both motifs link the authenticity and power of the writer to the aesthetic of a properly rendered cultural—perhaps even *spiritual*—reality. A relation to a certain *terre paternelle,* whether atavistic or broadly racial-existential, is forged. As well, this proper rendering makes the transition to the world to come possible,

whether that be the purely aesthetic space of Lamming's writerly men or
Césaire's more broadly cultural and political space of a new Africanness. It
is here that land and alienation come together. The Caribbean is alienated
land, blackness is alienated in any land, and so the task of the future, *for the
black writer*, is a transformation of the aesthetics of geography—reaching
to Africa or writing to writerly space—in order to reclaim the newness of
the New World. The *terre paternelle* (literal or figurative) is simultaneously
a here and an elsewhere. Thinking and writing that paradoxical spatiality
is fundamentally an aesthetic task of testimony *and* writing the future. A
task that, for Césaire and Lamming both, makes a strange and new sense
of home possible from out of a deep and traumatic spiritual homelessness.

The Other Exile

In the paradoxical space and time of home, doubled between the past and
future, Césaire and Lamming are drawn into a common theoretical geography with Glissant. Most fundamentally, all three understand the global
character of Caribbeanness. This global character situates the aesthetic
between a here and an elsewhere. What we are to make of this global character, however, hinges on the problem of the *relation* between here and
elsewhere. Namely, how—in memory, history, and futurity—*ought* the
experience of the Caribbean to be translated into poetic language? We
begin with a descriptive problem (how does the Caribbean find itself?),
which then becomes a normative problem (how ought the Caribbean articulate itself as an address to alienation?). A common space of discussion
for sure, and one bequeathed to the postcolonial moment as a crisis for
critical consciousness. This is fundamentally an aesthetic crisis: How can
and how ought the affects of alienation, exile, and hope be transmitted,
represented, and brought to palpable affective presence?

It is precisely this common theoretical space that draws out the important sites of distinction, which in turn shape the frame *out of which*
Glissant tries to think. The global space of world history in Césaire stands
in no small bit of contrast to Lamming's concern with the human condition. That is, in order for Césaire's discrete arguments concerning the
memory of Africa, traces of homeland, and other component parts of a
Négritude-rooted aesthetics of culture to work, he needs a larger story
about historical experience and race. Indeed, that is the entire purchase

of the distinction between civilization and culture in the 1956 essay. Civilization provides the meta- and non-temporal ground of any claims about race, language, aesthetics, and so culture. Civilization is also a metaphysical category, a sort of Nation-being that logically and temporally precedes the being of a given culture. This is why civilization, especially in a diasporic context, has no location; civilization is detected in the traces and spirit deposited in a given culture. *Sedimentation against the sedentary.* Like all metaphysical notions, materiality serves as exemplary, not the thing itself. The writer-artist is a reader of traces, and every reading is or ought to be oriented toward the reactivation of those traces. Lamming's existential rewriting of the problem of race, racism, and identity takes blackness seriously but alters the aspirations of the question. In place of Césaire's metaphysical story of black Atlantic history, Lamming, whose work refuses Négritude's atavism, conceives the black writer as the exemplary aesthetician of alienation. Alienation is the human condition, and it is the particularly and excessively alienated life of postcolonial Africa-descended peoples that, by way of a kind of *lived hyperbole*, serves as the paradigmatic study of what it means to be human. Rather than in a metaphysical story of history, Lamming locates the globalizing of discourse in the problem of human existence: the search for meaning, the conflict between inner life and sociality, and so on. The problem of human existence is fundamentally anti-systematic, countering grand narratives with the small stories, writ large by the great artist, of alienation and struggle. *In the castle of my skin.* The globalization of Césaire leads back to Africa, then again forward to the West Indies. The globalization of Lamming leads the particular consideration of black existence and alienation in relation to the general problem of human meaning, a condition in every world. The difference here between the metaphysical language of civilization and the discrete, particular language of human existence is, at bottom, a question of what it means to read and render aesthetic sensibility in a New World context. The pain of history bears on that context, *on this place*, and the metaphysical and existential languages of globalization in Césaire and Lamming—a converging, then diverging geography of universalization—mark two different paths for an aesthetics coming to terms with those affects, the traces at work in them, and the meaning that *ought to be* transmitted by the writer. Land and alienation, again. Spread across the globe, this difference between Césaire and Lamming is negotiated across two sorts of land in order to write against alienation and to arrive, for the first time, at home—a new land. Two senses of exile, two senses of globalizing territory, and one aesthetic land-to-come. *Home*.

The distinction between Césaire and Lamming, then, is ultimately a variation on what it means to account for the particular form of alienation—an obligating alienation—common to black people. As well, that alienation is always negotiated in relation to some sense of land, ranging from the land-relation lost in historical violence, to the rendering of all land as alienating in a racist social order, to the virtual land of the human condition, to, in the end, the Caribbean landscape of renewal, revitalization, and re-arrival. A critical question: What is the status of the history that produces such alienation, and how does an aesthetic simultaneously manifest and work against that alienation? Négritude or existentialism? The disjunctive hinges on the common space bordered by and saturated with alienation, futurity, and aesthetic sensibility. The disjunctive also marks two ways of telling the story of stories, namely, the story of a people, their land, and how an authentic relation to self and world obtains in a configuration of all of these terms. In this conceptual context, Césaire and Lamming share a certain theoretical conceit. Césaire's conceit is clear in the metaphysics of civilization and the dependent status of culture; this is a Hegelian story of History and Spirit through and through, no matter Césaire's radical critique and rewriting of Hegel's claims about Africa. For both, some version of Spirit moves across the particulars of history and culture. Lamming's conceit is subtler, and in this way he shares that enigmatic place in the history of ideas particular to other existential thinkers. His conception of the black writer is anti-systematic, appealing always to the situatedness of racial identity and to the author's constant turn to the inner self (even as it is saturated with the social). At the same time, Lamming argues first and foremost that the black writer's great contribution, given the exceptional character of anti-black racism, is his or her special access the human condition as such. Thus, in terms of lofty aspirations, there is a peculiar, even oblique, shared affect between Césaire and Lamming: the feeling of a globalizing universality, of the discovery of origins and original structures, *even as they both advocate an aesthetic committed to the new*. Both are certainly aware of the tension between universality and the new. But the question is whether or not they have thought through that tension with sufficient attention to the Caribbean context. It is precisely here that Glissant's aesthetics sheds a suspicious, critical light.

Glissant's aesthetic proposal rejoins his familiar philosophical motifs of nomad, rhizome, and abyssal beginning to a sense of land. Alienation is, of course, the guiding problematic against which the aesthetic motif, just like with the wider philosophical motifs, labors. The Caribbean context has to reckon with the particularities of historical experience—this brings Césaire, Lamming, and Glissant into a common place of critical beginning. Yet, in Glissant's hands, this common critical place is dismantled by the question of fragmentation. In particular, the question of how we are to work with the cultural, metaphysical, and epistemological fragmentation produced by forced migration—atavistic, a sign of a wider human condition, or the grounds of another cultural signification—breaks up the common place of critical beginning. Fragmentation is fraught for Césaire and Lamming. Indeed, one could read each of their aesthetic sensibilities in terms of a reconciliation of fragmentation in the universal. Whether the local universalism of atavism in Négritude or the abstract universalism of black existentialism, we can see in Césaire and Lamming an anxious relation to fragmentation. Fragmentation alienates. Therefore, fragmentation must be overcome. But Glissant's commitment to composite cultural formations as what is uniquely Caribbean about Caribbeanness necessarily characterizes fragmentation as originary, irreducible, and central to the meaning and method of Antillanité. And so land and alienation—in a word, *exile*—comes to signify, for Glissant, a persistent and fundamentally productive fragmentation rather than a problem to be reconciled in a geographic (Césaire) or conceptual (Lamming) elsewhere. The aesthetics of Antillanité thinks *with* and *as* fragments—and here we can see the importance of the intimacy of Glissant's relation to Walcott's critical essays for theorizing the aesthetic. In this sense, we can frame Glissant's departure from—or perhaps advance on—Césaire and Lamming as a kind of postmodern critique of their metaphysical and existential conceit. In fact, it is precisely this conceit that Glissant wants to overcome by resetting and recalibrating *the very origins and grounds* of Caribbean thinking.

Thus, Glissant's is an immanent critique. The critique of Césaire's and Lamming's position is immanent because Glissant speaks from the same family of historical experiences and forms of alienation (language, tradition, roots, exile), but also because he asks the very same deeper, motivating question: How does the pain of history and promise of a future form a Caribbean aesthetic? Glissant's critical response is *postmodern*, by which I mean it is concerned with two key issues in postmodern theory: eschewal of metanarrative and the irreducibility of difference. First, Glissant's focus on the composite sense of culture emergent from the Plantation serves, among other things, as a sustained critique of the idea of a metanarrative— that wide story about origins and unities. Césaire and Lamming, whatever the difference between them, share an orientation toward just such a metanarrative. Glissant's postmodern perspective, however, is not undertaken for the sake of, say, Derrida's play or Lyotard's gaming. Rather, the postmodern emerges for Glissant out of a critical diagnosis of the Caribbean situation and an affirmation, even when it leads to paradoxical formulations of the pain of history, of the complexity of composite cultural life. That is, the postmodern is underpinned by a sense of beginning in and with fragments and creolization, not dismantling the suffocating edifice of tradition (*pace* Derrida et al.). This sense of beginning calls the very idea of metanarrative into question in both descriptive and normative senses. The Caribbean both *is* and *ought to understand itself* as creolizing. The movement of Relation, Glissant insistently and consistently points out, is not another name for Being, but rather the surpassing of Being in the becoming of beings. The second postmodern issue shows up here. As composite and creolizing, Caribbeanness, *sensu stricto*, cannot be named, if by naming we mean the establishment of an identity. Relation as creolization is not another name for Being, so Glissant's sense of fragmentation disrupts any chain of signification—any name—with detours and other forms of nomadic relay. The work of creolization is therefore driven by a movement of difference-without-resolution. Difference *as such*. The Caribbean, on this account, is neither exemplary of a civilization nor exemplary of an invariant human condition. This sense of fragmentation, fragmentation from the abyss, anti- and ante-atavistic through and through, can never render an origin or a unity without betraying the originary character of difference. Glissant's insistence on the *movement* of creolization—and so not *creoleness*—maintains fidelity to this sense of difference in conceptual and poetic practice.

This remains an immanent critique. For Glissant, difference in the Caribbean context begins under the very same conditions under which difference appears for Césaire and Lamming: the experience and condition of exile. Drawing from his "Culture and Colonisation" alone, we can understand Césaire's thinking in terms of the experience and condition of exile, modeled as it is on the movement from civilization to culture to alienation, then back again to the single origin, then, at its conceptual cli-

max, forward to the newness of Afro-Caribbean culture. Indeed, the journey documented in the looping temporality of *Notebook* mimics just this
sense of movement from exile to home, which, in the end, is a movement
from alienation to authenticity. The *authentic* is measured by the proximity of culture and aesthetic production to origins—that is, for Césaire,
the ability of French to speak an essential Africanness, a sort of linguistic
terre paternelle after alienation. For Lamming, exile itself is authenticity. If
Lamming argues that alienation is the human condition as such, and so is
lived in a particularly intense sense by black people across the globe, then
we should not be surprised to read him declaring that "the exile is a universal figure."[28] A universal figure, yes, but this does not lead Lamming to
despair—"to be an exile is to be alive"—nor does he ignore the Caribbean
specificity of exilic life. "When the exile is a man of colonial orientation,"
Lamming writes, "then there are certain complications" ranging from the
general problem of identity to matters of aesthetic judgment.[29] In the way
of being alive called exile, London (in Lamming's case) remains an anxious presence as the Other of measure (aesthetic and otherwise), but also
and in a productive sense derision and rebellion. The writer, in his movement toward Lamming's third sense of world, writes the particular exile
universal—toward that intellectual space to come. For both Césaire and
Lamming, then, exile is anxious and displaced into the aesthetic, splitting
the writer between two places where authenticity is measured by the ability or inability to render, then close, the conditions of that anxiety.

Glissant's theorization of exile makes important, nuanced criticisms of
this account of exilic thought. Glissant's work deploys two closely related
yet distinct senses of exile, both of which draw on nomadic subjectivity as
the figure of and vital force in exilic life. The first sense of exile, the one to
which Glissant juxtaposes his own, is exile as non-consent in the presence
of origin. This sense of exile has both internal and external manifestations.
Internal exile, which Glissant claims "tends toward material comfort,
which cannot really distract from anguish" (PR, 20), comes about in "living where solutions concerning the relationship of a community to its
surroundings are not, or at least not yet, consented to by this community
as a whole" (PR, 19). In the Caribbean context proper, the external sense
of exile is most significant. External exile is the forced abandonment of
home, where the exile is severed from roots and place and compelled to
wander—perhaps without the possibility of return, perhaps with a possible homecoming. One can think here of the West's two great figures of

exile, Abraham and Odysseus. The former bequeaths a tradition wandering without a homeland, which Glissant identifies as one of Judaism's flirtations with an aesthetic of errantry before settling Palestine (PR, 20), and the latter makes the journey back home across Homer's verse, which describes atavistic thinking in epic terms. Exile as the originary and originating loss of home resonates in the Caribbean context for obvious reasons. If, as Glissant argues in the opening pages of *Poetics of Relation*, abyssal beginning locates its first event in the Middle Passage, then beginning in the Caribbean context is a beginning with the loss of home. Exile as *terre maternelle*. This *maternal* event of loss, Glissant's articulation of the womb-abyss, changes the terms of exilic life.

Exile is simultaneously about loss of home and arrival. Indeed, the enigma of exile always lies in the meaning of arrival, for whatever the mournful relation one might have for a place lost, relocation—migration forced and unforced—makes another connection to time and space. Perhaps one resists assimilation. Perhaps one assimilates. Or, perhaps, the non-assimilation/assimilation dyad proves fantastical and, in fact, arrival creates an interstitial, hybrid-then-more subjectivity. Perhaps, then, this subjectivity and its mixed sensibilities carve out a new and unprecedented place in the sun, on the traumatized shoreline, in the abyssal place of what has been lost. In this last account, the composite cultural moment in its exilic origin, dis-location and re-location must be thought at one and the same time. That simultaneity describes how, for Glissant, exile is transformative of all three moments of individual and collective temporality. Dis-location breaks the *past* apart, lifting it from a living context and into the realm of memory (which is then subjected to the problem of trauma and traumatic remembrance); re-location places new demands on that memory for imagining a *future* (the trauma and unresolvable disorientation of arrival). The past is bound in new ways to the *present*—traces in memory, with or without original presences—and the question of how to best imagine the future against the oppressive, melancholic weight of the present is raised with special urgency. Each moment of this exilic time informs the other. Exile fundamentally alters, maybe even *curves* across and through, the flow of that temporal dynamic. Again, the question of the aesthetic is paramount.

It is at this point that Glissant poses the metaphysical question set aside in (or even eclipsed by) Césaire's and Lamming's work: How are we to make sense of the trauma of the Middle Passage in relation to questions of exile? Glissant situates that trauma in the present, marking the "agitated existence" under colonialism with the original experience of the abyss. "Martinicans," Glissant writes in *Caribbean Discourse*, "lead an agitated existence, violently and irrevocably severed from the motherland of Africa and painfully, inevitably, and improbably cut off from the dreamland of France" (CD, 9). Exile is doubled here, which marks an important sense of how exile makes two journeys in the Caribbean context: in relation to Africa, then in relation to France. Both journeys are crucial for understanding the meaning of dis-location and re-location, of course, and this doubling designates the intersection of the slave trade and the colonial relation. So, we have already gained a bit of specificity regarding exile and its movement toward reckoning or, perhaps, even a kind of homecoming. For Césaire, the meaning of all this is clear. The Caribbean cultural movement toward the retrieval and reactivation of African civilization through the aesthetic transformation of language reveals a straightforward sense of *external exile*. Négritude's prerogative depends on a sense of loss of home that makes a particular kind of homecoming possible (civilization as the precondition of cultural home). To be sure, Césaire's sense of Négritude has all the necessary caveats and hesitations regarding the place of Africanness in the New World. Those caveats bear out the doubled sense of exile Glissant describes. This is most evident in Césaire's commitment to French. If the task of an aesthetics lies in making French speak African traces in the Caribbean context, and this speaking resolves the seemingly unresolvable relation between two exilic forces, then we can see in Césaire's conception of the writer, with a couple of minor qualifications, an aesthetics of exile.

Against the exiles of Césaire and Lamming and the arrow-like nomadic character each manifests, Glissant proposes the notion of errancy. In a certain sense, we could say that errancy replaces the language of the exilic, and yet, even as Glissant ultimately gains some distance from the discourse of exile, exile and errancy keep an intimate relation. Exile, like errancy, is a site of beginning in which "roots are lacking" (PR, 11). Thus, Glissant remarks, in a certain register "exile can be seen as beneficial, when . . . experienced as a search for the Other (through circular nomadism) rather than as an expansion of territory (an arrowlike nomadism)" (PR, 18). This is to say, for Glissant exile makes detour a condition of living *after* arrival; exilic beginning gestures toward abyssal beginning. Yet, the ambivalence of exile in relation to roots pushes Glissant to supplant the language of exile with the more decisive notion of errancy. "Whereas exile may erode one's sense of identity," Glissant writes, "the thought of errantry—the thought of that which relates—usually reinforces this sense of identity" (PR, 20). In this sense, we can say that errancy takes the de-location and re-location of exile on its own terms by affirming the composite character of arrival, a character that closely aligns an errant exile with the circular nomad. *Exile without the thought of origin,* in other words. Glissant writes:

> Errantry, therefore, does not proceed from renunciation nor from frustration regarding a supposedly deteriorated (deterrritorial- ized) situation of origin; it is not a resolute act of rejection or an uncontrolled impulse of abandonment. . . . Because the thought of errantry is also the thought of what is relative, the thing relayed as well as the thing related. The thought of errantry is a poetics, which always infers that at some moment it is told. The tale of errantry is the tale of Relation. (PR, 18)

Glissant's evocation of the deteriorating origin is an obvious citation of Césaire's sense of errant and exilic thought, where the erosion of identity is linked to the distance of the root (civilization) from the land on which one stands (culture). The distinction is important. "In contrast to the situa- tion of exile," Glissant writes, "errantry gives-on-and-with the negation of every pole and every metropolis, whether connected or not to a conquer- or's voyaging act" (PR, 19).

At this point, Glissant's transformation of the experience of exile into the poetics of errantry mimics Lamming's remarks on the universal con- dition of exile. If there is no home, then every writer writes from a sense of exile. At the same time, however, Lamming's shift from the particular case of exilic consciousness in the Caribbean to the problem of root- lessness more generally—resonance with the thought of *tout-monde* notwithstanding—risks too much. That is, the anti-systematic thinking that initially drives Lamming's analysis in "The Negro Writer and His World" is recast as a quasi-system in his appeal to a universal human con- dition. As noted above, this is a nuanced and difficult issue. The existential motif and its privileging of lived experience over metaphysics *promises* so much more than it can fulfill. Glissant's reinterpretation of the problem of exile fulfills Lamming's promise. The thought of errantry—and this is the postmodern moment in Glissant's work—pushes the question of particularity and specificity fully forward without the presence of universality. Even an empty universality, such as "the human condition," is a generalizing force. And one loses sight of the specificity of the Caribbean context. But the thinker of errantry "challenges and discards the universal. . . . He plunges into the opacities of that part of the world to which he has access" (PR, 20). *To which he has access.* Glissant's delimitation of the question of access, which is the boundary of what comprises the tours and detours of errantry, takes Lamming's anti-systematic impulse to its radical conclusion: thinking *with* fragments, not above, below, or against them.

We might say, then, that the thought of errantry, framed by the two exilic thoughts of Césaire and Lamming, transforms exile into archipelagic thinking—and therefore an aesthetics of fragmentation. *Tout-monde* is an archipelago.

If we can track this transformation across his work on the aesthetic, then we can surely make a note of Glissant's general ethic of suspicion: there is perhaps a nascent continental thinking in both Césaire and Lamming. This is quite plain (and even quite literal) in Césaire, where the continent is Africa, mapped in relation to the Caribbean through the metaphysics of civilization and culture. Whatever the fragments of cultural difference and dispersion, the literal and trace figure of Africa reconciles those fragments with a continent. *Civilizational thinking is continental thinking.* With Lamming, things are a bit more complex. The continent for Lamming is a figure for the human person itself. The black writer becomes exemplary of a distant yet shared continent—a rooted sense of what it means to be. Whatever the particularities of alienation and subjection to the Other's gaze, the figurative conceptual continent of alienation or exile functions to reconcile one's existential situation with the human condition itself. *An abstract space of return.* For both Césaire and Lamming, then, we can say that fragments operate as mimetic traces, hearkening back (or forward) to a unity, a continent, in which firm roots are set. Against this, Glissant's postmodern insistence on the originary character of fragmentation, derived from his complex sense of beginning we have developed in previous chapters, places archipelagic thinking back at the center of aesthetics. The key turn in thinking lies in thinking with fragments outside the copy-original model that would seem to function, however nascently, in Césaire and Lamming.

And yet, from Glissant's perspective, Césaire and Lamming are right about this: alienation characterizes the relation of subject to land in the Caribbean context. An aesthetics must reckon with the painful history that gives rise to such alienation, as well as, insofar as the writer is concerned with futurity, how the work of art can transmit pain and hope at one and the same time. But further questions arise when held under Glissant's conceptual scrutiny: What sort of aesthetics reckons with painful history and its transmission to a future in fragments? Is continental thinking attentive to the abyss of beginning? If not, then how does Glissant negotiate the strange relation between overcoming alienation and fidelity to fragmentation? In these questions we see the necessity of a fully developed metaphysics and epistemology. For, Glissant's claim is that the ultimate reality of the archipelago is fragmentation and the peculiar knowing of the Caribbean—that complex method he terms Antillanité—demands its own epistemic conditions. Haunting these moments, and grounding the loftier aspirations of a philosophy of Antillanité, is the problem of transmission. What are origins to the present? What is the future to the past? Those haunting moments resolve themselves in perhaps the most enigmatic of practices: an aesthetics of the abyss.

Boundary, Time, Aesthetics

"The world's poetic force (its energy)," Glissant writes in *Poetics of Relation*, "kept alive within us, fastens itself by fleeting, delicate shivers, onto the rambling prescience of poetry in the depths of our being" (PR, 159). Prescience is time, force is the movement of time across the aesthetic and its manifold registers. What does Glissant mean when he describes poetic force as fastening *and* fleeting? Rambling, yet deep?

In preparation for theorizing this prescience and poetic force, let us begin by recasting the aesthetic motif. As noted above, a meta-question for the theory and practice of aesthetics is pointed and straightforward: How and why is aesthetics a legitimate form of philosophy? Or, to the contrary, is aesthetics merely an expression of other areas of thinking, such that aesthetic questions are more seriously addressed in, say, epistemology or ontology? Or subordinated to politics?

Among the many boundaries and contraries Glissant's work puts in question, it is just this kind of distinction, between the autonomous and the serious and their dependent stepchildren, that appears especially urgent and problematic. For, if, to evoke the epigraph from Walcott that introduces *Poetics of Relation*, memory and history lie drowned in the sea and, in that drowning, condition thinking with an abyssal absence, then the intellectual and political work of cultural transformation cannot be grounded in a single root. Nor can that work subordinate and measure sensibilities. Lacking a single root, there is no "original parentage," so to speak, on the basis of which one could designate the stepchild relation. Rather, the rhizomatic openness of a future, which Glissant contends is the only possible Caribbean future, folds the aesthetic back into the family of exigent questions clustered around the problem of postcolonial identity. And so aesthetic inquiry and production is, in some sense, nothing like what the Western tradition has called "aesthetic"; knowing and being are as much at stake in—if not at times dependent upon—aesthetics as they are on their natural, "by definition" companions: epistemology and metaphysics. In other words, Glissant's aesthetics gathers the whole world to itself, without ever becoming one and the same root of that world, that possibility, that *future*.

Beginning with *L'intention poétique* and up through *Poetics of Relation* and after, Glissant cast the aesthetic of gathering the world to itself, dispersed yet in contact, in terms of an opposition to the literary epic, an opposition that becomes, after important moments of creolization, an apposition of epic. Epics promise origins and founding. Indeed, even in those epic stories begun in wandering (Glissant cites the Hebrew Bible and Homer's *Odyssey* most often), movement is oriented by a desire for roots. The nostalgia or future-oriented or the combination of both for a rootedness in territory is what heightens the stakes of an epic. The journey *matters* because identities are made, unmade, then retrieved in movement and cross-cultural encounter. Tension and release pivot around this dynamic, which is difficult to conceive without atavistic desire. Those roots may be set for the first time at the end of a voyage, or they may be unexpected and rediscovered only at the moment of arrival, but the epic journey has roots as its central meaning. That is, the epic journey has its *vouloir-dire* in roots—in the sense that it both finds *meaning* in roots and *wants to say* roots. If we interpret the meaning of epic journey in this sense, according to the peculiar double meaning of *vouloir-dire*, then we can see how epic might suggest a bit of affinity with Glissant's notion of Relation. For, as Derrida argues in *La voix et le phénomène,* the structure of *vouloir-dire* implies, if not outright performs, deferral and delay. What is *said* is always structured by the *want*, so this activity, in principle, never calcifies, but rather always pushes into a future. A future, of course, that by definition cannot be anticipated. So, if the aesthetic of epic is entwined with deferral and delay, then the movement of epic would seem to be an example of the sorts of aesthetic sensibility expected from a poetics of Relation.

And yet Glissant does not affirm epic in this sense. Whatever the deferrals and delays, the nascent atavistic desire in the literary epic remains incompatible with abyssal beginning. For, if abyssal beginning means the loss of origin and the construction of memory, history, and identity in the Plantation, then atavism betrays the geography of Caribbean becoming. Shoreline thinking is lost and forgotten in nascent structures of identity when those structures have an atavistic character, rather than manifesting as traces. Epic, bluntly put, is the betrayal of Glissant's notion of difference. That said, a transfiguration of epic is always possible; Caribbeanness is a method, after all, which means that it is capable of effecting the creolization that makes epic important in the Antillean context. Deferral and delay are no small parts of that creolization. Glissant does not want to dispense with the notion of epic, but rather activate the deconstructive aspects of it in order to dismantle the atavistic dimensions while also preserving epic's commitment to movement and (or as) the sacred. As well, the relation between exile and exilic speech is important here, where Glissant writes that "while one can communicate through errantry's imaginary vision, the experiences of exiles are incommunicable" (PR, 20). Epic gives an imaginary to the experience of exile and so gives first words to that experience. The decision at that moment, at the level of the imaginary, is absolutely critical. In fact, everything is decided. This is an aesthetic question through and through. The decision for the atavistic desire of epic frames questions of exile—and so the meaning of errant imaginaries and speech—with a language of discovery and homecoming. This is precisely what animates Césaire's notion of exile. For Glissant this is the political moment in an aesthetics, one that overwhelms a properly Caribbean aesthetic sensibility with a mismatched sense of arrival. In *Poetics of Relation* he writes:

> I began wondering if we would no longer need such founding works today, ones that would use a similar dialectics of rerouting, asserting, for example, political strength but, simultaneously, the rhizome of a multiple relationship with the Other and basing every community's reasons for existence on a modern form of the sacred, which would be, all in all, a Poetics of Relation. (PR, 16)

This arrow-like nomadism is the wandering errantry of discovery and conquest, seeking, even in the rhizomatic moment(s), a destiny and founding.

To recall the discussion above, Césaire's interpretation of exile would seem to fall under this sense of epic; indeed, it is quite easy to read *Notebook* under the rubric of epic, seeing the very notion of return—that double movement of reactivation and reinvention—as a story about founding.

Glissant's rejection of the aesthetic of literary epic draws out an important point of critical contrast with both Césaire and Lamming. In particular, I have in mind how the poetics of Relation—that sacred space of world-making and aesthetic intensity—works by way of apposition. Set alongside one another and in contact through irreducible opacity, discourses, ideas, and cultures produce the unexpected. Césaire's "Culture and Colonisation," as we have seen, deploys the aesthetics of Négritude in order to *oppose* Western humanism and its aesthetics of reason. As well, we can read Lamming's movement from the particularist character of alienation and exile toward the exemplary status of the black writer, which measures the aesthetic of the writer with the universal affective condition, as a certain kind of *deposing*. What both Césaire and Lamming miss, in this case, is the productive and dynamic character of a sense of relation that neither seeks the exclusion of its Other nor seeks to neutralize difference. Glissant's notion of difference functions otherwise, and the aesthetics of appositional relation makes that alternative structure of difference apparent.

The apposition of epic, exile, and errantry promises another sense of epic—a sense emergent from two sites of creolization. The first of these sites is the Caribbean itself. As we have seen in our long exploration of the abyssal sense of beginning, the problem of atavism and non-rhizomatic roots is ill-suited to the historical experience of the Caribbean. The trauma of the Middle Passage and the creation of composite cultural forms unroot subjectivity in the name of a nomadic, curved time and space. The archipelago is elevated from geography to deconstructive figure in this experience. Epic is fundamentally different in this context; delay and deferral shift from dramatic narrative to the content of identity and proper aesthetic sensibility. The second of these sites is the shift Glissant makes in his later work from the archipelagic thinking of the Caribbean to the archipelagic thinking of *tout-monde*. Glissant is decisive on this, even when it is declared as a programmatic normativity, an *ought* that is just now coming into being. The world *itself* is creolizing. Creolization in a global context, to recall a passage we discussed above, comes about at the *end of the world*. Once the voyage-discovery-conquest sequence has come to an end, new possibilities are suddenly opened up. It is now a question of what it means to *understand* the Other, rather than discover and conquer—at least as a

possible horizon of thinking. This is why Glissant will claim that "the poetics of Relation remains forever conjectural and presupposes no ideological stability," a claim that leads to the remark that poetry and a poetics "no
longer conjecture a given people but the evolution of the planet Earth"
(PR, 32). This is at once aesthetic, historical, and political, for the historical and political always follow from an aesthetic claim on or about the
world. *Historically*, the aesthetic of errancy and Relation as a claim on
and about *tout-monde* marks the end of the world. Such an aesthetic is
unthinkable without the end of the brutal historical epics of voyage and
conquest. *Politically,* the aesthetic of errancy and Relation fundamentally
changes our relation to difference through the elimination of atavistic desire and the single root. (Recall here that Glissant, in a speculative and
equally provocative assertion, links genocidal violence to the ideological
stability of roots.) The aesthetic claim of *tout-monde* therefore opens new
historical and political horizons. Glissant writes:

> The founding books have taught us that the sacred dimension
> consists always of going deeper into the mystery of the root,
> shaded with variations of errantry. In reality errant thinking is the
> postulation of an unyielding and unfading sacred. We remember
> that Plato, who understood the power of Myth, had hoped to ban-
> ish the poets, those who force obscurity, far from the Republic. He
> distrusted the fathomless word. Are we not returning here, in the
> unforeseeable meanders of Relation, to this abyssal word? (PR, 21)

The answer to this final question is of course affirmative. Glissant's poetic
word is errant and committed to opacity, which means that it does not
yield to identity at the expense of difference. *Tout-monde* is a commitment
to radical difference. There is an opacity to myth, for sure, and therefore
to epic itself when left to the poets. That is, the aesthetic of the voyage
and the journey takes full account of what is encountered as difference;
the political intervention is what "transmutes," to use Glissant's word,
the poetic word. The word is transformed or deformed, moving from an
opaque moment of contact with the world to a consumable articulation of
identity by political intervention. This is Césaire's compromise on difference; his postcolonial politics bleeds over into poetics and aesthetics becomes a carrier of a (however righteous) political position. The insistence
on the irreducibility of alienation is perhaps what ensures the enduring

significance and relevance of Lamming's existentialism for the thought of errantry. Perhaps if we are all errant, then *tout-monde,* having transformed the story through a more robust account of historical sensibility, is (or could be) at least in part a narrative of the human condition.

The relation of the aesthetic to myth, especially when considered as a form of opacity outside of and resistant to the political dimensions of epic, raises again the matter of Creole language, *créolité,* and processes of creolization. The epic imaginary invokes and provokes what Wilson Harris, in a discussion of creoleness, calls "involuntary association."[30] For Harris, and this parallels exactly Glissant's critique of the atavistic, anti-rhizomatic desires of epic narrative, the purity of identity claims (racial and/or ethnic) fundamentally misapprehends New World experience, where mixture is a founding, not a fallen principle. The errant character of creoleness in Harris's essay, and indeed in his critical and creative work as a whole, frees myth from its dependency on epic. This liberation from the desires of epic opens important new creative horizons in which the geography of reading and appropriation *reinvents* the meaning of a myth; Harris cites the figure of Legba as an example.[31] Such reinvention is what is meant by creoleness, but it would be shortsighted to conceive such reading as merely an analogy of creole-as-bloodline. Rather, and here Glissant's notion of *tout-monde* is enormously instructive, the geography of ideas is already creole *in the act of reading.* That is, to creolize myth is to enact explicitly what is already implicit in any act of interpretation as appropriation. The only objection to such appropriation, the only resistance to creoleness and creolization, is the function of the epic aesthetic in myth.

Glissant's conception of creolization is committed to becoming. For this reason, he avoids the term *créolité* and keeps a bit of distance from the creoleness movement initiated by Bernabé, Chamoiseau, and Confiant in their famed manifesto *In Praise of Creoleness.* Glissant's hesitations about the term *creoleness* are fairly well known but are worth briefly rehearsing here in order to garner some clarity about his break with epic in the formation of an aesthetics and poetics of Relation. *In Praise of Creoleness* makes a straightforward argument that draws heavily from Glissant's own theory of Antillanité. Antillanité marks a break with the nostalgic overtones of Négritude by affirming the fecundity of fragmentation in a New World context. This fragmentation is then written further into the structure of the postmodern, globalizing world; creoleness opens "the routes of the world."[32] Just as Glissant's notion of composite cultural forms and formation marks the first distance of a shoreline thinking from Négritude, creoleness, the authors argue, "liberates us from the ancient world" and affirms the very opacity of creole *parts* made *whole* in aesthetic production. They write:

> We call Creole the work of art which, celebrating within its coherence the diversity of meanings, will preserve the mark which justifies its pertinence regardless of how it is understood, where it is culturally perceived, or to what issues it is associated. Our submersion into Creoleness will not be incommunicable, but neither will it be completely communicable.[33]

In Praise of Creoleness makes its appeal here to opacity, drawing on the power of the opaque to contain its meaning even as it traffics across borders, making itself global. But what concerns Glissant about the formulation of Creoleness in Bernabé et al. is the rhetoric (and perhaps even practice) of identity. For, as we have seen, Glissant's transformation of Deleuze and Guattari's conceptions of rhizome and nomad complicates the very notion of identity, which, in turn, locates creole in movement, not in principles. Glissant writes:

> Creolization, one of the ways of forming a complex mix—and not merely a linguistic result—is only exemplified by its processes and certainly not by the "contents" on which these operate. This is where we depart from the concept of creoleness. (PR, 89)

Forming a complex mix. Just as Caribbeanness is for Glissant a method, not an ontological claim, creolization is a way of making meaning, an aesthetic in the purest and most abyssal sense. Creolization's articulation of mixture and movement as such, rather than "defining or identities" or "humanity's Being" (Glissant's phrasing in *Poetics of Relation*), takes the abyss of beginning seriously in its caution before, even interdiction on, atavistic desire and single-root thinking. Creolization insists on the becoming of the unexpected, and this insistence on movement complicates, if not uproots, the declarative, identitarian language of creoleness. This nuance is quite significant, for it establishes the critical role of Relation in thinking about creole identities and the aesthetic of Creoleness. While it *may* seem to be a point of emphasis rather than crucial difference, in fact the whole of Glissant's project in *Poetics of Relation* and after is at stake. In particular, fidelity to abyssal beginnings. This is why, for all of his intimacy with the *créolité* movement, Glissant worries about the possibly regressive character of that movement and the essentialisms it would seem to need for its conceptual and cultural programme.

Creolization, then, lies at the heart of the movement of Glissant's notion of Relation. The structure of Relation operates according to the ethics of the Other discussed above in our reflections on subjectivity, an ethics in which the relation to the Other sustains opacity *even in contact*. Contact signifies the initiation of mixture, but the persistence of opacity changes the meaning of what it is to know and understand in that mixture; contact between opacities begins the formation of mixture. Glissant overturns the sense of knowing as a grasping or seizing (*comprendre*) in the sorts of relations comprising Relation, relations that are not *relationships* and function rather more like an intransitive verb (PR, 27). Without a direct object, Relation cannot be thought as correlation, summation, or grouping under a common concept. Thus, the central role played by creolization. Creolization highlights one of the central features of Relation: the production (aesthetic or otherwise) of new and unexpected cultural forms. Relation names the structure of that process, attentive to both what is produced and given in contact *and* what is left, lost, withdrawn, or remainder in moments of opaque resistance. Relation is "active within itself" and "movement" (PR, 171), but a given relation or creolization created in contact "neither relays nor links afferents that can be assimilated or allied only in their principle, for the simple reason that it always differentiates among them concretely and diverts them from the totalitarian" (PR, 172). Relation, Glissant writes,

> informs not simply what is relayed, but also the relative and the related. It's always approximate truth that is given in a narrative. For, though the world is not a book, it is nonetheless true that the silence of the world would, in turn, make us deaf. . . . But because what it relates, in reality, proceeds from no absolute, it proves to be the totality of relatives, put in touch and told. (PR, 27–28)

Totality is made spatial by contact and what Glissant here calls telling or narrative, then made temporal by the approximations that characterize every site of contact. Relay, link/re-link, delay, and deferral. We must read this sense of delay, deferral, relay, link, and re-link in terms of time and space. Given what we have drawn out of Glissant's work thus far, the centrality of historical experience and commitment to opacity injects temporal and spatial characteristics into the structure of Relation.

The repetition of the terms link, re-link, and relay in *Poetics of Relation* highlights the spatial dimension of Relation, the "product that in turn produces" (PR, 160). I am here insisting on the language of delay and deferral for a specific reason: those terms attend to the withdrawal and withholding that is elemental to the movement of Relation. The temporal deferral of meaning, that delay on the margins of any givenness or site of contact, keeps opacity outside the reach of totality. Totality thereby remains open. "Relation is open totality," Glissant writes; "totality would be relation at rest" (PR, 171). If Relation is movement *and* is the product that produces, then every contact is both fecund and structured by forgetting. Relay and link/re-link make creolization produce cultural forms and expressions. Delay and deferral keep those forms and expressions open to their own critique, supplanting, transformation, or any other possible decisive alteration, for, as Glissant notes, the work of Relation "always changes all the elements composing it and, consequently, the resulting relationship, which then changes them all over again" (PR, 172). Poetry is the aesthetic of this sense of Relation. Indeed, Glissant aligns the poetic force (*la force poétique*) with the infinity of possibility. He writes in *Poetics of Relation*:

> This world force does not direct any line of force but infinitely reveals them. Like a landscape impossible to epitomize. It forces us to imagine it even while we stand there neutral and passive. . . . The expression of this force and its way of being is what we call Relation: what the world makes and expresses of itself. (PR, 159–60)

The infinite, patient revelation of the world in poetry turns on an aesthetic of relay, link/re-link, delay, and deferral. The impossibility of the poetic word, yet its constant and renewed address to the world, takes place in the space-time of Relation. The swirl of rhizome, nomad, and errantry against epic and its calcified myths.

Spacing Transmission

Glissant's aesthetic sensibility is charged with—and charges the writer with—a peculiar and complex task. While the critical distance he gains from the aesthetic of the epic is instructive and humbles the aspiration of art, the turn toward fragment work is by no means a simple contrary. For, as we have seen, Glissant does not eschew the significance of identity in theorizing the aesthetic. The Caribbean writer writes an individual and collective narrative, indicating the double imperative of Glissant's aesthetics: speak to existential fragmentation at one and the same time as taking the historical experience of the archipelago into account. Individual and collective. Glissant's repeating island.

As we have seen in the reflections above, Glissant's aesthetic shift away from the diversion and return *ethos* of Négritude and existentialism takes as its regulating idea the problem of fragmentation. Fragmentation, of course, must be thought in terms of contact, but always a contact without a reconciliation or neutralization of difference. Opacity and creolization sit at the heart of a poetics of Relation. That poetics—Glissant's aesthetic sensibility in shorthand form—functions as delay, deferral, relay, link, and re-link, which gives an important spatiotemporal dimension to Glissant's sense of Relation. The nuance of Glissant's difference from Derridean *différance* is instructive as well, underscoring how the structure of delay and deferral comes, not from the play of signs and the slack inherent in linguistic systems, but from the inner structure particular to composite cultures initiated by abyssal beginnings, bequeathed by the Middle Passage. So, the question quite naturally arises: What does an aesthetics of an abyssal subject look like in practice, both as a method of reading aesthetic objects and production of the same?

Glissant's novels, as well as his literary critical essays, are obvious places to turn in answering such a query. Indeed, one can see in a novel like *The Fourth Century* how attempts to render a single narrative about origins becomes, as a matter of the spatial distribution of historical experience (Plantation and *marronage*), a story of contradiction, mixture, fragmentation, and so on. Or one can see in Glissant's reflections on Faulkner how problems of filiation, incest, and miscegenation can be read as larger historical dramas particular to the womb of the Plantation. Glissant's readings of Perse, Lam, and others bring the thought of errantry to bear on poetic works and the plastic arts. But I want to set those texts aside and instead ask how Glissant can illuminate the meaning and significance of cinematic language in Raoul Peck's 1990 (U.S. release 1992) documentary *Lumumba, la mort du prophète*, how Glissant's aesthetic works as a normative claim and a frame for reading. In particular, I want to think about how Peck's film enacts the very sort of spacing of transmission articulated in Glissant's notion of Relation, a spacing that evokes time and space in the full context of historical experience. This spacing of transmission takes place in *Lumumba* in a personal story: Peck's attempt to return to multiple senses of origin. With Glissant as a frame for reading the film, we can see not only how Peck's cinematic language manifests the delay, deferral, relay, link, and re-link structure of Relation but also how the conceptual story of that film is a story about exile and errantry in the context of the Americas, and so a collective story at the very same time it is presented as an individual reflection.

Although Peck's feature-length biopic *Lumumba* (2000) stands as perhaps his best-known film, and is indeed an important cinematic work in its own right, the earlier, failed documentary stands as an altogether different aesthetic event.[34] And, I would claim, a more compelling one, at that. Whereas the feature-length film coherently and quite mournfully tells Lumumba's—and by extension Congo's—postcolonial moment, the documentary is from the outset fragmented and melancholic. The coherence of the feature length lends itself to mourning, insofar as it tells the kind of story to which one can attach a coherent sense of loss. The at times derailed incoherence of *Lumumba, la mort du prophète*, however, removes the object of attachment, and so the result is a wandering, melancholic collage of image and sound, memory and history thought in the cinematic medium. In this sense, and by Peck's own admission, the documentary is a failure; it can never document its theme. Lumumba, the Congo's postcolonial moment, even Peck's own relation to the various sites the film cites—everything dissolves at the moment a fully realized and intelligible approach to them is made. Yet, in its fragmented melancholy, the film is still *necessary. Lumumba, la mort du prophète*—it *must* be a film. What does it mean that Peck's first effort at rendering Lumumba's life fails? Why this necessity simultaneous with failure? Further, and most importantly, what might this designation "failure" tell us about the limits of a certain kind of aesthetic judgment, namely, the kind of judgment that is oriented (implicitly or explicitly) by the desire for a stable and repeatable object of mourning?

Peck's aesthetic—especially the aesthetic of blending failure and necessity—follows Glissant's conception of Caribbeanness as a methodology (and so not a state of being). As a method, this blending of "failure" and necessity is legitimized by the conditions under which Glissant claims the Caribbean intellectual labors. Method interrogates the world with an important purposefulness, guided in this case by a certain kind of subjectivity and its history that moves the purposeful back into a productive relation with Chaos and the Diverse. An aesthetics in this sense gives us, not a coherent story, but rather a necessary errancy and a notion of Relation. What does it mean, then, to think and create in this space? How is one to conceive, produce, and read aesthetic objects as rhizomatic? Dislocation and repudiation of the single root wreaks plenty of productive havoc on conceptual schemae, and so the translation of that same rhizomatic sensibility into aesthetic objects is nothing if not enigmatic. And it is here that Peck's documentary becomes important, as Peck brings exactly that rhizomatic sensibility to image and sound. How do image and sound, in Peck's hands, come to represent the rootless-cum-poly-rooted wake of traumatic history?

Lumumba, la mort du prophète is a failed documentary. So, a first question: What does it mean to call Peck's work a failure? It is a failure for the simple reason that it does not and cannot document its theme. Let us begin with the title: *Lumumba, la mort du prophète.* If Peck's aim in the film is to document the last days of Patrice Lumumba's life, and so also the beginning of the authoritarian catastrophe of what was to become Zaire, then the film does not accomplish that task. Indeed, to the extent that the film documents Lumumba's final days, the document is broken exactly where it should be declarative. This is perhaps most poignantly demonstrated in Peck's collage of image and sound comprising the documentation of Lumumba's last speech. Without a doubt, this is the pivot point of the film's success and/or failure. This decisive collage *promises* a root for the document, *promises* a fixed point in which the name Lumumba might become a single, founding ground for documentation. But of course the collage fails its promise.

The image in this decisive collage is a photograph, a still image in which Lumumba strikes an ambivalent pose. Peck's filming of the photograph initially lifts Lumumba to the status of prophet and bearer of hope. But the shot immediately becomes as troubled as it is reverential. The troubled character of the image—this other side of ambivalence—is borne by two aspects. First, there is Lumumba's own posture, which suggests a wavering of instability, a kind of stammering at the heart of his prophecy (in this sense, we might say that Lumumba's prophecy in the film takes on a Mosaic quality). Peck captures this in the slow pan across Lumumba's face and body, deliberately introducing the gathered crowd, and eventually bringing in the catastrophic specter of what is to come: the young Joseph-Désiré Mobutu, later Mobutu Sese Seko, standing alongside Lumumba.

Accompanying this ambivalent image, moving from hope to despair, from liberation to exploitation, is an audio recording of Lumumba's speech. The words stop suddenly, and the remainder of the speech is lost. Trailing off, Peck's shot lingers on Lumumba's face, a mood that marks a space of loss, abyss, and absence. Peck does not fill in the space with words. He refuses to explain the loss, except only to underscore it with the absence of sound. What remains of Lumumba, then, is silence, a silence made all the more striking and troubling by what preceded it: an articulation of hope. Juxtaposition becomes the space of loss and terror. This hope functioned in two directions. First, Lumumba's articulation of the moment of decision gathers the precolonial and colonial past into one moment, piecing back together what had been broken apart under colonial rule. Second, in gathering the two pasts into the moment, Lumumba's words and *persona* project a very different future than what would seem to spring from those pasts: anticolonialism, postcolonial moral and intellectual revolution, industrial to post-industrialization, socialism. In other words, and to repeat, Lumumba's words and *persona* sit at the decisive moment of Congo's history, which, as *Lumumba, la mort du prophète* would seem to claim, is inseparable from Haiti, the Americas, Peck himself. We might say that, as this crucial scene unfolds, the documentary flirts with the very best of Négritude.

But the words break off. And silence remains. Lumumba's death, then, does not come to presence as such; the death of the prophet is the death of prophetic presence itself, first stalled in the still image, then later, decisively, in the breaking off of the final words. There is no record, no documentation, of Lumumba's final words. If the film aims at documenting the final days of Lumumba's life, then it fails. The subject himself is incomplete, as the document is fractured by the very despair against which he, as a prophetic figure, labors. But this is only one layer of the film's deciding moment, and perhaps even the least compelling if read simply as a point of political despair. After all, *Lumumba, la mort du prophète* is as much about Peck as it is about Lumumba, which means that the film is as much about the trafficking across detoured existential geographies as it is about images and sounds of/from Lumumba's final days.

The moment we see the film as a documentary about Peck—and so about Haiti, the Americas, Africa, Négritude, postcolonialism, diaspora, south Atlantic movement and migrations forced and compelled, and so forth—the purchase of these stalled moments of image and sound comes into relief. The failure to document Lumumba's final days is the failure of return as such. What are we to make of this failure of return? Where, for Peck, does such a failure leave him? In a key scene, Peck gives us his answer. Mobutu's government, having been solicited for travel visas by Peck and his crew, refuses them entry at the airport in Brussels. *Lumumba, la mort du prophète* does not investigate, explain, or even muse over the refusal of entry. Rather, the camera stares down empty airport hallways with mediocre lighting. Sound is minimal, only ambient. And so Peck's film, in many ways, resolves its failure at this very moment. The empty hallways stand in for the literal and figurative question of passage. Literally, Peck's collection of shots only tells us about him and his crew, how they are stranded, waiting in the airport. Figuratively, however, they tell us so much more. Brussels airport is the interval between places, the transition point between Haiti, the Americas, and Africa, as well as of course the interval between policy and massacre under colonial rule. Stalled in the interval, there is no home, no terrain, no density of place in which something meaningful might take root. The hallways figure what the documentary has documented all along: passage, lack of a single fixed root, and therefore a nomadic subject. Errant, movement in and through the abyss. Indeed, how better to resolve the failure of the document (Lumumba's last days) than to find, in that failure, what fated failure in the first place: the irreducible movement and chaos of errantry. Stranded on first glance, Peck's image and sound, when read with Glissant, manifest the nomadic character of subjectivity, while at the same time reminding, always, of the poly-rooted rhizome: Haiti, the Americas, Africa, Europe, and the intervals between.

One last remark. In the end, when taken as an aesthetic object, what is so forceful about reading Peck's documentary as a necessary failure is how that object repudiates the logic of repetition. This repudiation is already implicit in Glissant's conception of subjectivity as rhizomatic, but the rendering of that rootless openness in an aesthetic object poses an even deeper question to white Western aesthetic theory. To what extent is white Western aesthetic theory and practice dependent upon the logic of repetition? To be sure, the problem of *mimesis* has been systematically contested in the West for over a century, yet posing (or reposing) this question in terms of repetition widens the scope of critique. To wit: authorship, political import, and other origins and destinies of the artwork turn on a certain presupposition of the logic (albeit a slackened one) of repetition. Repetition of vision (the cult of genius), repetition of style (the cult of icon), and various repetitions of political ideas reify an expanded (and, frankly, expended) sense of *mimesis*. But *Lumumba, la mort du prophète* cannot be understood as a variant of this logic; as the crucial scene in the Brussels airport makes clear, there is no repetition possible in emptiness, in the abyss that spaces times of relation and Relation. Peck's work blends so many incompatibles into conceptions of place, affect, and image and sound that the work repeats nothing. Rather, the film affirms the productive space of dislocation; again, the ghosts of an abyssal sea sustain life with the disastrously won gift of *diversité*. Cinema as method, not narrative. Cinema as an articulation of the condition of thinking, not the repetition of a state of being. *Lumumba, la mort du prophète*, when read as an enactment of this first moment of Diversity (that is, before the fully developed labor of a national literature), reminds us that the aesthetics of Relation are painful. And we should not expect otherwise. After all, a ghost who sustains life is still a ghost. The geography of the Caribbean, across which he sees the open future of Relation, is always, for Glissant, as tortured as it is lovely.

It is precisely this initially (and perhaps persistently) painful rendering of the space of Diversity that calls us to rethink the resonance of failure. Is the failure of *Lumumba, la mort du prophète* only its inability (or unwillingness) to tell a continuous story? If that lack of continuum—which is nothing other than laboring through what Glissant calls non-history—is failure, then we bring the presupposition of repetition out into the clear. And further, with Glissant's critique of linearity as a totalitarian approach to *Histoire* (history and story) in view, this presupposition cannot but trouble. In that troubled presupposition and the subsequent giving way of the same, we glimpse just what the poetics of Relation, on the shoulders of the rhizomatic subject, carry *into* the project of a national literature: errantry, chaos, detour, nomad, and, ultimately, opacity. For, if Glissant demands the right to opacity as the condition of rendering the traumatic wake of the Middle Passage productive (PR, 189), then what does it mean to say that an aesthetic object fails? The meaning of failure is in some sense reversed here. The quasi-totalitarian trajectory of coherence and the continual is itself a failure, whereas the affirmation of the poly-rooted writer, the one exploring the obsessive presence of painful history in the present, is successful in its productive engagement with chaos and its myriad detours. The Brussels airport, coupled with lost audio, expose poly-rootedness at the very moment the single root is lost. The film draws life from the space of alleged failure. An ethical reversal, no doubt, as detours through chaos refuse domination and nostalgia while confirming, in Glissant's very peculiar sense, difference as *creolization*. Peck's title, then, becomes no small irony: the death of the prophet is the birth of another sort of prophecy, what Glissant calls in *Caribbean Discourse* "a prophetic vision of the past" (CD, 64). What, then, do we want from an aesthetics? Perhaps a prophecy of the abyssal past from and through which, however haunted by pain, there is a sustaining moment of articulation.

In other words, the whole world gathered to itself, disparate.

If Glissant's aesthetics responds to the prophetic vision of the past characteristic of an abyssal subject, creative and created as the legacy of the Middle Passage, in the mode of critique, then we must attend to the fecundity of critique. In the same measure that critique puts representation in question and dismantles modes of rooted transmission, critique *produces* something new. Indeed, Césaire understood this above all: the aesthetics of Négritude were not expression alone, but the transformation of a people.

What, then, is the meaning of the Caribbean, not just as a method, but as a people? That is the most perplexing question. Glissant's work is so deeply committed to the anti-authoritarian work of war against the despot, rhizomatic and nomadic subjects against the single root and plotted territorialization, so the meaning of collectivity is nothing if not fraught. And perhaps impossible. The simple answer is that Glissant is interested in fragmentation and the possibilities of cross-cultural contact to the radical end of dissolving national identities. Indeed, that is the lesson of the Caribbean, the repeating island: you can have a dismantled identity, affirm the chaos of difference, and still appeal to *place*.

What does it mean to think *in place*?

Who thinks *in place*?

What is *placed* intellectual work?

Who is that intellectual?

· CHAPTER 5 ·

Thinking and Building

What Is an Intellectual?

The mimetic trap is everywhere.

—Glissant, *Caribbean Discourse*

AN ABYSSAL BEGINNING makes everything precarious. Indeed, as figured in the epigraph to this book's introduction, language and its companion identities are akin to words in chalk, always perched between becoming-word and genocidal erasure. It is worth recalling our epigraph, for in it Patrick Chamoiseau captures what, for Glissant, is the simultaneous risk and urgency of writing. In *School Days*, Chamoiseau writes, observing his protagonist:

> He saw himself there, captured whole within a chalk mark. *Which meant he could be erased from the world!* . . . [H]e began to copy out his first name a thousand times, in order to proliferate and avoid a genocide.[1]

The chalk mark captures what has not yet calcified in language, for there is always distance and drift between the colonial word and the identity of the postcolonial subject, which is here cited as the boy's proper name. And yet there is the *necessary* risk of writing. There *must* be a name. Writing is risky, for Chamoiseau, because something about the instrument and its mark renders the proper name erasable. Legibility is not in question, but rather the solidity of the sign. *How can it endure and carry meaning?* A chalk mark is unsecured, after all, perhaps irreducibly so. Everything is at stake for the postcolonial subject; the evocation of proliferation against genocide is only small (or maybe even no) hyperbole. Genocide is possible because writing has brought the subaltern to a sort of presence in words, resetting identity in a promise, which then initiates a struggle for voice, for recognition, for participation. Erasure takes all of that becoming away in a flash, no matter how caught in fits and starts such becoming, born of an abyssal beginning, might be. Chamoiseau puts the proper name at risk in order to both underscore and elevate the already sizable stakes of discussion. Not only the boy's identity is precarious. He also, and foremost, wants to avoid *genocide*. The postcolonial Caribbean itself is a coming to chalky language and a risking of erasure.

Writing identity as a between. Chamoiseau's protagonist is placed between word and death. This between, this utterly precarious and fraught space, is precisely what prompts Glissant to characterize national literature—"writing identity" writ large—as *struggle*, and so not merely play or expression or decadent enjoyment. For Glissant, national literature ought not be oriented toward the re-enchantment of a lost past or the political articulation of alienation alone. Rather, Glissant's conception of national literature is firstly located in a space prior to reactive nostalgia and political need, which is precisely the space of fragmentation affirmed in his notion of Antillanité. It is also a space in which survival is a constant question and demand, the continuous pressure of the new against a past saturated with disaster and exploitation. Survival is thus located between the becoming of word and the encroachment of death, which leads Glissant to write in *Caribbean Discourse* that a literature formed in this between writes from "the urge for each group to assert itself: that is, the need not to disappear from the world scene and on the contrary to share in its diversification." (CD, 99). Becoming word *against* genocidal erasure. National literature is taken up, ever precarious, in this very between. Chamoiseau calls this terrifying between—with no small smirk in his prose—a "fine predicament."

Intertwined with this fine predicament is another, companion motif, the motif of an antechamber to the word written in chalk. Another motif, that is, that answers to the enigma of beginning: What is creation from the abyss? How is it possible to think at an abyssal beginning, to create and build where repetition and *mimesis* are betrayals, rather than resources? What is the name for this possibility of thinking at the interval of beginning?

A terminological suggestion, then, which structures the outset of the present meditations: *poiesis*. The term is sensitive to the demands of an abyssal beginning, for it captures the art of thinking, naming a sense of intellectual work not beholden to precedent and continuity in historical thought. What does *poiesis* have to say to Glissant's work—in particular, what does it say to how he conceives both "the intellectual" and the companion notion "national literature"? And, as context for such a question, how is Glissant's intellectual to be distinguished from Fanon's militant conception of the same? This distinction, as we shall see, brings important aspects of both thinkers to the fore, and, from those aspects, much can be discerned about national literature as its own kind of revolution. To get at these questions, I want to begin with a short reflection on Martin Heidegger's rendering of *poiesis*. In *poiesis*, Heidegger discovers the character of *building* in thinking. This notion of building is crucial for conceiving *the new*, which, for my purposes here, is the key to intellectual work undertaken under the rubric of Antillanité. No matter the critical hesitations one might make regarding Heidegger's Eurocentrism (and there are plenty), his reflections on *poiesis* as a response to a crisis of loss prove to be an especially rich and instructive resource for working through the question raised in this chapter: What is the character and significance of the intellectual?

Beginning, *Poiesis*

Heidegger's long meditation on the problem of *poiesis* is profound for both its insight and its circumscription. In drawing a boundary between what is thought and what must be thought, Heidegger brings the difficulty of intellectual work in late modernity into bold and often disconcerting relief. Heidegger takes the crisis of the West seriously and offers, in an interval, a provocative future for thinking *after*. This interval also makes *poiesis* a particularly interesting site for creolization. For creolization, as we have seen, performs its work in the interstitial spaces of meaning. This is precisely the space of *poietic* work: *poiesis* is a transformation of the given and an opening upon the new at one and the same time. Further, as we have seen in previous chapters, this interval between transformation and opening is critical for an abyssal beginning. So, two opening questions: How does *poiesis* locate discourse in interstitial space? And, how is creolization of this space made possible in Glissant's critical work?

Poiesis emerges as a key theme for Heidegger at the border of the history of Being, that fault line between calculative thinking in the epoch of technology and the task of thinking at the end of philosophy. Thinking, as Heidegger conceives it, functions as a response to a massive crisis in the West: one is no longer at home in one's home. Language, the home of our being, has become alien. We do not know how to dwell. In "Building, Dwelling, Thinking," Heidegger writes:

> The real dwelling plight lies in this, that mortals ever search anew for the nature of dwelling, that they *must ever learn to dwell*. What if man's homelessness consisted in this, that man still does not even think of the *real* plight of dwelling as *the* plight?[2]

The great insight gathered from this crisis lies in Heidegger's account of *poiesis* as the necessity of the new in response to an impossibly stifling history. One cannot breathe at the end of metaphysics. Nothing is offered to philosophy except repetition of the same form of life, language, and thinking, whose variations are informed by an alienated and alienating ideality. Calculative thinking suffocates philosophy, so the charge of the task of thinking at the end of metaphysics, of catching one's breath in intellectual work, is tantamount to conceiving an aesthetics of the new. Thinking must open up the possibility for transmission of that newness, wherein the new is conceived as the irreducible and incalculable transcendence that cannot be (re-)possessed by the reductive character of calculative thinking. *Poiesis* defines itself, at least in part, as a *counter* to given forms of life, language, and thought. Heidegger responds to the decadence of his own geography of reason, a decadence that resonates very differently, yet also in important ways, in a south Atlantic context.

Thinking at the end of metaphysics has a very particular context for Heidegger—and perhaps this is true for any and every endeavor of *poietic* intellectual work. Heidegger's work responds to a crisis that is rooted in a very particular experience of history. That is, we can only conceive its end if metaphysics is located on a trajectory of thinking, one determined in that trajectory by specific epochs and (very) particular forms of thought. *Poiesis* as a counter-practice *responds* to the end of a particular way of thinking. And so labeling Heidegger's notion of thinking-as-*poiesis* "Eurocentric" is neither controversial nor simply a critique. It is plainly and indisputably true. Heidegger's articulation of the question to which *poiesis* is an answer focuses explicitly on the trajectory of the white (even just Germanic) West, working from the ancient Greeks through contemporary philosophy's troubling mimicry of natural science. Heidegger's circumscriptive work therefore attends to historical experience as *this* historical experience, not historical experience *as such*. At the same time, I think we can read *poiesis* as something that functions—or at least *ought* to function—more generally as a name for the task of thinking as building, as a fashioning of the new out of the ruins at the end.

That is to say: Does Heidegger's account of thinking and building function only for those thinking at the end of a particular metaphysics? Or might *poiesis* as a generalized problematic of thinking exceed the Eurocentric horizon within which it emerges for Heidegger, thereby becoming a transformed and transformative notion for the intellectual of Antillanité?[3] Is there a promise to *poiesis* that Heidegger helps us see such that we can place a claim on this notion for thinking through the process of creolization?

Let us consider a famous remark from Heidegger's 1953 lecture "The Question Concerning Technology." In this remark, Heidegger underscores both the limits and the fecundity of his account of *poiesis*. Heidegger argues that the Enframing—his term for modernity's orientation as calculative thinking—"blocks *poiesis*," and so, in the famous turn of phrase, "conceals the revealing which, in the sense of *poiesis*, lets what presences come forth into appearance."[4] Heidegger captures something important about the destiny of the West in this remark. Working from Heidegger's insight, there are many stories to be told about such destiny. At least since the advent of modern science and scientism in the West, which arguably has its roots in particular ancient Greek conceptions of the *logos*, one could say that philosophy has censored what comes to concept and word—a sort of totalitarianism at the level of ideas. As well, this blocking, this thinking of totality, can be linked to forms of exploitation in general and perhaps specifically, as Enrique Dussel has argued, to the economy of conquest and the subsequent transatlantic slave trade.[5] Perhaps one could also develop a story about the link between the blocking of *poiesis* and the eclipse of the humanity of another. Horkheimer, Adorno, Levinas, and others have so much to say on these matters.

But debating the story of stories is not my concern here. My question instead is: What can be said about the reductive character of Heidegger's account? It is surely too much to say that his is a totalizing narrative about *poiesis* and Enframing or a story about the human, History, and Being as such. In fact, I am not convinced that Heidegger himself makes such a claim. Of course, the question would always remain to be asked: *Whose* humanity, History, and place in Being's home is being addressed? This very question already names the limit and narrows the scope of Heidegger's claim about thinking and philosophy's end. However, naming the limit and narrowed scope does not simply lead to the rather banal claim that Eurocentrism is confined to something called "Europe." Heidegger's location of his work on the trajectory of the (white, perhaps even just Germanic) West is both self-conscious and productive for thinking about a central demographic in Europe's historical experience (it does exclude Romani experiences, as well as black Europe, wider immigrant Europe, etc., and Heidegger has no pretensions to speak to such experiences). Such an explicit declaration of location *might* be taken as an affirming hesitation in theoretical discourse, a way of setting a given discourse in its proper place, rather than a nostalgic lament about a lack of universality. And, to that extent, this provides an important link to Glissant's work. Indeed, one of the most consistent and powerful motifs in Glissant's work is the rejection of the very project of universalization in the insistence on a geography of reason. Thinking the geography of reason needs, as well as provides, this kind of rejection. "Eurocentrism" would then function as a caveat, as it were, for thinking, a decisive caution and qualification of a given discourse about humanity, History, and Being. Setting aside for a moment the question of how Heidegger conceives the unity and disunity of the West (an enormous question), and instead directing focus on how thinking at the end of philosophy might be said to either tear apart or suture Western philosophy, it is enough here to simply observe that Heidegger's account of *poiesis*, and indeed the very concept of *poiesis* itself, draws by necessity upon a particular historical experience. It is an experience of loss, to be sure, but if we attend to its particularity and specificity, the kind of crisis that provokes *poietic* intellectual work ought to remind us firstly of where thinking *has already been*. This is exactly how Heidegger marks the authenticity of the *poietic*, especially in how the dwelling of the human as built out of what "has a liking for man" is so inextricably linked to the site of thinking and its crisis. He writes:

> The poetic is the basic capacity for human dwelling. But man is capable of poetry at any time only to the degree to which his being is appropriate to that which itself has a liking for man and therefore needs his presence. Poetry is authentic or inauthentic according to the degree of this appropriation.[6]

Thinking in this conception of Europe has its own story, even with occasional or even persistent breaks and fissures, and so loss is never abyssal for Heidegger. Loss is rather a matter of oblivion, a forgetting that reminds us of how deeply indebted philosophy is to memory, as well as of how the rights to memory operate, however nascently, as a privilege, not a presupposition. The root fades, and in one way or another European philosophical practice is the work of retrieval—even if as a failure to retrieve. This last lesson is to be gleaned from Glissant's meditations on beginning as abyssal. One cannot presuppose the coherence, even in its incoherence or disorientation, of the memory of historical experience. Historical experience in the Caribbean begins *otherwise*. An abyss is not a variant or event of the continuum between coherence and incoherence.

A further claim, then: Historical experience intersects with the exigency of *poiesis* when the intersection is a *site of memory*—namely, conceptual, existential, or political memory (often all at once). *Poiesis* issues its call for another beginning to thinking, that building of the new out of the ruins of the old on the basis of what is *remembered* in historical experience. Historical experience, after all, outstrips any rendering in a single narrative. The experience of bureaucratic reason, for example, might evoke the impoverishment of philosophical thinking for one, the fate of millions in mechanized man-made mass death for another, or an efficiency model that would underwrite genocidal conquest and slavery for yet another. And so on. Memory, we might say, gives contour and shade to what already has shape, and this nuance comes to mean everything. At the crossroads of history and memory, Eurocentrism then becomes something quite different from mere ideological critique. Rather, and alternatively, Eurocentrism's positivity directs us back to the geography of reason, locating historical experience in a place, which means that the intellectual functions as a diagnostic or even productive response to crisis and loss in *this* landscape. Heidegger's ponderings at the Greek temple are Eurocentric, even Germanicentric, in the precise and rigorous sense of the term(s). And further, if memory attaches itself to historical experience, and if that attachment compels certain modalities of *poietic* labor, then the *geos* of memory—that *centrism* constitutive of any remembering—ought to found not only the condition of writing but also the condition of that condition: *poiesis*. *Poiesis* is just that: the condition that facilitates the relation between historical experience and writing by giving to both the possibility of another saying, another beginning, and so the possibility of the creation of a different order. Put another way, if *poiesis* is a response to loss and its initiation of crisis, then how that loss *registers* in memory of history *ought* to figure prominently in configuring the force and possibility of thinking in the wake of (or at the shoreline of) crisis. A geographic grounding or locating of the intellectual therefore emerges as constitutive of the very idea of intellectual work. The crisis and loss that saturates Caribbean memory would break with Eurocentrism as a matter of creative positivity instead of critique, opening up new possibilities poly-rooted in the archipelagic and south Atlantic historical experience, and so would bring *poiesis* into different focus, placing different demands on thinking. Discerning this geographic character of *poietic* labor, then, begins to provide us an answer the question of the meaning of the intellectual.

Our previous exploration of Glissant's aesthetics deployed the nomadic and rhizomatic character of Caribbean subjectivity in accounting for the transmission of affect in objects structured by detour and opacity. A notion of *poiesis* is already operative in this aesthetics. That is, to the extent that aesthetic objects simultaneously produce and reproduce identity, Glissant's aesthetics of the abyssal subject mirrors and creates Relation. In that interval between production and reproduction, between mirroring and creation, sites of memory gather: creolized language, thresholds of departure and return, and the beginnings of and toward another future. This gathering begins with what is ruined, but it also commences with a radical openness that refuses, upon opening into a future, any sense of closure. Even if the earth is wounded, it is still the site of roots—no matter how thoroughly rhizomatic we theorize that sense of roots. The meaning and significance of a *Caribbean* loss thus appeals, from the very first, to a geographically rooted *poiesis* with roots in a wounded earth, a tortured geography. This geography is both abyssal and irreducibly plural—a creolization of Deleuze and Guattari's sense of the multiple and of difference—precisely because it is a *poiesis* that looks to its sites of painful, archipelagic memory and not backward to another, dreamed world. Glissant writes in "Tomorrows," a bit from the *Black Salt* collection:

No hinterland [*arrière-pays*] at all. You, unable to withdraw behind your face.
Reasons to unfold this running dry to plunge into all the absence, till through twisting detours you revive, black in the rock. (BS, 156)

Glissant writes these lines at the close of sequence of six poem-clusters gathered under the title "Yokes [*Boises*]." This final poem, "Tomorrows," gets out from under the *garrotte* of history and memory in order to set *poiesis* out into a future that says yes to historical experience, yes to the memory of pain, and so takes up an epistemology of loss without the mediation or neutralization of nostalgia. There can be no reproduction here in the sense of a repetition of the past. There is no *arrière-pays*—literally, no backward-looking land—which means, in our present context, that intellectual production must always "plunge into absence."[7] There is therefore the production of the new in the reproduction of absence and fragmentation. So begins *poiesis* as an abyssal beginning, this *other* centrism, this certain centrism engaged with Antillanité. Afro-Caribbeancentrism, perhaps.

The double function of *poiesis* as production and reproduction helps us focus the question of the intellectual and note, too, how production and reproduction in the context of the intellectual *might* move away from Althusserian models of ideology, that is, how the archipelagic intellectual and its sense of *poiesis* works against the institutional construction of meaning and the embedding of that meaning in sites of reproduction. Relation is no small part of this difference in conceiving production and reproduction. An aesthetics of an abyssal subject *creates* Relation at the very moment such an aesthetics *mirrors* the archipelago. Just as geography is rendered Being, Being is rendered geography—a reversal that structures Glissant's aesthetics. And so the aesthetics of an abyssal subject, rooted as it is (paradoxically) in the geography of the archipelago, places us at the site of *poiesis*. *Poiesis*, however, is not an aesthetics proper. That is, *poiesis* does not point us to figures of transmission and quasi-dictations of form. Now, while aesthetics might function as an *element* of *poiesis*, as in cases where traumatic experience haunts (for better or worse) the imagining of a new social order, the element can never reduce that which operates within it. *Poiesis* both operates within and exceeds an aesthetics of loss. To be sure, *poiesis* is rooted first in questions of absence, those questions of history and memory and so of the fate of a community as a people, a nation, or any sense of collectivity whatsoever.[8] This means that, at the moment of production from out of the reproduction of absence and fragmentation, Glissant's *poiesis* crosses the interval of past and future without forgetting the saturating element of loss. And yet, whereas an aesthetics of loss articulates that sense in the context of affective transmission and form, the intellectual labor of *poiesis* places transmission within what Glissant calls, in a non-Lacanian register, "the imaginary." The imaginary raises the stakes of intellectual labor. Glissant writes in *Poetics of Relation*:

> Thinking thought usually amounts to withdrawing into a dimensionless place in which the idea of thought alone persists. But thought in reality spaces itself out into the world. It informs the imaginary of peoples, their varied poetics, which it then transforms, meaning, in them its risk becomes realized. (PR, 1)

This imaginary, which Glissant nicely defines here as how a people transforms meaning in a poetics, emboldens intellectual labor at the very moment it "plunges into absence" and sets in motion "a knowledge becoming" (PR, 1). Intellectual labor is rooted in history and memory and bears the fate of those addressed by intellectual work in an important shift of horizon: away from the *arrière-pays,* toward the new. To be sure, the pain of history, which saturates the aesthetics of loss with an irreducible sadness, would seem to suggest a *poietic* work dedicated to mourning. This is a significant feature of Heidegger's work.[9] Glissant, however, places the intellectual in two very different historical and memorial sites than Heidegger, which is due, as I have argued here, to the *-centrism* inherent in any *poietic* work. First, the intellectual is plunged into loss, into abyssal beginning— the Antillanité of commencement. The abyss is other than the spastic white Western dialectic of coherence and incoherence. Second, and most important for our considerations here, Glissant places the intellectual in the complicated place of the emergence and creation of the new. This is a sense of place at once renewed (literature is its own reactivation of traces, no matter how faded) and imagined (literature speaks to the possible, to the imaginary of a collectivity).

Poiesis is always concerned with the new, even when that concern carries with it very specific shifts and turns in accounting for the historical and memorial context of intellectual labor. Retrieval, after all, is still an event of the new. In the Caribbean context, raising Glissant's conception of the new cannot but evoke that other great Martinican thinker of the same: Frantz Fanon. The philosophical relation between Fanon and Glissant is surely fraught, traversing the complex terrain of the Négritude movement and pan-African solidarity, but in that often-agonistic space between them, so much is brought to clarity. What does the convergence and conflict of ideas in this relation tell us about the intellectual, about the possibilities of *poiesis* for transformation, and so also about the geography of reason? Two questions are critical. First and most generally, what is the meaning of national literature and national culture? That meaning lies at the heart of any postcolonial intellectual practice. Second, the intellectual as the site of literature and culture, beginning with the peculiar alienation of the abyssal, raises the broader historical question: What is Glissant's relation to Fanon? The question of this relation functions as something of an antechamber to the problematic of national literature and culture by drawing out the characteristics of the intellectual laboring toward literary and cultural ends.

So, who is Fanon to Glissant? Fanon casts a long and imposing shadow on Caribbean intellectual life, as Glissant's own words attest. Along with Césaire, Fanon created a rich and productive midcentury moment of anticolonial theory in the francophone Caribbean, and so much that follows from that era is in response to the sorts of questions Fanon raises. As a theoretical horizon, and this is a crucial part of his legacy in the Caribbean, Fanon's work opens up the question of the relation between the old and the new, the past and the future, that cannot be thought without creolization. Fanon's own relation to language and culture is not yet *créolité*, to be sure. In fact, Fanon's work is explicitly hostile to linguistic and cultural practices of pidgin and creole, linking them to lament, abjection, and appeal to white domination.[10] Yet, I want to argue here that Fanon's work *must* become creolization, even when his own words pull us in an often very different—at best only ambivalent—direction. That is, I want to argue that Glissant's critique of Fanon's conception of the intellectual exposes a conceptual impossibility (in the worst sense) at the heart of Fanon's conception of the new. If beginning is abyssal, something on which Fanon and Glissant quite readily agree in their shared critique of Négritude, then questions of the new must be thought through with close attention to how the pain of history informs not just our account of the past but also the interval to the new. In that interval to the new we can discern the character of the intellectual and intellectual work and, by extension, the meaning of national literature and culture. In other words, the full significance of the new is the accomplishment and practice of *poiesis*.

Let us turn to a well-known passage from Glissant's *Caribbean Discourse*. The passage comes from the opening chapter of that work, in which Glissant articulates the terms of Caribbean *dispossession*. Dispossession is doubled as both the violence of the Middle Passage and the terror of colonialism, where the latter finds Martinique, in Glissant's words, at a "loss of personality, cultural consumption not accompanied by creativity, derisory substitutes: devitalized folklore, etc." (CD, 379). Whole clusters of other terms and issues are folded into the notion of dispossession, for sure, but it is enough here to read dispossession as an event that obligates the intellectual in terms of both the pain of history and the openness of the new. Dispossession is the ground of a certain regulation of thinking; *poietic* labor always keeps history and memory in view, just as history and memory always keep *poiesis* in view, which means that *poiesis* is constrained (accomplished) and directed (practiced) by its relation to history and memory. The Middle Passage and colonialism work as regulative ideals rather than moments of pain. Dispossession sets the ground of thinking. What it means to create moves on this geography.

Intellectual labor is always rooted somewhere. Every thinking has a *geos*, literally and figuratively. But dispossession removes the terms of stable rootedness, offering to *poiesis* neither a familiar soil of experience nor that comfortable connection to the soil we often call history. Although dispossession largely issues from the pain of history, and so would suggest only alienation and despair, Glissant conceives dispossession as also a gift of possibility—a gift so profound that he will write in *Traité du monde*, "my proposal is that, today, the entire world archipelagize and creolize itself [*s'archipélise et se créolise*]" (TTM, 194). The archipelago becomes *verbal*, a way of being. This is why Glissant will say that dispossession tempts (or even compels) the intellectual—both the colonized and the postcolonial—to seek an *elsewhere*. The compulsion to seek an elsewhere is lodged deeply within the painful experience of history and its intertwined relationship to geography, and so Glissant's distance from Fanon, as we shall see, begins with a re-articulation of the meaning of the pain of history as dispossession. To begin with dispossession is therefore to begin intellectual work with a sense of unrootedness and alienation, which means, as well, to respond to loss without conceding to either nihilism or nostalgia. Fanon's intellectual begins with the crisis of language. *The Wretched of the Earth*, in particular the fourth chapter, "On National Culture," attempts to reground thinking in the terrain of struggle—a form, perhaps, of militant self-dispossession, uprooting from conventions of the present or nostalgia about the past. Glissant's intellectual begins with the abyss. This is why *dispossession* functions as central, both as a motif and critical term, to the multifaceted aims of *Caribbean Discourse*. As a *motif*, dispossession motivates Glissant's articulation of subjectivity-as-nomad, which in turn generates the logic of the poetics of Relation. As a *critical term*, dispossession functions as a crucial site for Glissant's transformation of Caribbeanness from content or pathology *to* method. And so for both Fanon and Glissant, dispossession names a doubled sense of propriety: the rights to what has been lost and the rights to loss itself. It is a moment of claiming for the first time what it means to start with nothing. The relation between Fanon and Glissant, then, begins here and, next, hinges on how differently the pain of history registers in the rights to what has been lost. That is, Fanon and Glissant *begin* as intellectuals at the very moment they register the rights to what one retains in loss and the future such rights make possible.

Now, let us turn to the passage in question. In *Caribbean Discourse*, Glissant reads Fanon the thinker and the mythic figure as a flight from hauntology. This is why Glissant's remark on Fanon begins with the claim that "Martinique is the land of ghosts." Fanon's work is perfectly well attuned to the ghostly character of Martinique, noting at every turn how colonialism produces myriad neuroses (and worse) and leaves the landscape riddled with zombified bodies and psyches. The postcolonial body and consciousness in Fanon's work is possessed by what it *cannot be*, a possession that is always a pathology and existentially fated to the zone of nonbeing. Glissant underscores this shared diagnosis of the Martinican situation when he writes in *Caribbean Discourse* that "the mimetic impulse is a kind of insidious violence." But whereas this diagnosis leads Glissant to long meditations on the haunted terrain of the archipelago, Fanon is remarkably indifferent to the ghostly character of the land. The haunted terrain, for Fanon, produces pathologies to be treated by a certain combination of *assertion* and *return*. Something of the human remains, and in that remainder there is the movement toward the new, the moment of *poiesis*. But Fanon does not think dispossession itself, does not think the ghosts and how they might form, de-form, or re-form the very terms of one's address to haunted space—the specifically Caribbean geography. Now, as we shall see, Fanon will in fact later link landscape to intellectual work, binding that work to the senses of relation to land and place. But how seriously does Fanon take his own understanding of that bound relation? That is the crucial question. For, as Glissant makes clear in this passage, Fanon's work is ultimately realized only in its complete break with the present, which comes to mean, in the end, a break with the archipelago as an imaginary and as land:

> It is difficult for a French Caribbean individual to be the brother, the friend, or quite simply the associate or fellow countryman of Fanon. Because, of all the French Caribbean intellectuals, he is the only one to have *acted on his ideas*, through his involvement in the Algerian struggle; this was so even if . . . the Martinican problem . . . retains its complete ambiguity. It is clear that in this case *to act on one's ideas* does not only mean to fight, to make demands, to give free rein to the language of defiance, but to take full responsibility for *a complete break.* (CD, 25)

When Glissant writes here that Fanon *acted on his ideas,* we might be tempted to read this as a kind of hagiographic moment. *Surely Fanon is a hero—and so perhaps all the more "right" as a thinker—for blending action and theory.* Is not this sort of praxis *precisely* what is most demanded in the postcolonial moment? To act with militancy and destroy the world as we know it? And so, is the problem with intellectual life not precisely the divide between theorizing and acting, where only the latter is an effective and effectual intervention in history?

And yet, Glissant notes, the Martinican problem "retains its complete ambiguity."

What are we to make of Glissant's identification of Fanon's defining characteristic: the transnational actor? The one who left the archipelago for the continent? How is such action related to reckoning with the land of ghosts? And, further, what does such a relationship to land and its ghosts say about the potency and limitations of Fanon's intellectual? An answer to these questions requires a precise formulation of the relation between the intellectual, rootedness, and the question of postcolonial identity.

Organicity; or, Fanon the (Unexpected) African

For both Fanon and Glissant, the function of the intellectual is key for theorizing matters of identity, meaning, and the transformation of history. But the very notion of the intellectual is fraught in the postcolonial moment, for the terms of intellectual work are always laden with the force of what has already enacted dispossession. How can one decolonize intellectual work? Antonio Gramsci's work on the meaning of the intellectual—the formation of intellectuals and the origins of their work—is important here, especially his famed distinction between corporative and organic senses of the intellectual. The corporative intellectual cannot but labor *for* the dominant social order; language, concept formation, and the diagnoses that follow are intractably ideological. This becomes the colonized intellectual in a global South context. Moral and intellectual reform, however, which Gramsci understands to be at the heart of authentic revolutionary hegemony, fundamentally alters the meaning of thinking. If thinking is always already ideologically fraught, and moral and intellectual reform must be *counter*-ideological in order to exercise a hegemony that is new, and so not a repetition, then radical intellectual work must break with mimesis at every level. This is no small task, for, as Glissant puts it in a footnote to *Caribbean Discourse,* "the mimetic trap is everywhere" (CD, 38n1). Intellectual work is therefore charged with bringing non-mimetic senses of creation into being and becoming. For Gramsci, of course, this is the question of making a history out of the erasure of subaltern classes from history's story, which means that the *creative* intellectual brings something into being for the first time. The subaltern becomes historical for the first time in that work, perhaps breaking through as what, with Caribbean specificity, Glissant calls "our irruption into modernity" (CD, 100). For Gramsci, it is the *organic* intellectual who enacts this irruption without sacrificing the meaning of the subaltern classes. Such enactment is a tricky business, requiring the intellectual to have a sense of the past and present, but also the will and capacity to enter a different future. In "The Formation of Intellectuals," Gramsci writes:

> It can be seen that the "organic" intellectuals which each new class creates with itself and elaborates in its own progressive development are for the most part "specializations" of partial aspects of the primitive activity of the new social type which the new class has brought to light.[11]

"Class," which for Gramsci is expanded to encompass the web of social and cultural forces constitutive of life, settles the ground in which the organic intellectual has *and* grows roots. And so the organic intellectual is sprouted, as it were, from the fertile (if subaltern) memory and forgotten history of the class in question. Every corporative class is articulated by intellectuals of that class, even when, laboring under the fantasy of root-less inquiry, intellectual work imagines universality. Now, this intellec-tual work is not without its complexity, for it is always already (at least typically) naive about its origins. That is, the very language of intellectual work, the form and matter with which creation labors, is already institu-tional and therefore already ideological. Again, the problem of the relation of "the new" to economies of social reproduction. The organicity of the intellectual is key here, insofar as it functions as both a description (we all come from somewhere) and a normative call (we *ought* to understand our rootedness on its own terms, not as interpreted by dominant ideological forms).

The Caribbean context alters this sense of an ideologically laden form and matter of creation. Whereas the subaltern class, for Gramsci, has failed to enter its own language and meaning into (Italian) history, yet retains that history in its memory, the Caribbean context begins with an altogether more catastrophic sense of absence. "The first step toward mad-ness," as Glissant puts it, is that moment in which history is lost, not for-gotten. And this difference is everything. Gramsci's sense of the subaltern is far from history, but only because the story of history forgets what is marginal, or, perhaps more precisely, has yet to recognize the marginal as already historical. For Gramsci's subaltern, there is always the continuity of memory—the soil nourishing the organic intellectual's roots—upon which a narrative might be made historical. The Middle Passage imposes a different sense of loss. This is why Caribbean intellectual work proceeds from an abyssal beginning. Fanon's work is positioned somewhere be-tween these sites of beginning.

With that position in mind: What might a conception of *poiesis* mean in Fanon's thinking? And how might that conception frame a reading of Fanon's account of the intellectual?

These questions bring a concept and aesthetic sensibility not present in Fanon to bear on reading his texts. At the same time, the nuances that drive Fanon's break with Négritude and his imagining another sort of hu-manism both hinge on a conception of the new. The new emerges out of two fundamental experiences. First, there is the impasse of the postcolo-nial subject, caught between Parisian French and what Fanon calls "pid-gin" or "creole." Parisian French, of course, is contaminated by both the alienating interpellation of the colonized and its anxious relation to the epidermal conception of race. The black man, as Fanon repeats so often in

Black Skin, White Masks, is never at home in (a particular kind of) French. Second, and perhaps less appreciated, is the sense in which the break with the colonial past and present initiates an experience of nihilism, rooted in what we might call his race realism. Fanon's relationship with the Négritude movement is complicated—the significance of which occupies much of what follows—but the very fact of that complication removes one of the blocks to nihilism. To wit: if decolonization is tasked with the formulation of an identity disentangled from the colonial psychic and cultural infrastructure, then surely the shortest path to that identity is *return*. But Fanon's hesitation regarding Négritude's return to Africanness forestalls this short path. Nihilism begins at the moment of hesitation, both because it blocks return to the past and, when coupled with the alienating interpellation of language, halts the present. Blocking and halting—whence meaning, if not from a past passed on in the fragmentary present?

In the introduction to the collection *A Dying Colonialism*, Fanon offers a glimpse into this experience of nihilism. He relays a remark made by an Algerian in the moment of postcolonial struggle, a remark that links nihilism to the necessity violence:

> Having a gun, being a member of the National Army of Liberation, is the only chance the Algerian still has of giving a meaning to his death. Life under the domination has long been devoid of meaning.[12]

Let us set aside the question of violence for a moment. This sense of nihilism is strict. Fanon is not simply reiterating the problems of despair and the inferiority complex. Meaning saturates the body and psyche; life under domination knows no boundaries, nothing is left untouched. Despair and the inferiority complex take root in the present, in this moment of reckoning with colonialism's shadow, a shadow that structures the interior *and* exterior life of the postcolonial subject. Epidermal racism and language structure the first phase of postcolonial subjectivity as *anxious*. Anxious, that is, as being not-at-home in one's home. Fanon is surely right when he writes in *Black Skin, White Masks* that "a man who has a language consequently possesses the world expressed and implied by that language,"[13] and then later that "to speak a language is to take on a world, a culture."[14] And so the problem of diction dominates the opening chapter of *Black Skin, White Masks*, documenting in often painful detail how the inhabitation of French makes the postcolonial subject un-at-home in France (the despair of epidermal racism) *and* in the West Indies (the vicissitudes of the inferiority complex). Diction makes the blocking of the past and halting in the present incarnate, marking the body with the anxiety of subjectivity both black and French. Without return—without the fantasy of *arrière-pays,* perhaps—there is no past language to recover or even just to move from margin to center. Diction in the present is for Fanon either the inferiority complex of "pidgin" and "creole" (in which speaking is identification with what it derivative) or the impossible racialized measure of whiteness (in which speaking with perfect diction is mediated by black skin). Thus, a spasm of nihilism.

Glissant's work, in particular his centering of the question of the Middle Passage, exposes a gap in Fanon's thinking: a lack of rigorous interrogation of the meaning of forced migration and enslavement. What is the Middle Passage to Fanon? I do not think this question appears in any significant way in his work. Rather, Fanon begins with colonialism. His backward glance, however resistant to "the great mirage" of Négritude, as he puts it in a 1958 essay, is always and only about the lessons of the African past. Césaire's work, for all of the ways in which it falls under critique from Fanon, is still that reminder. Whatever has been said about black people, there is the falsehood of the roots of that degradation in an abjection of Africa and Africanness. Césaire makes that clear for the Caribbean context. And the truth of African nobility, even greatness, is comfort in refutation of a sinister myth. This is Fanon's thinking in *Black Skin, White Masks* and a few essays in the years following its publication. And so there is Fanon's leap: from Africa to the colonial Americas *after* enslavement. In that context, the *after* of enslavement, what we call colonialism in its later stage, Fanon begins with aspiration (belonging through diction) and the racialized structure of its failure (black and white people are locked in identities forged in oppressive structures of measure). Indeed, Fanon's conception of inferiority only works in an economy structured by superiority. Fanon has no taste for the interstitial, the practices at the margin, *the vernacular* of black life. Glissant's work is exactly the retrieval of such life in its geographic specificity *against* Fanon, a speaking back to Fanon's own anxiety about speaking, a retrieval of the Caribbean landscape *as such*, of pidgins and creoles (they are plural) on their own terms, and thus an indulgence and exploration of the vernacular character of everyday life *in*, *at*, and *as* the margins. And then, from that retrieval, the transformation of the margins as margins in the dissolving of the very idea of a single root. The abyssal subject. The aesthetics of the abyss. There is no measure after the abyss, and both subjectivity and its aesthetics are rooted in what trauma means for a future folded into, then created out of, the past. All of that begins with the abyss. Arrival as absence. The Middle Passage as origin. What is the Middle Passage to Fanon? It is his shadow. Fanon thinks without seeing the shadow talk back—pidgins and creoles all the way up, all the way down—in his own formation as an intellectual. In his conception of what forms the revolutionary (violent struggle, apocalyptic[15] through and through), the organicity of a Promethean intellectual comes into being.

This original absence, this abyssal sense of beginning, is doubled by the experience of colonialism. The traumatic loss of the Middle Passage sustains a second blow in colonialism, as the loss of life and roots is supplemented by a structure of life not only foreign, but wholly and irredeemably alienating. This is firstly an existential alienation; the very meaning of existence is not just touched, but structured from the inside by what is foreign and alienating. "The colonized," for Fanon, names a kind of person, not just a social and cultural artifact, habit, or affect. *Colonialism as typological and typographical.* This elevates the stakes for the organic, transformative intellectual. For, as Fanon writes:

> National liberation, national reawakening, restoration of the nation to the people or Commonwealth, whatever the name used, whatever the latest expression, decolonization is always a violent event . . . quite simply the substitution of one "species" of mankind by another.[16]

Decolonization's existential charge—this violence that is ethical, epistemological, aesthetic, and ontological in the very same measure that it is political—marks the very break with the past that Glissant notes in *Caribbean Discourse.* The logic of Fanon's appeal to violence is both obvious and nuanced. The obviousness comes from the desire for another kind of recognition, a desire so lucidly and dramatically documented in *Black Skin, White Masks.* The nuance, however, is what makes that *other recognition* so very difficult. Substitution of one species for another requires a total and complete transformation of being, knowing, feeling, and acting; this is why the intellectual works with such elevated stakes. The violence of the twice-rendered blow—that violence of the Middle Passage *cum* colonialism—is countered, not by a third blow, but rather by the counter-hegemony of *newness*. The new is a violent irruption and eruption into the known world. What it is and what comes after departs from the economy of known and knowable things. It is a pure future.

There is so much to be said about this newness. To begin, it is important to underscore Fanon's commitment to a certain, albeit very limited, kind of geography of reason. That commitment links important motifs and arguments in Fanon to Glissant's poetics, of course, and it also put the question of life at the center of thinking. How can a geographic theory and practice of reason generate a relation to place capable of sustaining life? Fanon's answer, as is typical, proceeds by way of contrast. His remarks on the colonized painter in *The Wretched of the Earth* are especially instructive. The painter depicts two intertwined concepts: landscape and life. The *national* character of landscape intertwines the question of life with that of geography—something captured nicely in the term *place*—by marking what is ontologically at stake in painting. Painting is never innocent. That is, aesthetics both presents and reproduces an ideologically fraught conception of the being of the human *in place*. Fanon writes:

> Before independence the colonized painter was insensitive to the national landscape. He favored therefore the nonrepresentational or, more often, specialized in still life. After independence, his desire to reunite with the people confines him to a point by point representation of national reality which is flat, untroubled, motionless, reminiscent of death rather than life.[17]

Without mentioning him by name, Fanon invokes Freud's conception of the death drive as a desire for stasis, an untroubled sense of the psyche and reality. The reminiscence of death in the painting of national landscape, however, is not simply an example of an alienated aesthetic. Rather, the alienated aesthetic reproduces a particular kind of relation to geography, one that cannot make space for the substitution of one type of human for another—and so the geography of reason becomes an articulation of possibilities for a future. Another sense of rootedness, an authentic sense of the organicity of intellectual work, is necessary, and so an aesthetics of landscape must break with, rather than reiterate, in order to sustain life. The painted landscape cannot describe. Fanon says the same of the poet, claiming that the poet "who insists on describing his people, misses his mark, because before setting pen to paper he is in no fit state to make that fundamental concession."[18] The landscape, painted or put in verse, must *raise and sustain a question*, to evoke the closing remark of *Black Skin, White Masks*. The painter and the poet practice, then surmount, what Fanon examines in *The Wretched of the Earth* under the generalized category of the colonized intellectual. The de- and postcolonial intellectual blends the interrogative with the task of forming identity—the question of "the people" in and after revolutionary struggle.

Raising and sustaining a *question* (rather than declaring an answer, the vanguard's putative advance on struggle) defines a people by placing alienation at the origin of intellectual work, work that is that always in response to the doubled loss of place: displacement (the Middle Passage) and misplacement (colonialism). The creativity, the charge to make something new, comes out of this origin in alienation. Alienation gives nothing to thought, and so Fanon writes:

> Yes, the first duty of the colonized poet is to clearly define the people, the subject of his creation. We cannot go resolutely forward unless we first realize our alienation. We have taken everything from the other side. Yet the other side has given us nothing except to sway us in its direction through a thousand twists, except lure us, seduce us, and imprison us by ten thousand devices, by a hundred thousand tricks. To take also means on several levels being taken.[19]

This "being taken," as Fanon puts it, saturates the body and its relation to the world. "It is here," he writes, "that their souls are crystallized and their perception and respiration transfigured."[20] Overcoming this tranfiguration is of course the task of decolonialization. The intellectual sits at the interval of that task, brings both critique to the past and present and imagination to the future. Fanon locates the task wholly within the body. It is not only what and how the body sees, but how the body breathes. The prayer that closes *Black Skin, White Masks*, asking to be made a man and body who questions, is reiterated in *The Wretched of the Earth* in the call for new sight and breath.

What, then, are we to make of the organicity of intellectual life? Fanon is at least clear about what constitutes *false* roots. There is nothing *here* for Fanon, as *his* humanism is still yet to come, the new human deferred into the future as an intellectual imperative of revolutionary action. This translates into an enigmatic conceptual move from pathology to violence to novelty-as-transformation. But it also says something important about the geography of reason. In the *Black Salt* poems, Glissant calls the Caribbean a "tortured geography," which, for him, means that the history and memory of the landscape give pain to thought. We can surely say the same for Fanon, except that for him pain gives thought the imperative of *relocation*. There is nothing worth *thinking* in the Caribbean as such. Like V. S. Naipaul in *The Middle Passage*, where the melancholic writer declared that "history is built around achievement and creation; and nothing was created in the West Indies,"[21] Fanon sees only abjection in the languages of the Caribbean, rather than the possibility of sublime poetry of which Walcott caught sight in Felicity. Fanon's relationship to the Négritude movement, however nuanced, tells us (perhaps ironically) this story: it is the spirit of revolutionary Africa—that *other* geography becoming home, making home in armed struggle—that animates the new humanism by declaring its first possibility. Martinique was not enough. He had to struggle in Algeria. That is, I think it is fair to say that Fanon still thinks of intellectual work as connected to place, to the earth, for it is constitutive, and so not just an aesthetic accident, of the intellectual's authenticity and revolutionary potential—those two features of organicity. Violence is part of landscape. Everything looks different, everyone breathes differently, on an earth saturated with revolution. That is still a landscape. At the same time, and this is where Glissant's comment that Fanon acted on his ideas takes up, it is important to note that Fanon's geographic conception of intellectual work begins in a *relocation*, or what Glissant calls *diversion*. Glissant writes:

> The thrust of Négritude among Caribbean intellectuals was a
> response perhaps to the need, by relating to a common origin, to
> rediscover unity (equilibrium) beyond dispersion. (CD, 5)

This is where Glissant's contrast with Négritude, and particularly with Fanon's (perhaps ironic) transformation of it into a fetishization of revolutionary (rather than vitalist) Africa, becomes important. The *need*, and this is such a peculiar word for Glissant to use, for unity fails to take up the possibilities dispersion gives to thinking. Nostalgia for a prior unity *or* a unity to come, which is nothing other than seeking a temporal space in which to set stable roots of organicity for intellectual work, cannot take the archipelagic geography of reason seriously as a figurative and literal condition of the Caribbean.

Archipelagic Thinking, Vernacular Intellectuals

Fanon, like Naipaul, departs from the Caribbean in order to find meaningful identity formation, marking the abjection of the West Indian landscape with an Afro-pessimist characterization. But of course the Caribbean speaks and has spoken, and that speaking across time(s), the vicissitudes of pidgins and creoles in every iteration and figuration, speaks a world into existence, then infuses that speaking and world with forms of multiplicity governed by productive chaos and curves of time. This relocates the intellectual in the dynamics of the Caribbean geography, with all the figures, metaphors, and incarnate life of the landscape. Glissant's work takes this geography seriously, something most clearly articulated in the notion of the rhizome in *Poetics of Relation*. The rhizome is able to sustain a relation to geography and is also sufficiently mobile to negotiate across the fragmented history bequeathed by pain and the multiplicity of cultures, languages, and relations constitutive of the Caribbean. While Glissant will not elaborate the notion of rhizome until *Poetics of Relation,* senses of multiplicity, horizontality, and repetition without calcification are already present in *Caribbean Discourse* at the very moment he marks distance from Fanon on the meaning of the intellectual. Glissant writes:

> . . . *to pull together all levels of experience.* This piling-up is the most suitable technique for exposing a reality that is itself being scattered. Its evolution is like a repetition of a few obsessions that *take root,* tied to realities that *keep slipping away.* The intellectual journey is destined to have a geographical itinerary, through which the 'intention' within the Discourse explores its space and into which it is woven. . . . We need those stubborn shadows where repetition leads to perpetual concealment, which is our form of resistance. (CD, 4)

Perpetual concealment embeds so many of the interesting themes from Glissant's conceptions of memory, subjectivity, and the aesthetic. In a retrieval of the notion of repetition, wresting it free of the logic of mimesis,

Glissant sites intellectual work inside opacity, deployed as ethical and political resistance.

The zigzag movement between taking root and slipping away places the formation of meaning, the work of the intellectual, in "stubborn shadows"—a sense of the marginal that is not measured by the center, but instead resistant and self-forming through concealment. A noncontinental, wholly archipelagic intellectual. *Opacity.* At the same time, this does not mean that Glissant's intellectual repudiates every last insight of the Négritude movement. This is important. Glissant writes:

> Today the French Caribbean individual does not deny the African part of himself; he does not have, in relation, to go to the extreme of celebrating it exclusively. He must *recognize* it. He understands that from all this history (even if we lived it like a nonhistory), *another reality* has come about. He is no longer forced to reject strategically the European elements in his composition. (CD, 8)

This is complicated conceptual stuff, and I would say that only the notion of rhizome as the rhizomatic intellectual clarifies the relation of recognition to "another reality," and in this Glissant recognizes what Fanon articulated so clearly and with such transformative force as the second traumatizing blow of colonialism. But here is where we find the other reality, the intellectual work in the shadows rather than zone of nonbeing, a root that is forever uprooted and re-rooted/re-routed. The rhizome is nomadic, never at home, yet always finds dwelling space within and between the fragments of lived nonhistory. *Lived nonhistory as productive anxiety.* It is the very anxiety of this composition that makes Caribbean unity "a form of cultural self-discovery" (CD, 8). Cultural self-discovery is anxious in that it does not settle in a home (thinking is archipelagic) and because, like Fanon, Glissant's intellectual begins with alienation. And so Glissant writes that the Caribbean intellectual

> can see that alienation first and foremost resides in the impossibility of choice, in the arbitrary imposition of values, and, perhaps, in the concept of value itself. He can conceive that synthesis is not a process of bastardization as he used to be told, but a productive activity through which each element is enriched. (CD, 8)

The rhizome negotiates a liberatory relation to what, for Fanon, was irredeemably alienating. The need to return, the diversion of Negritude, concedes too much—namely, it concedes the geography of—however tortured—the Caribbean. Glissant's intellectual sets roots in the European, but not as a bastardization, and so not without rhizomatic transformation, contact, Relation, and what Glissant here calls "enrichment." The existential conditions of intellectual work trump strategic relations to or epistemological threats from "European elements," something that evokes Léopold Senghor's early work on appropriation and assimilation.[22] With this, then, we can say that Glissant—as he said of Fanon—acts on his ideas. Commencing from (or with) the abyss, Glissant's intellectual works—rhizomatically—between Europe and the Americas, creating and enriching the humanity that has been, that has survived, and that has built and builds a future for thinking out of the fragmented physical and spiritual geography of reason.

The organicity of this transformative intellectual labor emerges, for both Fanon and Glissant, as a figurative and literal condition of thinking in the very terms of dispossession: the loss of place, the loss of earth. The trauma of that loss is fully registered in the moment of facing dispossession, which means, in the postcolonial moment, facing the abyssal sense of beginning. This is a larger story about trauma, memory, and history, of course, but it is enough to say here that the loss of root infuses intellectual labor with the problem of what might be meant by *another* root. In this case, the Caribbean sense of root, uprooted from the colonial territory and in search of both another site (the insight of Négritude) and another way of seeing this alienated site (Diversity, nomadic relation), always in the service of identifying and thinking what is capable of sustaining life.

What are we to make of this shift between Fanon and Glissant regarding the geographic character of intellectual work? Let me say just a few words, for I think that this shift means everything. It means everything because gathered to it are all the central motifs of philosophy: language, subjectivity, space, time, history, memory, and thus the conditions under and through which meaning emerges and registers. The matter of sustaining life, as well, is absolutely crucial. The colonial territory, left to itself, means only that spiritual death we call, with such a timid word, *alienation*.

It is important here to understand Fanon and Glissant as *threshold* thinkers. That is, they are thinkers both *of* and *at* the interval of the movement of memory and history into the future. Abyssal beginning registers in a traumatized memory of the past as well as in the (radically) subaltern relation to history. The intellectual works from this abyss in order to make history possible as an irruption into modernity, perhaps for the first time, and so to make of memory something more than the privacy of life's pleasures and pains. But thinking the threshold also means saying something about the *character* and *significance* of the pain of the past. What is the meaning of that pain? How does that pain inform one's thinking about the future? The question of diversion, which Glissant raises so critically against Fanon and his repetition of Négritude's intellectual geography, turns on the first question of the meaning of history's pain. That critical question ought to provoke a critical reproach of Fanon and his obsessive return to the pure future as the site of revolutionary meaning, rather than, as with Glissant and others, a treatment of the past and its sedimentation in vernacular culture as already a site of resistance (past), resilience (past and present), existential and cultural meaning (present), and transformation of globalized and globalizing cultural formation in the age of *tout-monde* (past, present, and future). Like Césaire and his iteration of Négritude, Fanon has a real distaste for impurities. The intellectual as impure, archipelagic, and *Caribbean without qualification* has to be reconceived in this moment, precisely because the intellectual, for Glissant, is less a kind of agent from the future—unlike Fanon's new humanist, who is a time traveler of sorts—than an agent who works carefully with vernacular cultural forms that have already been places of meaning and unicity in the black Americas. Those cultural forms are sites of remembrance, to be sure, but they are also sites for cultivation and re-imagination. Thinking is embedded in those forms as shadows, concealments, and resistance, but also cultivations of the life of the rhizomatic subject and abyssal aesthetics. Glissant's intellectual, whether the *djobber* or the author of national literatures or more likely both at once, is tasked with expanding the imaginary *inside* history and memory—a sort of honoring of boats as one sets sail. The archipelagic imaginary is already every possibility, never a single necessity. Chaos. Rhizome. The swirl of meaning that radicalizes becoming and de-links it from Being and beings. There is no need for diversion. *Pace* Naipaul's phrasing, *everything was created in the West Indies.* Glissant starts with this claim. Therein lies his organicity. Not as soil or a root, but as a mangrove and shoreline thinker risking roots in order to make the *tout* in *tout-monde* the condition of sublime intellectual work. *Everything was created in the West Indies. Salt in the roots, mangrove poetics.*

How do we characterize this kind of intellectual and her work? That is, if everything was created in the West Indies and the West Indies is always already, from the moment of its irruption into modernity, *tout-monde,* then what is the intellectual on this model? It is worth considering here, as a final word or two, Grant Farred's conception of the vernacular intellectual in his 2003 work *What's My Name? Black Vernacular Intellectuals.* In this work, Farred lays out the logic and conditions of the vernacular intellectual in order to fundamentally alter the meaning of the figure of the thinker, particularly in the context of black Atlantic theory. What emerges is a folding of thinking into idiomatic expressive life—what Glissant calls creole or creoleness, put in motion by the *djobber*'s creolizing fragment-work of Relation. In developing his compelling readings of C. L. R. James, Stuart Hall, Bob Marley, and Muhammad Ali, Farred reconfigures our vision of the intellectual, moving from vanguardist or genius-modeled figures of thinking to the figure of a *vernacular* thought and thinker:

> Vernacularity marks that sociopolitical occasion when the conventional intellectual speaks less as a product of a hegemonic cultural-economic system than as a thinker capable of translating the disenfranchised experience of subjugation as an oppositional, ideologically recognizable, vernacularized discourse. Vernacularity represents the moment of a significant, palimpsestic transformation. Vernacularity signals the discursive turning away from the accepted, dominant intellectual modality and vocabulary and the adoption of a new positioning and idiomatic language.[23]

This notion of *palimpsestic transformation,* as Farred puts it, is critical for thinking through vernacularity in a black diasporic context, precisely because it recalls the bit from Chamoiseau above. Erasure and traces describe the precarity of vernacular work and identity; traces are given to the labor of thinking—the *djobber* as theorist, poieticist, the one who brings into being—and those traces are made out of and conditioned by the terrifying erasure of the Middle Passage. That is Glissant. To think *with* and *after* Glissant, to show fidelity to or perhaps intervene in order to embellish, is to situate the intellectual in vernacular space. Creole and creolizing space.

Are *creole* and *creolization* words for vernacularity in Caribbean spaces? Of course they are, and they are also names for the space Fanon could not imagine outside the humiliation of the oppressed, the space Césaire caught sight of but promptly turned away from in an apocalyptic gesture. Fanon and Césaire so loved the future that they sacrificed their only begotten past. Orphans who would reproduce orphans, but do not speak the orphan's language and see how the orphan has created an entire world that is the measure to itself, a world that is two halves sutured with bitterness and also love. The vernacular intellectual, in his translation of the disenfranchised experience of the subjugated, collapses whatever distance there is between language and that experience in the full embrace of creole and creolization. This sense of the vernacular intellectual is one that sustains the life of Chamoiseau's chalk mark—and postpones or even denies the second trauma, the second genocidal effort we call coloniality. In this frame, I think the *créolité* theorists can be folded more tightly back into Glissant's notion of the *tout-monde* and the thought of creolization. The vernacular, creole intellectual makes contact possible; exchange proceeds from what is stable and bold and identified with the landscape and tongue of the people. National words, rather than nation literature, perhaps.

Glissant's conception of archipelagic thinking, a thinking in fragments that indulges the profundity and fecundity of what is not whole, gathers and creates with voracious force. The relation of margin to center, of colony to center to other periphery, is taken outside the logic and affects of pathology, not in a leap forward but in a deep dive into abyssal beginning, the Plantation, and the bustle of everyday resistance and meaning. Who is this intellectual? This is the intellectual who moves back to community—understood by Glissant not as a people formed in resistance (*pace* Fanon) but as a collectivity made in languages and expressive forms that emerge out of a shoreline thinking. The shoreline, when taken seriously as a world-made and world-making site of beginning and after, shifts the entire logic of center and measure. Let me rewrite that sentence in order to collapse any distance between world and word. The shoreline, when taken seriously as a word-made and word-making site of beginning and after, shifts the entire logic of center and measure. Resistance then becomes less an imperative for collective formation and more an element embedded deeply within the already rich cultural formations of a repeating island. The intellectual of the repeating island works in an already reconstituted space and set of linguistic, expressive practices. This is the *local* intellectual made *global* at every turn, yet, in that making global, moves through senses of community made bold and strong through an already negotiated precarity. Precarity as trace, rather than precarity as the compulsion to struggle against and resistance. Precarity as a transcendental condition, not existential experience or ontology of the worldly subject. Shoreline thinking does not deny precarity. Rather, it only argues that precarity has been negotiated and transformed by and in the shadows and in movements of concealment.[24] Center and periphery look very different in the wake of that work of negotiation and transformation, and so too does the figure of the vernacular intellectual. Farred writes further:

> It also signals a turning toward, not in a nostalgic but in a considered and deliberate fashion, and (re)connection to an originary—but not necessary umbilical—community: it marks the initiation of that process when the conventionally trained intellectual is ideologically remade through culture—the culture of the subjugated, diasporic community, those cultural practices that signify an intersection between the dominant and the subjugated, those practices that while being marked as Other, have transformed both the periphery and the metropolis, that have affected relations between the (erstwhile) colonizer and the colonized, those practices that have reconstituted the diasporized constituencies and the metropolis as a whole.[25]

The originary community, the vernacular space of intellectual work, is the archipelago. Archipelago as figure. Archipelago as regulative ideal. Archipelago of our already *tout-monde* world. Glissant's reflections on the intellectual and the foundations of Caribbean vernacular culture add a sense of motion and peculiar repetition to Farred's notion of originary community. This is a creolization of his phrase, for sure, but it also importantly draws on the important qualifier Farred puts in front of community: originary. The origin, and so the ground of the originary, is critical for understanding both the shape and ethics of the originary: to what are we obligated as intellectuals, in what measure, and from what site and citation of history and memory? Glissant's reservation of the right to opacity, which surely informs the shadow and concealment structure of intellectual work, flows from the origin and the originary. It is fidelity. Faithful to the people, to the community. Embedded in that community and sustained by all the comforts and possibilities offered by creole forms. Doing the work of what Walcott called the bitter juice that seams two halves of fruit, or the glue, the love stronger than loss, that bonds fragments together. Glissant's vernacular intellectual.[26]

In this shift, Glissant breaks with organicity of any non-rhizomatic model, of course, but always in the mode of saying yes to the life of those marked Other, those who still practice the vicissitudes of becoming, saying yes, hearing now, beginning again, beginning without authoritarianism. And so the vernacular intellectual in Glissant's conceptual scheme is in some ways the dismantling of the very idea of the intellectual: plural and disassembling to the point of non-return, a nomad whose work returns erratically to the *djobber* taking the role of storyteller. That decisive swerve and shift that repudiates paternal lines. I am thinking here of how Walcott ends his essay "The Muse of History," speaking back against both the African and European fathers who would lay claim to his life and legacy. Walcott lets them go and says yes to the orphaned life. His life's work is in many ways testimony to that moment, lived in the epic beauty of *Omeros* or the discrete archaeology of the ocean floor in "The Sea Is History" or the wandering witness to reassembly in the Nobel Lecture "The Antilles." Walcott's reckoning is always melancholic. Orphan narratives have a right to their sadness. But orphans play with language and place and make worlds. Orphans are not abject. And that brings us back to Glissant's great poem, his *Omeros* we might say, his epic and anti-epic "The Indies." Glissant ends the poem with the intractable sea, older than the new world Caribbean and its memory and history, its womb-abyss, the anti-origin of thinking and building, and so we end here as well:

> O journey! These forests, these virgin suns, these waves
> Are one and the same efflorescence! Our Indies are
> Beyond all rage and acclamation, these are left behind on the shore,
> Dawn, radiance sailing the wave henceforth
> Its Sun, of splendor, inured mystery, O ship,
> Rugged calm of the horizon amid an uproar of currents,
> And the eternal fixity of days and tears. (CP, 100)

Acknowledgments

I WON'T EVER FORGET my first day on St. John. We'd arrived the evening prior in Concordia and set up for a meal, then to sleep. I woke up in the middle of the night to use the bathroom, and when I walked outside—the sleeping area was separate from the eco-toilets—I was staggered by the sky. The stars seemed on top of me, like the sky had fallen most of the way to earth. My eyes and balance took a few minutes to adjust. I'd never seen anything so gorgeous or overwhelming.

The next morning, we walked down a path to a rock beach, just below our eco-tent. I'd fallen asleep to the rhythms of the waves pushing up, then withdrawing over the rocks—an incredible, hypnotic sound. I remember thinking as I drifted off to sleep how this is a part of the sea making the rocks into sand and wondering what it meant to hear sand as a future memory, so far before it became pebbles and grains. But now the sun was brilliant and the sea had that wild, seductive shimmer. Some small islands just off on the horizon. A sailboat. Birds. Gentle waves. Breeze. Yes, breeze. I was overwhelmed by the beauty. There is no more beautiful place on earth.

As we got to the rock beach, I saw a plaque. I read it. It described how the trade winds blow directly from West Africa to this exact point—so directly, in fact, that a sandstorm in the Sahara will often create a haze a few days later on that very spot. And that also means this was a place for disembarking slave ships. The plaque outright said that. Human bodies were delivered as points of sale on this spot. It gave shape to memory's ruin and the ghosts of the archipelago.

I still do not have words for this moment. The mixture of sublime beauty and sublime violence was just too much. I do not have the words, but of course this very experience, this moment that folds history into one person's moment standing on the beach and summons traumatic pasts, which is really just everyone's every moment walking in the Americas, is at the heart of Édouard Glissant's poetry and poetics. We walk among this memory in very different ways—the history of race and racism is about that different walk—but the folding of history and trauma into landscape is exactly what Glissant calls our shared "tortured geography." There is no escape from this mixture, this tortured ground, even as the history of so much of the white Americas has been the erection of visual, institutional, and ideological denials and evasions of this inescapable geography. I'd been writing a couple of essays as test exercises for a possible book project, and this moment brought home the importance of writing on Glissant. It frankly terrified me, because the experience to which he speaks is too much for any writer. I wrote this book in order to bring my best thinking and capacities to what is one of the foundations of our very being in the Americas: traumatic beginning, beginning again, and the mixture of terror and beauty. It is a cruel logic, lived as histories and legacies of race and racism. But it must be said out loud. I don't know that this book is a success. That's really up to the readers. I think it's pretty good. I do know that I've tried very hard at every turn to be my best philosophical self across all the pages. I wrote it in many ways to honor Édouard Glissant. The twentieth century did not host a better or more profound thinker.

Writing a book is a lonely process. This book has been particularly so, written a handful-plus years ago as I hurried to get words on the page before my second son was born, then I shelved it, then I brought it back after quite some time at the urging of a couple of friends. I composed, then edited, then edited again, the entirety of this book in the cracks and breaks of my days. None of this was written in those long spurts we always imagine makes good writing possible. Quite literally, I wrote and edited as eggs cooked and my sons got dressed for a school day, or as I waited in the car to pick them up after school, or on my phone in line at the grocery store, and so on. It is how I work. Not always the most graceful, but it is efficient and I like the result. I never really had a choice, anyway. Life is what it is. This book is good enough. In fact, I'm writing this acknowledgment in the dark as my sons sleep on the plane, exhausted by this endlessly delayed flight we're traveling on to see their grandmothers. I find this acknowledgment-writing scenario hilarious, typical, and fitting.

I do want to thank Catherine Epstein, dean of faculty at Amherst College, for supporting so many things I do. Time off, time to gather colleagues for lectures and symposia on campus, big and small events both—I appreciate your support, Catherine, I really do. And thank you to the folks who endowed the Charles Hamilton Houston 1915 Chair, my professorial appointment. He is arguably the most important graduate in the history of Amherst College. It's an honor to work under the name Charles Hamilton Houston, especially in the Department of Black Studies. *Glissant and the Middle Passage* is my first book with this professorship, and I want to acknowledge that it means a lot to me.

After I drafted this, I put it aside so that I could teach Glissant's work and related stuff. The pressure and demands of explaining these ideas to students really clarified my understanding, and this book is immeasurably better for it. I wanted to write out the names of my students from my spring 2010 course "The AfroPostmodern" because they were just so good and we did fabulous work together. Also, I promised them I would. You all probably thought I'd forget, but I didn't. I told you I'd remember. Shanika Audige, Venise Crawford, Joyia Echols, Michelle Huynh, Carlissa King, Laken King, Kenneth Sentamu, Max Suechting, Brooks Turner, Sasha White, Alexandra Futty, and Austin Gregory—you all are still my favorite class ever. Don't tell the others.

Thank you to student assistants—Michelle Huynh, Amina Taylor for the first go-round with this manuscript, then Rachael Abernethy, Savannah West, Gabrielle Francois, Renai Foster, Trenati Baker, and Mia Nicholson—for a lot of little things that added up to big things. To Krishna Lewis at Harvard, for being brilliant and kind. Though I was writing a different project while at the Du Bois Institute, our conversations over that year found their way into this plenty quick.

And Rhonda Cobham-Sander, one of the best readers of Caribbean poetry in the game and my co-teacher, colleague, and dear friend. Thank you, Rhonda. You'll notice I don't talk much about poetry here. That's because you set too high a standard. Seriously. I appreciate every last one of your insights. You introduced me to Brathwaite's "The Dust," and I will be forever grateful for that alone. *Why is that? What does it mean?*

In particular, I want to single out my good friend and many times collaborator Grant Farred. I would say a lot of things, but I know you prefer it short and direct. There aren't many people out here who engage the best of theory with real rigor and with a deep ethical sense. Certainly none who do it like you, my friend. Respect.

Also, just a short word about my family people. My sisters Emily, Hannah, and Katie are always kind and hilarious. I need both. They are always happy for me when good things happen. That matters too. And a special thank you to Tracy Jarrett and Katrina Gonzalez. You two are as much our family as anyone, which has taught me so much about how we re-make family relations in love and affection and soulfulness, and how many things are possible when you break with conventions of how we imagine that family. I love you both. Countless times, your random messages and hellos and photos and need for an advice or two and visits to eat with us, to play with our sons, to talk about work and all of the things of being human—it has made my whole life better, every single time.

Mostly, a thank you to Marisa Parham—love of my life, the one critic who matters to me. I wonder what you will think of what I've written here.

This book is for my babies. Miles Henry, you are my firstborn. You are a warm, sublime New Mexico sunset, all bigness and calm and amazing and overwhelming. My Buddha, mommy's Bean. There is nothing on earth like your eyes. And Satchel Bee, our littlest, you are all sparkle and shine and happiness and the biggest sky of stars. There is nothing on earth like your whole body smile. Let's be real: you two got in the way of this book so many times that I couldn't count if I wanted to, but I wouldn't have it any other way. If it ain't a struggle, it ain't worth doing.

And finally, with still teary eyes three and a half years later: I offer this all as a small gesture in memory of Gene Drabinski and Denise Woods. Both suddenly gone, in a flash. We miss you.

Notes

Preface

1. For this reason, I think Eric Prieto's characterization of Glissant as a post-postcolonial thinker is both intriguing and largely accurate—though I would categorize much of what he names as "postcolonial" (characterized by militancy and nationalist politics) as "anticolonial." But that is a small terminological matter, and Prieto is right in this naming, then renaming, of Glissant's work in the context of what "postcolonial" means in our academic idiom. See Eric Prieto, "Édouard Glissant, *Littérature-monde,* and *Tout-monde,*" *Small Axe* 33, no. 3 (November 2010): 111–20. As well, on the distinction in Glissant's work between anticolonial and postcolonial in terms of language and the people, see the short but insightful remarks by Florian Alix, "Je, tu, nous et les autres: Le 'versant subjectif' des essais d'Édouard Glissant," *Presence Africaine* 184, no. 2 (2011): 37.

2. The meaning of the term "philosophy" and its mode of thinking is simultaneously the crucial and the impossible question here. It is crucial because this book is an argument about the possibilities of philosophical thinking after the Middle Passage, which suggests that we ought to know what "philosophy" means before beginning reflection. And of course the meaning of philosophy as an approach or term will inevitably be entangled with histories of colonialism, violence, and specters of white Eurocentrism. I let this issue settle here, in the preface, as "engagement with the conditions of knowing, being, and creating in the mode of the interrogative" in order to keep the boundaries of philosophy open. Non-white Eurocentric engagement with philosophy is for me about two shifts. First, *away* from philosophy as an inherent characteristic of a given text (rational argumentation, adherence to contemporaneous conventions of formal and informal logic—something, by the way, that has never strictly applied to even the foundations of "Western" thought in the Presocratics and Plato) and toward philosophy as a method of reading. Philosophy is a way of discerning conceptual moves in a given text, which is of course what philosophers in the Eurocentric traditions have always done (while often calling it something different, then deploying that difference as a form of intellectual imperialism). Second, *toward* multiple genres of texts and traditions of rendering thought public, from poetry to drama to language innovation to vernacular culture to cuisine and fashion. These are all

interventions in questions of knowing, being, and creating, every bit as philosophical as a Kantian deduction or formal argument in Searle, and they ought to be read as such.

At the same time, while saying at least that much about what "philosophy" means, we cannot know what is meant by philosophical thinking outside the experience of reading the text (thought broadly, beyond the written word to encompass mediums of meaning-making) itself. That is, the readings of Glissant in this book demonstrate philosophical significance inside the readings themselves; only the most general shape of their meaning can be described ahead of time. This is what it means to say that philosophy is not an inherent characteristic of a text, but rather a method of reading. Philosophy is *displayed in the act of reading*, drawn out in a philosophical *treatment* of a text, as staining a piece of wood makes otherwise hidden or subtle grains bold and striking. Reading philosophically—with an eye for questions of knowing, being, and creating—discerns the philosophical dimension. Intertwining the frame of reading with the innovations of the text— therein lies the transformation of what is meant by philosophy and how notions of knowing, being, and creating emerge as new, provocative, and capable of altering how we think about thinking.

3. This is a centerpiece of my *Levinas and the Postcolonial: Race, Nation, Other* (Edinburgh: Edinburgh University Press, 2011), asking how Europe is thought *after* entangling it in its entanglements.

4. Michael Wiedorn, *Think Like an Archipelago: Paradox in the Work of Édouard Glissant* (Albany: State University of New York Press, 2017). Wiedorn's book draws out the notion of paradox in Glissant's work, but in many ways I think it does not think hard enough about the paradoxical function of paradox. Glissant employs paradox as a deconstructive method; it halts the movement of arrow-like thinking. But the halt is always surpassed by the fecundity of Chaos—the paradoxical function of paradox is that it makes perfect sense, rather than simply confounding sense. My argument here is thus an extension and modification of Wiedorn's motif, neither a critique nor an affirmation.

5. Hugues Azéradt, "Édouard Glissant and the Test of Faulkner's Modernism," in *American Creoles: The Francophone Caribbean and the American South*, ed. Celia Britton and Martin Munro (Liverpool: Liverpool University Press, 2012), 204.

6. Alexandre Leupin, *Édouard Glissant, philosophe: Héraclite et Hegel dans le Tout-Monde* (Paris: Hartmann, 2016).

7. See also Georges Desportes, *La paraphilosophie d'Édouard Glissant* (Paris: L'Harmattan, 2008). While largely impressionistic and suggestive, Desportes offers an interesting and convincing sketch of both how Glissant's work is philosophical and how para-philosophy is not, as he says, "philosophy *tout court*" (8). Part of my argument in the present work, however, is that Glissant's theoretical

writings are more broadly philosophical than Desportes allows in the programmatic passages from his book, even as the content of *La paraphilosophie d'Édouard Glissant* seems to make a case for a wide-ranging resonance of Glissant's work as philosophy.

Introduction

1. It is noteworthy here both how Glissant's nonfiction writings move between Europe and the Americas, with little attention to Africa or Africanness (his fiction and poetry are a bit different, in particular his novel *The Fourth Century*), and how my own hermeneutic throughout brackets the question of Africa. This is an interpretative decision, one that, I would note, sets aside the important question of the meaning of Africa and Africanness for theorizing creolization in Glissant's work—a limit to my project, no question, and really a matter of focus.

On the place of Africa in Glissant's poetry, see the short and insightful essay by Michel Bernier, "L'Afrique dans la poésie d'Édouard Glissant," in *Horizons d'Édouard Glissant*, ed. Yves-Alain Favre and Antonio Ferreira de Brito (Biarritz: J&D Editions, 1992), 255–64.

2. I have argued for the necessity of decolonizing Europe in a number of contexts, most systematically in *Levinas and the Postcolonial: Race, Nation, Other* (Edinburgh: Edinburgh University Press, 2011)—see especially the Introduction and chapter 5.

3. See my "Elsewhere of Home" in *Between Levinas and Heidegger*, ed. John E. Drabinski and Eric Nelson (Albany: State University of New York Press, 2015), 245–60, where I explore the important notions of home and homelessness in European theory and the New World context, with special emphasis on the problem of language.

4. Celia Britton's *Édouard Glissant and Postcolonial Theory: Strategies of Language and Resistance* (Charlottesville: University of Virginia Press, 1999) makes a long and convincing argument for the centrality of language to questions of identity in Glissant's work, and is also sensitive to the shifts and nuances in his engagement with those issues across the 1970s, 1980s, and 1990s.

5. Martin Heidegger, *Identity and Difference*, trans. and intro. Joan Stambaugh (Chicago: University of Chicago Press, 2002), 48.

6. Martin Heidegger, "The Origin of the Work of Art," trans. Albert Hofstadter, in *Poetry, Language, Thought* (New York: Harper and Row, 1975), 42.

7. Gayatri Chakravorty Spivak, "Subaltern Studies: Deconstructing Historiography," in *In Other Worlds: Essays in Cultural Politics* (New York: Routledge, 1988), 209.

8. Walter Mignolo, *The Idea of Latin America* (Oxford: Basil Blackwell, 2005), 119.

9. On the question of Glissant and Africa, see, for example, Sanyu Ruth Mulira, "Édouard Glissant and the African Roots of Creolization," *Ufahamu: A Journal of African Studies* 38, no. 2 (2015): 115–28. While I do not quite agree with the assertion that Caribbean culture shares a *cultural root*, Mulira's essay demonstrates nicely both how "a source and a mirage" is the proper characterization here and how important Glissant's poetry is to the question.

10. On the method of apposition see Seanna Summalee Oakley, "Commonplaces: Figures of Difference in Heidegger and Glissant," *Philosophy and Rhetoric* 41, no. 1 (2008): 2ff.

11. Michael Wiedorn, *Think Like an Archipelago: Paradox in the Work of Édouard Glissant* (Albany: State University of New York Press, 2017), xxvi and following. Wiedorn's claim is especially relevant for understanding the relation of Glissant to literature—both his own literary production and his critical commentary on other authors (William Faulkner, in this context).

12. Frantz Fanon, "Racisme et culture," in *Pour la revolution africaine* (Paris: Éditions La Découverte, 2006), 52; "Racism and Culture," in *Toward the African Revolution*, trans. Haakon Chevalier (New York: Grove Press, 1967), 44.

13. Peter Hallward's critique of Glissant in *Absolutely Postcolonial: Writing between the Singular and the Specific* (Manchester: Manchester University Press, 2002) is both subtle and polemical, but in many ways it hinges on a distinction between the descriptive (what he characterizes as the aesthetic) and the normative (what he characterizes as politics or the political). Part of my claim here, programmatic as it is, is that the distinction is untenable in any philosophical appreciation of Glissant's work. That is, the aesthetic possibilities opened up by the notion of opacity—and everything that flows from and underpins it—are inextricably linked to cultural politics and other forms of the political. If read in this frame, I think there is an interesting continuity between Glissant's earlier work, with its more explicitly political aims, and the aesthetic dimension of the later explorations of poetry, art, and *tout-monde*. I would extend this response to Chris Bongie's very similar critique of Glissant in the concluding chapter of his *Friends and Enemies: The Scribal Politics of Post/colonial Literature* (Liverpool: Liverpool University Press, 2008).

It is also worth noting, as Sam Coombes does in *Édouard Glissant: A Poetics of Resistance* (London: Bloomsbury, 2018), that Hallward and Bongie published their critical books before (Hallward) or just as (Bongie) Glissant issued a series of pamphlets directly addressing the history and memory of slavery, multicultural politics, and anti-black racism. One would certainly have to revisit those pamphlets in a full response. But I think Coombes is exactly right when he notes, and this comment includes the work from *Poetics of Relation* forward, that "the imaginary for Glissant, although vital to a poetic outlook, is not severed from political concerns. On the contrary, it is crucial to envisaging an alternative *political* future" (91).

1. Origins I

1. I here want to sharpen my focus, which is the philosophical question of beginning coupled to the intensification of existential and transgenerational memory. But Glissant is of course also concerned with larger, broader questions of memorialization. For consideration of that aspect of his work, especially regarding his writings on the memory of the slave trade, see the excellent work by Bonnie Thomas in her "Édouard Glissant and the Art of Memory," *Small Axe* 30, no. 3 (November 2009): 25–36.

2. Bessel A. van der Kolk and Onno van der Hart, "The Intrusive Past: The Flexibility of Memory and the Engraving of Trauma," in *Trauma: Explorations in Memory,* ed. Cathy Caruth (Baltimore: Johns Hopkins University Press, 1990), 177.

3. Dori Laub, "Truth and Testimony," in Caruth, *Trauma,* 73.

4. Maurice Blanchot, *The Writing of the Disaster,* trans. Anne Smock (Lincoln: University of Nebraska Press, 1995), 47.

5. "Die Welt is fort, ich muß dich tragen." Paul Celan, "Vast, glowing vault," trans. Michael Hamburger (New York: Persea, 1988), 267. Jacques Derrida has given this line much attention, but my invocation of it here should not be read as an allusion to Derridean motifs.

6. Blanchot, *The Writing of the Disaster,* 61.

7. Walter Benjamin, "Theses on the Philosophy of History," trans. Harry Zohn, in *Illuminations* (New York: Schocken, 1968), 257–58.

8. G. W. F. Hegel, *Lectures on Philosophy of History,* trans. C. J. Friedrich (New York: Dover, 1990), 36.

9. Benjamin, "Theses on the Philosophy of History," 256.

10. Benjamin, "Theses on the Philosophy of History," 256.

11. Benjamin, "Theses on the Philosophy of History," 257.

12. I am thinking of course of Althusser's classic account of ideology and reproduction in "Ideology and Ideological State Apparatuses," in *Lenin and Philosophy* (New York: Monthly Review Press, 2001).

13. Theodor Adorno, *Negative Dialectics* (New York: Continuum, 2000), 365. See also his "Education after Auschwitz," in *Can One Live after Auschwitz?* trans. Henry W. Pickford (Stanford: Stanford University Press, 2003), 19–33.

14. On the relation between opacity and poetry, a productive site for thinking through the notion of the opaque, see Daniel Aranjo's largely evocative but compelling essay "L'opacité chez Édouard Glissant ou la poétique de la souche," in *Horizons d'Édouard Glissant,* ed. Yves-Alain Favre and Antonio Ferreira de Brito (Biarritz: J&D Editions, 1992), 93–114.

15. Derek Walcott, "The Sea Is History," in *Collected Poems* (New York: Farrar, Straus & Giroux, 1986), 364.

16. See Valérie Loichot's fantastic work on orphan narratives in Glissant's work

alongside the work of Toni Morrison, William Faulkner, and, importantly, Saint-Jean Perse in her *Orphan Narratives: The Postplantation Literature of Faulkner, Glissant, Morrison, and Saint-John Perse* (Charlottesville: University of Virginia Press, 2007).

17. Derek Walcott, "The Muse of History," in *What the Twilight Says: Essays* (New York: Farrar, Straus & Giroux, 1998), 64.

18. Bernadette Callier has treated the memory of Carthage in great detail in her *Carthage ou la flamme du brasier* (Amsterdam: Rodopoi, 2007), examining the resonance of loss and trauma across the diaspora. Her treatment of Glissant's poetic engagement is provocative and important, and in many ways informs my reflections here. I owe a great debt to this short and very under-read book. As well, the pages dedicated to Carthage in Samia Kassab-Charfi's *"Et l'une et l'autre face des choses": La déconstruction poétique de l'histoire dans les Indes et le sel noir d'Edouard Glissant* (Paris: Honoré Champion, 2011) are extremely important, especially around the figure of salt in Glissant's poetry. My own theorization of Glissant and the memory of Carthage moves quickly where Callier and Kassab-Charfi are patient and have sharper literary eyes, so I want to point to their work for more elaborate exploration of the issue in the context of Glissant's poetry.

19. J. Michael Dash, "Ile Rocher/Ile Mangrove: Éléments d'une pensée archipélique dans l'œuvre d'Édouard Glissant," in *Poétiques d'Édouard Glissant*, ed. Jacques Chevrier (Paris: Presses de l'Université de Paris-Sorbonne, 1999), 17–24.

20. This opens up a compelling question about gendered language in Glissant (and Walcott). It is a complicated question and too big for either this occasion or this footnote. But I think it is important to locate the maternal body, Glissant's *feminine*, perhaps, at the intersection of pain and pleasure—the trauma of birthing, the beauty of the born. That is to say, the maternal for Glissant is not simply a carriage of or container for pain. The mother is not melancholic, but rather fecund under melancholic conditions. The paternal is absent here, and I suspect it is due to Walcott's "Muse of History" essay, which associates the paternal, not with fecundity, but with the passage of the proper name, the name that links the present to history. Eschewing that relation, Glissant renders the feminine nameless even in the moment of profound *production*, then *reproduction*—unless Caribbeanness is to be understood as a proper name.

On the question of women, violence, and the language of womb-abyss, see the interesting and important reflections in Cilas Kemedjio's "Rape of Bodies, Rape of Souls: From the Surgeon to the Psychiatrist, from the Slave Trade to the Slavery of Comfort in the Work of Édouard Glissant," *Research in African Literatures* 25, no. 2 (Summer 1994): 51–79.

21. Aliocha Wald Lasowski, *Édouard Glissant, penseur des archipels* (Paris: Pocket, 2015), 68.

22. My focus here is on the figure of birth, the shoreline, and the recurrence of trauma, which leaves aside consideration of the slave ship as such. On the ship and its place in the question of beginning, see the opening pages of Stanka Radović's "The Birthplace of Relation: Édouard Glissant's *Poétique de la relation*," *Callaloo* 30, no. 2 (2007): 475–81.

2. Origins II

1. On the end of history and Glissant's move against it, see Alain Ménil's *Les voies de la créolisation* (Lille: De L'incidence éditeur, 2011), 90ff. While Ménil's treatment of the end of history refers to neoliberal models of end, the form of his analysis encompasses the apocalyptic and messianic senses of end as well. This is of course especially important when history is linked to traumatic memory and how it draws out a distinction between Glissant and Benjamin and Gershom Scholem, that other profound thinker of apocalypse and life after.

2. What follows concerns ruins and their relation to landscape and the abyss, but this sets aside the utterly compelling question of gravesites in Glissant's work and his own life. On this, see Valérie Loichot's remarkable essay "Édouard Glissant's Graves," *Callaloo* 36, no. 4 (2013): 1014–32.

3. Walter Benjamin, *The Origin of German Tragic Drama*, trans. John Osbourne (New York: Verso, 2003), 178.

4. Walter Benjamin, "The Storyteller," in *Illuminations,* trans. Harry Zohn (New York: Schocken, 2007), 108.

5. Derek Walcott, "The Antilles: Fragments of Epic Memory," in *What the Twilight Says: Essays* (New York: Farrar, Straus, and Giroux, 1998), 68.

6. Walcott, "The Antilles," 69.

7. Frantz Fanon, *Peau noir, masques blanc* (Paris: Éditions du Seuil, 2001), 13; *Black Skin, White Masks,* trans. Charles Lam Markmann (New York: Grove Press, 1967), 17–18.

8. Walcott, "The Antilles," 69.

9. It is important to note here how the relation between the sea as history and the borderless space of the Plantation is *not* a discourse about slavery but instead a very different engagement with history and memory. Glissant's *Mémoires des esclavages* (Paris: Gallimard, 2007) is a very different kind of reflection on these same issues, framed as it is by slavery *as such*—the work of the system, the geography of its scope (including France, most prominently), and the struggle of abolition. This opens up fascinating new dimensions of Glissant's thought that exceed my concerns here. For a fantastic treatment of this text and its implications, see Cilas Kemedjio, "Mémoires des esclavages: Le dernier chantier d'Édouard Glissant," *Revue des Sciences Humaines* (*Entours d'Édouard Glissant*, ed. Valérie Loichot) 309, no. 1 (January–March 2013): 203–21.

10. On this particular resonance and function of the trace, see Ménil, *Les voies de la créolisation*, 197–206, especially 198–200.

11. Frantz Fanon, "West Indians and Africans," in *Toward the African Revolution*, trans. Haakon Chevalier (New York: Grove Press, 1988), 27.

12. J. Michael Dash, *Édouard Glissant* (Cambridge: Cambridge University Press, 1995), 6.

13. Valérie Loichot, *Orphan Narratives: The Postplantation Literature of Faulkner, Glissant, Morrison, and Saint-John Perse* (Charlottesville: University of Virginia Press, 2007), 41.

14. Romuald Fonkoua, "Édouard Glissant: Poétique et littérature: Essai sur un art poétique," *Littérature* 174 (June 2014): 11.

15. Derek Walcott, "The Muse of History," in *What the Twilight Says*, 64.

16. It is worth noting here how this account of beginning—which, for me, is central to the entire arc of Glissant's career, from the early engagement with surrealism to late work on *tout-monde*—calls for a rethinking of some of Peter Hallward's critical interventions in his *Absolutely Postcolonial* (Manchester: Manchester University Press, 2001). Hallward's distinction between the singular and the specific is deployed for a range of compelling insights, and I think it is a useful frame for reading a good bit of postcolonial theory. However, in the case of Glissant, I think it is a difficult distinction to maintain with full force if we theorize beginning as interval. The past in the future sustains the language of singularity, for sure, but Glissant's embrace of the pain of past and present (the Caribbean as crossroads of the world, as the Plantation and mixing of cultures in chaos) is also the language of the specific and its capacity to relay singularity into a sense of the collective. And so the turn to the aesthetic is for Glissant always simultaneously material and political. Abyssal beginning collapses this otherwise fascinating and productive distinction and, in that collapse, shifts some of Hallward's critical conclusions—in particular, that the political is in tension with the aesthetic generally (something we will take up in chapter 5).

3. Ontology of an Abyssal Subject

1. Peter Hallward, *Absolutely Postcolonial: Writing between the Singular and Specific* (Manchester: Manchester University Press, 2001), 67.

2. François Paré has nicely shown how Glissant's interest in fragmentation is co-extensive with his practice as a poet. "Throughout his intellectual career," Paré writes, "Glissant remained fascinated by the fragmental character of the poem." This observation, with all that follows in Paré's essay, adds an interesting literary critical dimension (especially around Glissant's relation to genre and breaking apart poetry) to my largely philosophical meditation on subjectivity—the *djobber*'s practice as an originary poetry, perhaps. See François Paré, "Édouard Glis-

sant: A Poetics of Shorelines," *Sites: The Journal of 20th Century/Contemporary French Studies* 7, no. 2 (2003): 271.

3. Gilles Deleuze and Félix Guattari, *A Thousand Plateaus: Capitalism and Schizophrenia*, trans. Brian Massumi (Minneapolis: University of Minnesota Press, 1987), 3.

4. Deleuze and Guattari, *A Thousand Plateaus*, 3.

5. Deleuze and Guattari, *A Thousand Plateaus*, 6.

6. Deleuze and Guattari, *A Thousand Plateaus*, 7.

7. Deleuze and Guattari, *A Thousand Plateaus*, 8.

8. Deleuze and Guattari, *A Thousand Plateaus*, 9.

9. Deleuze and Guattari, *A Thousand Plateaus*, 10.

10. Natalie Melas, *All the Difference in the World: Postcoloniality and the Ends of Comparison* (Stanford: Stanford University Press, 2007), 36.

11. This struggle to create the new is the vitality (without vitalism) of rhizomatic subjectivity, and in this vitality Glissant, like Deleuze and Guattari, envisions difference as the intensification of qualities, rather than mere proliferation of differences. This is at the heart of a dispute among a number of commentators— Nesbitt, Hallward, Bongie, and others—around the critical frames with which to read Glissant's philosophical dimension. I think the strength of Glissant's work is his creolization of the intensification of qualities. What this means, for me, is not a sense of multiculturalism or multiplicity of cultures, which is what Kamil Lipinski argues in "Une pensée d'archipel face aux orientations mondiales selon Édouard Glissant," *French Cultural Studies* 28, no. 2 (2017): 209–17. While "multicultural space," as Lipinski puts it, is certainly a feature of *tout-monde* and the cluster of concepts that lead up to it, I want to claim that Glissant's ultimate concern, his endgame, as it were, is really poly-rooted subjectivity (see present chapter) and the creolizing production of the people (see chapter 5).

For further discussion and exploration of the question of multiculturalism in Glissant's work, see also Alain Ménil's *Les voies de la créolisation* (Lille: De L'incidence éditeur, 2011), 531–56.

12. Deleuze and Guattari, *A Thousand Plateaus*, 380.

13. Deleuze and Guattari, *A Thousand Plateaus*, 387.

14. Deleuze and Guattari, *A Thousand Plateaus*, 381.

15. Deleuze and Guattari, *A Thousand Plateaus*, 381.

16. Celia Britton, *Édouard Glissant and Postcolonial Theory* (Charlottesville: University of Virginia Press, 1999). In her final chapter, "The Weave of the Text," Britton takes note of how the language-identity coupling finds its final destabilization, even as it continues to describe (rhizomatic) identity, in the thought of Relation.

17. As well, and this is a much broader question, thinking nomad and the presence of world languages gives us an important and interesting frame for reading

the very idea of the 2010 project *Terre le feu l'eau et les vents: Une anthologie de la poésie du tout-monde* (Paris: Galaade Éditions, 2010), which gathers together such an eclectic bunch of poets. Rather than simply a *representation* of *tout-monde* (which is itself plenty important), the collection draws the reader out as nomadic in the act of reading. The errantry of reading then becomes the nomadic movement into Glissant's sense of subjectivity. And then puts the question to us: are we sufficiently rhizomatic in our readerly practice?

18. For a nice overview of the preoccupation with Chaos in Caribbean theory, see Jeannine Murray-Román, "Rereading the Diminutive: Caribbean Chaos Theory in Antonio Benítez-Rojo, Édouard Glissant, and Wilson Harris," *Small Axe* 19, no. 1 (2015): 20–36.

19. Antonio Benítez-Rojo, *The Repeating Island,* trans. James E. Maraniss (Durham: Duke University Press, 1992), 291n24.

20. Benítez-Rojo, *The Repeating Island,* 255.

21. Benítez-Rojo, *The Repeating Island,* 24. See also Celia Britton's remarks on this same passage in *Édouard Glissant and Postcolonial Theory,* 14.

22. For more on the critical relationship of Glissant and Levinas, see my *Levinas and the Postcolonial: Race, Nation, Other* (Edinburgh: Edinburgh University Press, 2011), especially the final two chapters. My concern there is how Glissant might intervene to expose the colonial logic of the Levinasian text, whereas here I am concerned with the nuances of thinking alterity in its most radical sense.

23. H. Adlai Murdoch notes that Relation is largely aimed at contesting the coercive character of the Occident and its deployment of universality to those ends. See his "L'Identité-Résistance: Antillanité, Relation, Opacité," *Revue des Sciences Humaines* (*Entours d'Édouard Glissant,* ed. Valérie Loichot) 309, no. 1 (January–March 2013): 196.

24. Celia Britton, *The Sense of Community in Caribbean Fiction* (Liverpool: Liverpool University Press, 2008), 37.

25. Gilles Deleuze, "Nomadic Thought," in *Desert Islands and Other Texts: 1953–1974* (New York: Semiotext(e), 2004), 259.

26. This raises for me an interesting question about the role of Louis Althusser's conception of ideology in both Deleuze and Guattari and Glissant, in particular as a site of strategic intervention. Deleuze and Guattari speak directly to this issue; the nomad is anti-ideology in Althusser's sense, insofar as the nomad's radical intervention is to disrupt (or deny) the very terms of ideological reproduction: the bureaucratic, administrative state. But for Glissant, ideological reproduction is nothing other than the colonial relation. The nomad is anticolonial, for sure, to the extent that it disrupts the colonial administration and reproduction of alienation (namely, the colonial school system). But the nomad also expresses life as it is already lived on and after the Plantation—mixed, chaotic, creolizing forms of

life as *existing* ways of being that are in search of name. This, for me, shows how embedded Deleuze and Guattari's nomad and rhizome are in the question of ideology and the reproduction of society, whereas Glissant's creolization of the same notions aims at describing subaltern life amid the (always colonial) state apparatus and its expressions in ideology.

4. Aesthetics of an Abyssal Subject

1. G. W. F. Hegel, *Aesthetics: Lectures on Fine Art, Volume One,* trans. T. M. Knox (Oxford: Oxford University Press, 1998), 94.

2. W. E. B. Du Bois, "The Conservation of Races," in *W. E. B. DuBois: A Reader,* ed. David Levering Lewis (New York: Henry Holt, 1995), 26.

3. Du Bois, "The Conservation of Races," 25.

4. For details on this moment in Glissant's life, see François Noudelmann, *Édouard Glissant: L'identité généreuse* (Paris: Flammarion, 2018), 143–47.

5. Aimé Césaire, *Discourse on Colonialism,* trans. Joan Pinkham (New York: Monthly Review Press, 2000), 73.

6. Césaire, *Discourse on Colonialism,* 32.

7. Césaire, *Discourse on Colonialism,* 31.

8. Aimé Césaire, *Notebook of a Return to My Native Land,* trans. Mireille Rosello and Annie Pritchard (Newcastle upon Tyne: Bloodaxe Books, 1995), 93.

9. Césaire, *Notebook,* 101–3.

10. Césaire, *Notebook,* 127.

11. Césaire, *Notebook,* 127.

12. Césaire, *Discourse on Colonialism,* 51–52.

13. Aimé Césaire, "Interview with René Depestre," trans. Maro Riofrancos, in *Discourse,* 82.

14. Césaire, *Notebook,* 115.

15. Aimé Césaire, "Culture and Colonisation," *Presence Africaine,* nos. 8–9–10 (June–November 1956): 195.

16. Césaire, "Culture and Colonisation," 196.

17. Césaire, "Culture and Colonisation," 207.

18. Césaire, "Culture and Colonisation," 207.

19. George Lamming, "The Negro Writer and His World," *Presence Africaine,* nos. 8–9–10 (June–November 1956): 325.

20. Lamming, "The Negro Writer," 327.

21. Lamming, "The Negro Writer," 331.

22. Lamming, "The Negro Writer," 331.

23. Lamming, "The Negro Writer," 332.

24. Lamming, "The Negro Writer," 332.

25. George Lamming, "The Occasion for Speaking," in *The Pleasures of Exile* (New York: Schocken, 1984).

26. Lamming, "The Negro Writer," 332.

27. Césaire, "Culture and Colonisation," 207.

28. Lamming, "The Occasion for Speaking," 24.

29. Lamming, "The Occasion for Speaking," 24–25.

30. Wilson Harris, "Creoleness: Crossroads of a Civilization?" in *Selected Essays of Wilson Harris,* ed. Andrew Bundy (New York: Routledge, 1999), 237–47.

31. Harris, "Creoleness," 246–47.

32. Jean Bernabé, Patrick Chamoiseau, and Raphaël Confiant, *Éloge de la créolité (Édition bilingue)* (Paris: Gallimard, 1989), 13; *In Praise of Creoleness (Bilingual edition),* trans. M. B. Taleb-Khyar (Paris: Gallimard, 1993), 74.

33. Bernabé et al., *Éloge de la créolité,* 52–53; *In Praise of Creoleness,* 113.

34. On the critical tension between Peck's two films on Lumumba, see Burlin Barr, "Raoul Peck's 'Lumumba' and 'Lumumba: La mort du prophète': On Cultural Amnesia and Historical Erasure," *African Studies Review* 54, no. 2 (April 2011): 85–116.

5. Thinking and Building

1. Patrick Chamoiseau, *School Days,* trans. Linda Coverdale (Lincoln: University of Nebraska Press, 1997), 21.

2. Martin Heidegger, "Building, Dwelling, Thinking," trans. Alfred Hofstadter, in *Poetry, Language, Thought* (New York: Harper & Row, 1971), 159.

3. It is worth referring here to Grant Farred's short piece *Martin Heidegger Saved My Life* (Minneapolis: University of Minnesota Press, 2017) as an exemplary (and direct) engagement with the fecundity of Heidegger's thinking about thinking around the question of anti-black racism.

4. Martin Heidegger, "The Question Concerning Technology," in *The Question Concerning Technology and Other Essays,* trans. William Lovitt (New York: Harper & Row, 1982), 27.

5. I am thinking in particular of Dussel's remarkable essay "The 'World-System': Europe as 'Center' and Its 'Periphery' beyond Eurocentrism," in *Beyond Philosophy* (Lanham, Md.: Rowman and Littlefield, 2003), 53–84.

6. Martin Heidegger, ". . . Poetically Man Dwells . . . ," trans. Alfred Hofstadter, in *Poetry, Language, Thought,* 227.

7. See also Glissant's remarks on the Caribbean and the "hinterland" in CD, 102ff.

8. Alain Ménil's *Les voies de la créolisation* (Lille: De L'incidence éditeur, 2011) has a nice overview of this particular movement, identifying what we have

here discussed as the *between* of between Europe and the Americas, in particular the distance from Africa and rendering the continent as trace, and folding it into the question of creolization and the political problem of identity—which, he points out, is always also an existential and linguistic problematic bequeathed by history (see 517–24).

9. For an excellent account of mourning in Heidegger's work, see Dennis Schmidt, "Ruins and Roses: Hegel and Heidegger on Sacrifice, Mourning, and Memory," in *Endings*, ed. Rebecca Comay and John McCumber (Evanston: Northwestern University Press, 2000), 97–113.

10. See, for example, Fanon's remark in "Racism and Culture" (in *Toward the African Revolution* [New York: Grove Press, 1998]) that "the blues—the black slave lament—was offered up for admiration of the oppressors" (37), which renders cultural production abject under regimes of anti-black racism. This is the result, inevitably, of Fanon's iteration of what has come to be called Afropessimism—the broad claim that an ontology of anti-blackness stains all cultural production undertaken in the context or midst of an anti-black world, and so that everything inside that ontology is fundamentally abject. The argument of the present book, of course, is that Glissant inverts this position in an affirmation of vernacular cultural forms: the *chaos-monde* of the Plantation and its afterlives produces worlds irreducible to the white racist gaze. This is something Fanon did not, and perhaps could not, conceive.

11. Antonio Gramsci, "The Formation of Intellectuals," trans. Louis Marks, in *The Modern Prince and Other Essays* (New York: International Publishers, 1992), 118.

12. Frantz Fanon, *A Dying Colonialism,* trans. Haakon Chevalier (New York: Grove Press, 1965), 27.

13. Frantz Fanon, *Black Skin, White Masks,* trans. Charles Lam Markmann (New York: Grove Press, 1967), 18.

14. Fanon, *Black Skin, White Masks,* 38.

15. On the question of the apocalyptic in Fanon's thought, see my "Césaire's Apocalyptic Word," *South Atlantic Quarterly* 115, no. 3 (July 2016): 567–84.

16. Frantz Fanon, *The Wretched of the Earth,* trans. Richard Philcox (New York: Grove Press, 2004), 1.

17. Fanon, *The Wretched of the Earth,* 161.

18. Fanon, *The Wretched of the Earth,* 162.

19. Fanon, *The Wretched of the Earth,* 163.

20. Fanon, *The Wretched of the Earth,* 163.

21. V. S. Naipaul, *The Middle Passage* (New York: Vintage, 1981), 29.

22. On the problem of influence in Senghor and the black Atlantic more broadly, see my "Senghor's Anxiety of Influence," *Journal of French and Francophone*

Philosophy 24, no. 1 (2016): 68–80 and "Anxieties of Influence and Origin in the Black Atlantic," in *The Global South and Literature,* ed. Russell West-Pavlov (Cambridge: Cambridge University Press, 2018), 94–107. Both essays explore the logic of productive relations between European ideas and black Atlantic thought. In particular, as with the present reflection, I argue that robust notions of thinking and particularities of tradition (African and Afro-Caribbean) create a relationship to traditions of former colonial powers that is fundamentally creative and transformative. This is the key to breaking with the sorts of Manichaean thought with which Fanon was so concerned, and which dominate his account of the postcolonial intellectual.

23. Grant Farred, *What's My Name? Black Vernacular Intellectuals* (Minneapolis: University of Minnesota Press, 2003), 11.

24. I am thinking here of how this complicates Nick Nesbitt's claim in *Caribbean Critique: Antillean Critical Theory from Toussaint to Glissant* (Liverpool: Liverpool University Press, 2013) that the later Glissant leaves the question of "fidelity to suffering" behind in what Nesbitt calls "the *Tout-monde* as aesthetic package tour" (244). The intellectual of *tout-monde*, written out of the Caribbean context, carries precarity and the abyss in the word itself—an important cultural politics that must always accompany other forms of political action. The difference here, between my claim and Nesbitt's, hinges on how one understands politics in relation to theorizing language as memory, then language as politics. On the carriage of pain in vernacular expression, see also my "Orality and the Slave Sublime" in *The Caribbean Oral Tradition: Literature, Performance, and Practice,* ed. Hanétha Vété-Congolo (New York: Palgrave, 2016), 109–28. As well, I would add here J. Michael Dash's remark that Glissant "shifts away from the 'flesh transfigured into word' to a new verbal carnality" in his "Writing the Body: Édouard Glissant's Poetics of Re-membering," *World Literature Today* 63, no. 4 (Autumn 1989): 610. Writing that carnality large, as the body of the people, is key to understanding Glissant's conception of, and the power he lends to, the intellectual.

25. Farred, *What's My Name?* 11–12.

26. We can here return to Hallward's and Bongie's critical concerns about Glissant's alleged aesthetic turn, in which he, according to these critiques, leaves politics behind. I don't think there is anything wrong with the aesthetic left to itself, but I do think the critiques miss some crucial elements and distinctions. The importance of the question of the intellectual lies in precisely this moment and space. Like Césaire and Fanon, Glissant understood the importance of formulating a notion of community or "the people," and the intellectual is a centerpiece of that formulation. Césaire and Fanon understood their work to be a facilitation of the kind of revolutionary action that would make the possible people an actuality, whereas Glissant's vernacular turn, as I am phrasing it here, is responsive

and cultivating the everydayness of Caribbean world-making rather than absolutely creative. But all are cases of the aesthetic functioning as an originary form of politics—which, for me, exposes an often one-dimensional conception of politics in Hallward and Bongie. Hallward and Bongie, on my reading, confuse the political (extant forms of agonism) with politics (orders of identity and being), and this confusion shows up most clearly when we consider the question of the intellectual. Glissant's late pamphlets respond plenty to the former, if the critique was against him as an actor, and his practice of *poiesis* has always been deeply attuned to the formation of Caribbean identity out of abyssal beginning.

Index

abjection, 97, 147, 193, 200, 204, 205

absence, 8, 10, 12, 13, 26, 27, 36, 52–56, 69, 72, 73, 101, 114, 115, 166, 178, 190–92, 198, 201

abyss, x, xi, xv, xix, 3, 10, 16, 23–26, 41, 43, 45–65, 71–81, 91, 93, 96, 97, 99, 103, 108, 137–40, 160, 162, 163, 166, 172, 178–80, 184, 189, 192, 194, 201, 207, 208, 230n24

abyssal, xi, xix, 3, 4, 16, 19, 21, 24, 26, 38, 41, 45–51, 55–59, 62, 63, 70, 72, 73, 76, 78, 80, 81, 83, 85, 89, 91, 93, 97, 100–103, 108, 109–12, 115, 132, 133, 135–40, 145, 159, 162, 163, 166, 168–70, 172, 173, 175, 180, 181–85, 188–93, 198, 201, 207, 208, 210, 224n16, 231n26

accusative, 50, 124–27

Adorno, Theodor, xii, 10, 31, 37, 67, 187

aesthetic, ix, x, xii, xv, xvii, xviii, 2, 21, 29, 31, 59, 76, 81, 90, 133, 135, 137–81, 186, 190–92, 198, 201–5, 208, 220n13, 224n16, 230n26

affect, 17, 24, 26, 29, 33, 97, 126, 137, 139–42, 153–58, 180, 190, 201, 210

Africa, xi, 12, 24, 41, 45, 54, 55, 63, 76, 96, 111, 115, 138, 143, 145, 156–58, 163, 165, 178, 179, 200, 204, 213, 219n1, 220n9, 229n8

Africanness, 3, 84, 148–52, 156, 161, 163, 199, 200, 219n1

Afro-postmodern, 135

alienation, 16, 70, 75, 112, 137–39, 143, 144, 146, 148–52, 156–61, 165, 166, 169, 170, 184, 193, 194, 201, 203, 206, 207

allegory, 65–69, 78

alluvium, 65, 78

Althusser, Louis, 35, 191, 221, 226

ambivalence, 8, 29, 36, 83, 94, 135, 163, 177

Americas, x, xiii, xiv, xv, xix, 2, 3, 4, 12, 20–25, 32, 35, 41, 45, 50, 56, 61, 63, 64, 88, 92, 93, 96, 97, 118, 131, 145, 147, 176, 178, 179, 200, 207, 208, 213, 214, 219n1, 229n8

anticolonial, xi, xvi, xviii, 3, 13, 14, 16, 19, 80, 91, 92, 106, 109, 118, 120, 131, 149, 178, 193, 217n1, 226n26

Antillanité, x, 24, 46, 52, 98, 99, 159, 166, 171, 184, 185, 187, 191, 192

anti-Semitism, xii, 26

anxiety, xvi, 4, 14, 57, 76, 161, 200, 206, 229n22

appositional, 169

appropriation, xvi, xvii, 21, 44, 69, 100, 171, 188, 207

archipelagic, xv, xvii, 18, 40, 46, 55, 64, 88, 101, 106, 108, 113, 115, 121, 126, 138, 165, 169, 170, 190, 191, 205, 206, 208, 210

archipelago, ix, x, xi, xiii, xv, xvii, 4, 23, 24, 38–41, 46, 48, 50, 63, 64, 71, 76, 84, 91, 101, 104, 110, 118, 122, 123, 132, 134, 165, 166, 169, 175, 191, 194, 195, 211, 213 arrival, x, xix, 16, 20, 23, 45–51, 56, 58, 63, 64, 73–78, 81, 97, 98, 116, 117, 120, 122, 131, 150, 158, 162–64, 167, 168, 201

arrow-like, 118–20, 122, 123, 130–33, 163, 168

ashes, 31, 36–38, 40, 43, 44, 47, 52, 62

assemblage, 72, 113

atavism, 62, 70, 75, 84, 157, 159, 168, 169

atavistic, 62, 64, 68, 84, 85, 89, 91, 93, 98, 102, 105, 116, 133, 138, 151, 155, 159, 162, 167–72

Auschwitz, 31, 32, 37, 55, 221

authenticity, 138, 139, 144, 155, 161, 188, 204

authoritarian, 106, 125, 177

authoritarianism, xii, 105, 118, 131, 212

barbarism, 14, 15, 31, 35

beauty, ix, 19, 26, 39, 48, 65, 66, 71, 72, 77, 89, 142, 146, 212, 222n20

becoming, x, 3, 4, 6, 10, 14, 26, 46, 50, 51, 58, 61, 62, 68–72, 76, 81, 82, 84, 88, 93, 102, 104, 107, 108, 111, 126, 137, 140, 142, 143, 150, 160, 167, 168, 171, 172, 183, 184, 187, 192, 197, 204, 208, 212

beginning, ix–xiv, xix, 1, 2, 4, 16, 19, 21–26, 31, 38, 40, 41, 42, 46–58, 62–65, 70–96, 98, 100, 102–12, 115, 118, 130, 132, 139, 146, 148, 150, 159–69, 172, 173, 175, 177, 183–85, 189–93, 198, 201, 207, 208, 210, 212, 214, 217, 221–24, 231

Being, xvi, 6, 7, 14, 61, 68, 74, 75, 100–108, 112, 115, 117, 118, 123, 124, 160, 172, 185, 187, 188, 191, 208

beings, 19, 61, 81, 100–108, 160, 208

Benítez-Rojo, Antonio, xv, 48, 104, 122, 123, 126, 127, 129

Benjamin, Walter, xi, xii, xviii, 24, 31–39, 42–44, 47, 53, 62, 65–69, 76–78, 97, 223n1

birth, 4, 20, 24, 26, 49, 50–56, 65, 72, 73, 91–94, 109, 114, 131, 132, 139, 181, 223n22

BirthAbyss, 51, 57

Blanchot, Maurice, xiii, 9, 29, 31, 62

Brathwaite, Kamau, 62, 109, 215

Caribbeanness, ix–xi, xv, 2, 24–26, 41, 56, 57, 65, 72, 80, 83, 85, 87, 101, 108, 132–34, 144, 156, 159, 160, 168, 172, 176, 195, 222n20

Carthage, 25, 26, 33–38, 42–45, 47, 52, 55, 66, 75, 222n18

Celan, Paul, 30, 58

Césaire, Aimé, xi, xvi, xviii, 3, 4, 9, 16, 54, 62, 75, 84, 102, 131, 137–39, 143–51, 155–70, 181, 193, 200, 208, 210

Chamoiseau, Patrick, 1, 17, 19, 71, 171, 183, 184, 209, 210

chaos, xvii, 16, 18, 20, 48, 63, 73, 79, 95, 104, 106, 108, 113, 122, 123, 127, 133, 150, 177, 179, 180, 181, 205, 208, 218n4, 224n16, 226n18, 229n10

chaotic, ix, 13, 15, 20, 58, 68, 82, 92, 102, 109, 115, 121, 122, 226n26

chiasm, 127, 128, 129

chiasmic, 66, 128, 151

cinder, 36–38, 43, 52, 62

circular nomadism, 101, 118, 120, 122, 132, 133, 163

civilization, 34, 35, 70, 137, 142, 145, 149, 150, 157, 158, 160, 163–65

civilizational, 165

collective, xii, 8, 25, 30, 38, 39, 42, 43, 49, 50, 51, 58, 63, 65, 66, 68, 69, 74–76, 80, 81, 91, 94, 96–98, 100, 102, 109, 111–13, 126, 128, 130, 134, 138, 145, 162, 175, 176, 210, 224n16

colonial, xv–xvii, 2–4, 11, 14–19, 83, 85,
    90, 116, 119, 122, 130, 145, 149, 161,
    163, 178, 179, 183, 193, 199, 200, 207,
    226n22, 227n26, 230n22
colonialism, xiii, 4, 16, 23, 75, 81, 83, 94,
    98, 100, 105, 111, 115, 145, 155, 163, 194,
    195, 199, 200–203, 206, 217
commonality, 38
comparison, xvi, 16, 120, 123, 225
composite, xix, 3, 21, 68, 69, 84, 89, 90,
    91, 93, 98, 108, 113, 133, 138, 159, 160,
    162, 164, 169, 171, 175
contact, ix, x, xiv, xix, 2, 13, 14, 15, 16,
    17, 18, 19, 20, 61, 78, 79, 82, 92–94,
    99, 102, 110, 113, 116, 120–22, 125,
    127–29, 134, 138, 139, 140, 152, 155,
    167, 169, 170, 172, 174, 175, 181, 207,
    210
continuity, x, 41, 80, 81, 121, 184, 198,
    220n13
contradiction, xv, xvii, 41, 57, 79, 82, 92,
    95, 96, 110, 137, 140, 145, 175
corpse, 32, 36–40, 42, 43, 47, 147
cosmology, 93, 94, 98
counter-ideological, 197
creole, 3, 16, 17, 24, 83, 87, 93, 97, 101,
    108, 115, 118, 119, 132, 140, 171, 172, 193,
    198, 200, 209, 210, 212
créolité, xi, 17, 62, 70, 71, 87, 97, 115, 171,
    173, 193, 210
creolization, x, xi, xvi, xvii, 3, 4, 13–20,
    72, 75, 80, 82, 84, 94, 97, 100–102,
    108, 111, 112, 114–16, 118, 122, 125,
    129, 132, 139, 160, 167–75, 181, 185,
    187, 190, 193, 210, 211, 219n1, 220n9,
    225n11, 227n26, 229n8
creolizing, x, 1, 4, 17, 20, 42, 62, 81, 87,
    91, 98, 112–15, 119, 121, 132, 160, 169,
    209, 225n11, 226n26
cri, 96

curvature, 63, 120–22, 124, 126, 127, 137,
    139
curve, 63, 120, 121, 127, 134, 162, 169, 205

death, x, xix, 9, 26, 27, 32, 37, 45–47, 50,
    51, 53–55, 59, 66, 70, 72, 73, 79, 88,
    96, 107, 108, 111, 132, 135, 137, 147, 178,
    181, 184, 189, 199, 202, 207
DeathAbyss, 54–57
decolonial, 203
decolonize, 11, 196, 199, 201, 203
deconstruction, xi, 10, 117, 135, 222
deferral, 86–88, 95, 115, 117, 124, 135,
    167–69, 173–76
dehumanization, 4, 79
delay, 86, 115, 117, 124, 135, 167–69,
    173–76, 214
Deleuze, Gilles, x, xvi, xviii, 2, 49, 99,
    100, 103–9, 112–18, 122, 123, 130–33,
    172, 190, 225n11, 226n26
Derrida, Jacques, xiii, xvi, 5, 6, 9, 11,
    86–89, 111, 160, 167, 221n5
descriptive, 21, 101, 127, 134, 144, 150,
    160, 220n13
deterritorialization, 70, 72, 107, 108, 115,
    117, 120
detour, 58, 59, 70, 72, 89, 114, 133, 138,
    160, 163, 165, 180, 181, 190
diachronic, 17, 28, 111, 124, 125
dialectic, 13, 31, 58, 67, 73, 104, 118, 119,
    120, 140, 168, 192
dialectical, 67, 119
diction, 199, 200
différance, 11, 87, 93, 175
diffraction, 63, 82
digenesis, 92–94
disaster, xi, 5, 9, 12, 23–26, 30–32, 37, 38,
    50–52, 54, 68, 154, 184
dislocation, 24, 28, 41, 42, 112, 177, 180
displacement, x, 70, 137, 203

dispossession, 24, 112, 193–96, 207
diversity, 14, 15, 101, 108, 113, 127, 128, 134, 172, 180, 207
djobber, 80, 81, 91, 95–98, 208, 209, 212, 224n2
drown, 38, 39, 45, 49, 52, 54, 56, 62, 72, 73, 75, 84, 166
drowning, 38, 40, 50, 62–64, 73, 74, 110, 166
Du Bois, W. E. B., 2, 142, 143, 150
Dussel, Enrique, 187, 228

earth, 35, 38, 43, 45, 51, 66, 88, 90, 96, 100, 103–8, 110, 114, 117, 133, 149, 170, 190, 194, 204, 207
eliminationist, xii
Ellison, Ralph, 2
embodiment, x, xvi
empire, 3, 4, 25, 35, 118
enigma, xi, xii, 14, 23, 26, 27, 30, 40, 62, 76, 83, 90, 127, 141, 162, 184
Enlightenment, 61, 89, 133
entanglement, xiv, 3, 4, 20, 88, 217n2
entombment, 39, 62
epic, 44, 69, 70, 162, 167–71, 174, 212
erasure, 20, 40, 43, 73, 74, 106, 183, 184, 197, 209, 228
errant, 72, 119, 121, 131, 164, 168, 170, 171, 179
errantry, 38, 58, 101, 106, 113, 125, 131, 132, 162, 164, 165, 168–71, 174–76, 179, 180, 226n17
essentialist, 144, 146, 152
ethical, ix, xii, xvi, 6, 16, 18, 21, 26, 29, 30, 31, 36, 61, 68, 86, 113, 134, 139, 143, 144, 181, 201, 206
ethics, x, xii, 11, 15, 16, 17, 31, 47, 48, 113, 124, 128, 141, 143, 151, 173, 211
Eurocentrism, 185, 188–90
Europe, xiv–xvi, 2, 4, 5, 8, 9, 11, 12, 21, 25, 31, 35, 37, 38, 42, 43, 45, 62, 68,

77, 86, 111, 134, 145, 146, 178, 188, 207
European, x, xii–xvi, xix, 2, 4–6, 9–13, 18, 24, 25, 31, 37, 41–43, 62, 74, 86, 92, 102, 131, 142, 145, 146, 189, 206, 207, 212, 219n3, 230n22
excess, xvi–xvii, 12, 97, 111, 113, 115, 122, 128, 138, 139, 157
exile, 38, 58, 97, 120, 132–34, 155, 156, 158–65, 168, 169, 176
existentialism, ix, 21, 62, 144, 151, 152, 158, 159, 171, 175

Fanon, Frantz, xi, xviii, xix, 3, 4, 16, 17, 18, 58, 62, 65, 70, 75, 83, 105, 138, 152, 185, 192–210, 229n10, 230n22
Farred, Grant, 209, 211, 215, 228, 230
father, 41, 45, 52, 94, 148, 212
Faulkner, William, 79, 83, 85, 96, 175, 220n11, 222n16
filial, 41, 58, 59
filiation, 58, 94, 95, 112, 175
Flaubert, Gustave, 33, 34, 35, 43
flight, 40, 79, 80, 107, 119, 123, 129, 130, 134, 195
forced migration, x, xiii–xiv, 25, 38, 149, 159, 162, 178, 200
fractal, ix, 63, 82, 92, 98, 106, 108
fragmentation, xv–xvi, 43, 69, 88, 94, 97, 100, 101, 106, 107, 126, 135, 159, 160, 165, 166, 171, 175, 181, 184, 191, 224n2
fragments, xv, 12, 24, 63, 65, 71, 72, 75, 76, 79–85, 88, 96, 98, 101–3, 107, 108, 125, 127, 133, 150, 159, 160, 165, 166, 206, 210, 212
France, xv, 111, 163, 200, 223n9
Freud, Sigmund, 29, 83, 91, 202
future, xiii–xiv, 1, 2, 4, 10, 16, 17, 24, 26, 31, 32, 36–42, 48, 49, 55–65, 68–79, 82, 84, 86, 87, 90, 93, 96–98, 109,

114, 117, 144, 145, 147, 150, 151, 156, 159, 162, 166, 167, 178, 180, 185, 190, 191, 193, 195, 197, 201–8, 210, 220n13, 224n16

futurity, x, xi, 24, 51, 54, 55, 61, 63, 68, 71, 72, 74, 79, 81, 89, 90, 94, 96, 97, 98, 100, 137, 138, 156, 158, 166

garrotte, 53, 191
genesis, xv, 40, 50, 92, 93, 94
genocide, 1, 19, 23, 25, 58, 183, 184
geography, of reason, xiv, 11, 12, 18, 21, 23, 25, 27, 46, 68, 69, 76, 79, 83, 89, 97, 103, 131, 139, 145, 186, 188, 193, 202, 204, 205, 207
geos, 50, 56, 57, 68, 81, 83, 85, 89, 96, 189, 194
ghost, 26, 41, 48, 59, 63, 82, 90, 180, 195, 196, 213
Gilroy, Paul, xiii
Gramsci, Antonio, 51, 197, 198
Greek, 7, 8, 10, 12, 19, 186, 189
Guattari, Félix, x, xvi, 2, 49, 99–101, 104–9, 112–17, 122, 123, 130–33, 172, 190, 225n11, 226n26

Haiti, 77, 178, 179
Harris, Wilson, 171, 226, 228
haunted, 9, 47, 65, 77, 135, 181, 195
haunting, 9, 10, 28, 29, 30, 52, 65, 83, 86, 88, 166
Hegel, G. W. F., 5, 7, 33, 142, 143, 150, 158
Hegelian, xii, 142, 158
Heidegger, Martin, xvi, xviii, 2, 5–8, 10, 12, 19, 185–89, 192, 228n3, 229n9
hermeneutic, xviii, xix, 219n1
heterogeneity, 106, 108
historical experience, xi, xii, xiii, xix, 1, 2, 5, 6, 7, 8, 9, 10, 11, 12, 24, 25, 26, 27, 31, 33, 35, 36, 37, 38, 43, 66, 68, 69, 74,

77, 86, 89, 100, 114, 118, 133, 150, 152, 156, 159, 169, 174, 175, 176, 186, 188, 189, 190, 191
historical materialism, 33, 35, 42, 67
historicism, 33, 34, 42, 67
historicity, xiv, 7, 13
historiography, xii, 11, 29, 34, 36, 37, 42, 49
Holocaust, 9, 43
home, 5, 6, 14, 45, 85, 87, 93, 95, 117, 137, 146, 148, 149, 156, 158, 161–64, 167, 168, 179, 186, 187, 199, 200, 204, 206, 219n3
hope, xv, xix, 6, 7, 25, 48, 54, 57, 98, 140, 151, 156, 166, 170, 177, 178
Horkheimer, Max, xii, 187
humanism, xi, 4, 65, 145, 169, 203, 204
Husserl, Edmund, 7

identity, 2–7, 14, 15, 19, 23, 28, 39, 46, 50, 52, 58, 68, 71, 78–82, 88, 90, 91, 94, 97, 98, 100, 101, 104, 107–13, 120–28, 131–34, 143, 144, 149, 152–54, 157, 158, 160, 161, 164, 168, 169, 170–72, 175, 181, 183, 184, 190, 196, 199, 203, 205, 209, 225n16, 229n8, 231n26
illegible, 10, 13, 18, 19, 20, 37
imaginary, 15–17, 44, 45, 51, 56, 61, 84, 86, 110, 119, 125–27, 133, 140, 141, 151, 168, 171, 192, 196, 208, 220n13
imagination, xi, 5, 12, 23, 36, 45, 64, 80, 84, 105, 110, 116, 139, 144, 208
immanence, 99
imperial, xi, xiii, xiv, 11, 15, 18, 92, 122, 126, 130, 131, 217n2
indeterminacy, 106
inferiority complex, 146, 199, 200
inheritance, 26, 97
intelligibility, 25–28, 41, 64, 73
interdiction, 29, 31, 37, 172
intermezzo, 110, 116

interrogative, xi, 39, 203, 217n2
interstitial, 46, 162, 185, 200
intersubjectivity, 13, 155
intertidal, 46
interval, 9, 10, 23, 47, 61, 68, 69, 71, 78,
    82, 88, 90, 94, 96, 97, 109, 114, 116,
    117, 150, 179, 184, 185, 190, 191, 193,
    207, 224n16
iterability, xi

Johnson, Linton Kwesi, xvi

Kālā Pānī, 70
Kant, Immanuel, 4, 5, 6, 141, 217n2

Lacan, Jacques, 192
Lam, Wilfredo, 175
lament, 44, 48, 188, 193, 229
Lamming, George, iv, 137, 139, 143, 144,
    145, 151–65, 169, 171
land, 3, 19, 45, 47, 50, 55, 56, 65, 68, 76,
    77, 87–90, 108, 114, 117, 121, 127, 141,
    144, 148, 149, 156–59, 164, 165, 195,
    196
landscape, ix, 44, 45, 50, 58, 61, 62, 65,
    68–71, 76–78, 81, 83–85, 96, 104, 108,
    110, 114, 115, 119, 133, 137, 148, 158, 174,
    189, 195, 200, 202, 203, 204, 205, 210,
    223n2
language, ix–xi, xiii, xiv, 1–3, 5–10, 12,
    15, 17, 24, 28, 29, 31, 36, 37, 39, 41, 47,
    49, 53, 62, 68, 69–71, 75, 80–83, 86,
    87, 90, 92, 100–123, 125, 127, 131, 133,
    134, 138, 140, 148, 149, 151, 156–59,
    163, 168, 171–76, 183, 184, 186, 190,
    193, 194, 196–200, 204, 205, 207,
    209, 210, 212, 217nn1–2, 219nn3–4,
    222n20, 224n16, 225n17, 230n24
Laub, Dori, 28
legibility, 10, 12–16, 18–20, 37, 39, 65, 66,
    68, 77, 128, 183

Levinas, Emmanuel, xii, 6, 9, 11, 62, 86,
    87, 89, 123–29, 187, 226n22
lieu commun, 95
lifeworld, xii
localization, 102
loss, x, xi, xiii, xiv, xv, 5, 7–12, 16, 20,
    24–26, 29–46, 49–59, 62–64, 70, 71,
    78, 82, 83, 93, 94, 97, 103, 105, 107,
    109, 111, 140, 147, 162, 163, 168, 176,
    178, 185, 188–95, 198, 201, 203, 207,
    212, 222n18
love, xviii, 41, 71, 82, 180, 210, 212
Lumumba, Patrice, 138, 175, 176, 177,
    178, 179, 180, 228
Lyotard, Jean-François, xiii, 28, 160

mangrove, 46, 47, 51, 54, 73, 100, 107,
    113, 114, 133, 140, 208, 209
Manichaean, 105, 230
marronage, 79, 80, 81, 82, 91, 92, 96, 98,
    129, 133, 175
maternity, 49
Matta, Roberto, 121
measure, xv, xvi, 11, 12, 18, 19, 27, 68,
    82, 83, 102, 105, 106, 110, 117, 118,
    120, 122, 123, 128, 138, 145, 146, 151,
    155, 161, 167, 169, 181, 200, 201, 206,
    210, 211
melancholia, xiii, 29, 83, 91
melancholic, x, 29, 33, 49, 58, 72, 83, 91,
    162, 176, 204, 212, 222n20
memorial, 6, 7, 15, 16, 27, 29, 35, 38, 58,
    63, 86, 87, 144, 151, 192
memory, ix–xv, 1, 2, 4, 8–11, 16, 23–30,
    33, 35–49, 53–57, 61–98, 103, 109, 110,
    113, 114, 118, 129, 134, 137, 138, 144,
    147, 148, 150, 151, 156, 162, 166, 168,
    176, 189, 190, 191, 194, 197, 198, 204,
    205, 207, 208, 211, 212, 220n13, 221n1,
    222n18, 223n1, 230n24
Ménil, René, 2, 62

metaphysical, xiv, xviii, 2, 3, 5, 123, 144, 148, 149, 152, 157, 159, 162

metaphysics, x, xv, xvii, 5, 30, 49, 101, 122, 124, 141, 143, 144, 155, 158, 164–67, 186, 187

métissage, 4, 122

métropole, 75, 76, 132

Middle Passage, x, xi, xiii–xiv, xix, 1, 4, 16, 20, 24–26, 37–40, 42, 45, 47, 48, 52, 53, 55, 62, 63, 64, 70, 72, 73, 76, 78, 81, 84, 86, 92, 94, 103, 110, 118, 162, 169, 175, 180, 181, 194, 198, 200–209, 217n2

mimesis, 74, 75, 111, 179, 180, 184, 197, 205

Mobutu, Sésé Seko, 177, 179

modernity, ix, xiii, 1, 2, 12, 23, 79, 84, 134, 135, 185, 187, 197, 208, 209

monument, 39, 78, 97, 104

morne, 98

mourning, xii, 12, 24, 26, 53, 83, 91, 176, 192

myth, xii, 76, 85, 93, 170, 171, 174, 195, 200

Naipaul, V. S., 76, 205, 208

narrative, 11, 18, 29, 30, 34–36, 40, 42, 50, 67, 78, 83, 94–96, 134, 135, 148, 157, 160, 169, 171, 173, 175, 180, 187, 189, 198, 212, 221n16

nation, 1, 40, 145, 191, 210

nationalism, ix, 107

national literature, 180, 184, 185, 193

negation, 41, 42, 86, 129, 132, 164

negative sublime, 36, 37

Négritude, ix, 21, 46, 58, 62, 75, 80, 84, 89, 92, 102, 111, 138, 144, 148–51, 156–59, 163, 169, 172, 175, 178, 181, 192, 193, 198–200, 204, 206–8

New World, xiv, xv, xvii, 1, 2, 13, 17, 20, 23, 40, 44, 47, 52, 62–64, 68, 69, 75–78, 80, 81, 88, 91–93, 96, 98, 115, 138, 145–48, 156, 157, 163, 171, 212, 219n3

nihilism, 194, 199, 200

nomad, 2, 50, 56, 58, 95, 99, 100, 101, 115, 116, 117, 118, 119, 120, 121, 122, 123, 125, 127, 128, 129, 130, 131, 132, 133, 134, 135, 139, 159, 164, 172, 174, 180, 195, 212, 225, 226, 227

nomadic, 13, 24, 49–51, 58, 72, 102, 115–20, 122, 123, 125–28, 130, 133, 134, 137, 141, 160, 161, 163, 169, 179, 181, 207, 226n17, 227n26

nomadology, 99, 121, 130, 131–33

non-being, 103

non-filial, 58, 59

nonhistory, 42, 206

normative, 8, 21, 76, 77, 85, 101, 134, 138, 144, 151, 156, 160, 198

nostalgia, 7, 8, 10, 64, 80, 89–91, 93, 117, 129, 148, 151, 167, 181, 184, 191, 194, 204

Novalis, 5

ontological, xv, 16, 68, 116, 124, 139, 172, 201, 202

ontology, 16, 17, 71, 99–104, 108, 115–17, 124, 125, 141, 143, 154, 166, 211, 229n10

opacity, xvii, 13–20, 37, 57, 58, 80, 82, 88, 91, 94, 95, 103, 109, 110, 112, 113, 124–29, 137, 139, 140, 169, 170–75, 180, 190, 206, 211, 220n13, 221n14

organic, 46, 49–51, 56–58, 106, 197, 198, 201

origin, xv, 7, 8, 12, 18, 24, 26, 33, 34, 45, 51, 53, 62, 64, 65, 71, 72, 75, 76, 79, 81, 84, 87, 89–96, 102, 106, 107, 109, 110, 118, 120, 122, 124, 129, 130, 138, 153–55, 158–62, 164, 166–68, 175, 176, 179, 197, 198, 203, 204, 211, 212

originary, 16, 26, 27, 28, 88, 105, 130, 159, 160, 162, 165, 211, 224n2, 231n26
orphan, 40, 42, 94, 95, 96, 148, 210, 212

pain, ix, xii–xiv, 9, 10, 23–26, 31, 33, 36, 37, 40, 41, 43, 45, 61, 65–71, 74–79, 81, 86–91, 96–98, 111, 113, 114, 134, 137, 145–47, 150, 151, 157, 159, 160, 163, 165, 166, 180, 181, 190, 191–95, 199, 204, 208, 222n20, 224n16, 230n24
paradox, xv, xvii, 2, 14, 18, 26, 48, 49, 55, 72, 102, 106, 113, 119, 127, 128, 132, 154, 156, 160, 191, 218n4
para-origin, 153–55
para-philosophy, xvii–xviii, 218n7
parasitic, 100
paternity, 45, 49, 148
Peck, Raoul, 138, 175–81, 228n34
pensée archipélique, xvi, xvii, 3, 11, 14, 15, 17, 139
pensée continental, xv, xviii, 8, 11, 63, 139
Perse, Saint-John, 79, 119, 175, 222n16
pessimism, 10, 229n10
philosophy, ix–xix, 1–7, 10–12, 18, 29, 31, 33, 36, 37, 41–43, 53, 66, 67, 99, 100, 124, 141–44, 152, 166, 185–89, 207, 217n2, 219n7
pidgin, 16, 193, 200, 201, 205
place, xi, xiv, xviii, 1–4, 11, 12, 26, 47, 50, 52, 56, 58, 61, 65, 69, 71, 76–78, 81, 83–85, 88, 89, 92, 93, 96, 97, 104, 109, 110, 111, 113, 114, 116–19, 121, 122, 133, 137, 138–41, 143, 145, 148, 149, 157, 159, 161, 162, 179–81, 187, 189, 192, 195, 202–4, 207, 212
plantation, xiv, 16, 20, 63, 65, 72, 73, 77–83, 86–88, 91–98, 103, 109, 137, 148, 149, 160, 168, 175, 210, 223n9, 224n16, 226n26, 229n10

Platonic, xiii
poetics, ix, x, xvii–xix, 13, 14, 18, 24, 26, 37, 38, 41, 47, 49, 51, 55, 62, 63, 65, 70, 73, 77–80, 84, 92, 95, 100, 101, 103, 109, 111–21, 125, 126, 129, 140, 146, 147, 150, 164, 168–72, 175, 180, 192, 195, 202, 209, 230n24
poetry, x, xvii, 1, 10, 24, 30, 31, 59, 76, 81, 84, 100, 126, 134, 143, 166, 170, 174, 188, 204, 217n2, 219n1, 220n9, 221n14, 222n18, 224n2
poiesis, 2, 61, 68, 90, 114, 133, 184–95, 198, 231n26
polis, 151
political, ix, xi, xii, 3, 4, 6, 15, 21, 33, 58, 77, 89, 94, 143, 146, 149–51, 156, 167, 168, 170, 171, 178–80, 184, 189, 201, 209, 220n13, 224n16, 229n8, 230n24
politics, x, 12, 18, 140, 141, 150, 166, 170, 217n1, 220n13, 230n24, 230n26, 231n26
poly-lingualism, 121, 123
poly-rooted, 46, 103, 111–13, 122, 177, 179, 180, 190, 225n11
postcolonial, xi, xiii, xv, xviii, 3, 6, 18, 19, 21, 58, 99, 145, 149, 155–57, 167, 170, 176, 178, 183, 184, 193–96, 199, 200, 203, 207, 217n1, 224n16
postmodern, xv, xvi, 6, 21, 135, 159, 160, 164, 165
postmodernity, 1, 2, 23, 134, 135
prescriptive, 127, 134
presence, xi, xiii, 7–10, 12, 19, 24, 38, 47, 69, 72, 86, 90, 115, 120, 134, 138, 156, 161, 162, 165, 178, 180, 183, 187, 188
progress, 32, 33, 35, 37, 42, 66, 68, 197
prophecy, 177, 181
prophetic, 34, 178, 181

race, ix–xi, 1–3, 97, 142, 150, 152–57, 198, 199

racism, x, 17, 152, 155, 157, 158, 199, 200, 220n13, 228n3, 229n10

reactivation, 8, 10–13, 16, 19, 62, 93, 147, 150, 157, 163, 169, 192

regulative ideal, 6, 27, 33, 57, 72, 211

Relation, x, xvi–xviii, 13, 14, 17–20, 43, 47, 51, 58, 72–75, 78, 80, 85, 87, 88, 94–96, 98, 99, 101–4, 109, 110–13, 118, 120, 121, 125–30, 132, 139–41, 144, 145, 160, 164, 167, 168, 169, 170–77, 180, 190, 191, 195, 207, 209, 226n23

relay, 18, 68, 87, 88, 89, 95, 116, 129, 140, 141, 160, 164, 173, 174, 175, 176, 224n16

repetition, 13, 37, 48, 57, 73, 75, 89, 90, 109, 110–14, 120, 131, 174, 179, 180, 184, 186, 191, 197, 205, 208, 211

representation, x–xiii, 3, 26, 27, 29, 30, 35, 36, 39, 47, 123, 124, 137, 139, 181, 202, 226n17

reterritorialization, 104, 108, 115–17

reversion, 75–77, 138, 143

rhizomatic, 13, 17, 46, 51, 54, 59, 94, 102, 106, 107, 108, 112, 115, 122, 125, 126, 127, 133, 134, 137, 140, 167, 168, 169, 171, 177, 179, 180, 181, 190, 206, 207, 208, 212, 225, 226

rhizome, x, 2, 51, 56–59, 96, 99, 100, 101, 103, 104, 106–17, 121, 122, 123, 125, 127, 128, 132–35, 139, 159, 168, 172, 174, 179, 205–8, 227n26

Rimbaud, Arthur, 124–26, 129, 131

Rome, 33, 34, 35, 201

root, xiii, 4, 8, 17, 23, 26, 33, 38–43, 46, 47, 50, 53–56, 58, 64, 73–76, 89, 90, 94–96, 100, 102–7, 110–23, 125, 127, 129, 130, 133, 138, 139, 140, 149, 155, 159, 161, 164–67, 169, 170, 172, 177, 179, 181, 187, 189, 190, 197–201, 203–9, 220n9

RootAbyss, 52–54, 57

ruins, x, 8, 13, 15, 31, 35, 43, 53, 63, 65–73, 75–78, 87, 94, 96, 104, 187, 189, 223n2

rupture, 30, 41, 42, 56, 88, 107

sadness, 3, 25, 26, 33–36, 42, 43, 48, 66, 69, 74, 75, 89, 192, 212

salt, ix, 40, 43–46, 51–55, 57, 59, 77, 78, 190

sand, xix, 40, 49, 52, 88, 89

scent, 83, 85, 86

Scholem, Gershom, 223

sea, xii, 23, 38–52, 54, 56, 62, 64, 65, 71, 72, 73, 74, 77, 78, 103, 109, 110–14, 125, 139, 166, 180, 212, 223n9

sedentary, 108, 115–18, 121, 130, 131, 157

sedimentation, 120, 157, 208

Senghor, Léopold, xi, 207, 229n22

sensibility, 76, 93, 126, 133, 139, 142, 152, 154, 157, 158, 168, 169, 171, 174, 175, 177, 198

shackles, 53, 56, 140

Shoah, xi, xii, 26, 30, 31, 37, 42, 52, 62. See also Holocaust

shoreline, ix, x, xix, 16, 36, 51, 54, 56, 63–65, 68, 70, 73, 77–79, 81–83, 86, 88, 89, 92, 95, 97, 98, 108–10, 114, 131, 133–35, 137, 139, 162, 168, 172, 190, 208, 210, 211, 223n22

singular, xv, 1, 4, 10, 48, 100, 102, 107, 109, 110, 112, 121, 128, 130, 224n16

slavery, xiv, 75, 83, 85, 88, 146, 189, 220n13, 223n9

solidarity, 150, 192

space, x, xii, xiii, xviii, 2, 4, 5, 11, 14, 16, 17, 21, 23, 29, 30, 39, 46, 50, 51, 61, 64, 65, 78, 81–88, 91, 92, 94, 100–103, 110, 115, 117–27, 132–34, 137, 139, 140, 145, 148, 150, 151, 154–58, 161, 162, 165, 169, 174, 175, 177, 178, 180, 181, 184, 185, 192, 195, 202, 204–11, 223n9, 225n11 specter, xvi, 9, 47, 138, 177, 217n2

Spivak, Gayatri, 11

subaltern, 11, 29, 31, 183, 197, 198, 208, 227n26

subjectivity, x, xii, xiii, xviii, 2, 6, 7, 13, 16, 21, 27–29, 46, 49, 50, 55, 56, 58, 62, 63, 79, 81, 91, 99, 100–104, 106, 108, 109, 111–15, 118, 120–30, 133, 134, 137–39, 141, 150, 152–55, 161, 162, 169, 173, 179, 190, 195, 199, 200, 201, 205, 207, 224n2, 225n11, 226n17

sublime, 36, 37, 110, 204, 209, 230n24

sublimnity, 56

suffering, 9, 30, 36, 37, 47, 58, 65, 67, 72, 73, 85, 98, 145–47, 153, 230n24

surrealism, 2, 62

survival, 26, 30, 52, 55, 56, 65, 70, 73–76, 79, 80, 88–93, 97, 98, 103, 132, 184

synchrony, 30, 134

teleological, 29, 72, 102

territorialization, 89, 108, 115–18, 181

territory, 87–91, 103, 104, 108, 110, 115–17, 121, 132–34, 138, 163, 167, 207

terror, 51, 52–54, 178, 194

time, x, xii, xiii, xvi, xviii, 4, 7, 9–11, 14, 17, 21, 23, 25–31, 34, 35, 45–49, 51–56, 61–65, 67–69, 72, 74–76, 80, 82, 85–88, 90, 92, 96, 97, 100, 101, 103, 108, 112–22, 124, 126, 127, 131, 134, 135, 137, 139, 142, 144, 146, 147, 150, 151, 154–56, 158, 162, 164, 166, 167, 169, 173–76, 179, 185, 186, 188, 195, 197, 198, 204–7

tortured geography, 50, 51, 54, 57, 58, 96, 180, 190, 204, 207

totalitarian, 41, 42, 105, 130, 132, 133, 173, 180

totality, 18, 111, 113, 118, 124, 129, 133, 173, 174, 187

tout-monde, ix, x, xvi–xvii, 13, 18, 46, 86–88, 92, 93, 95, 96, 99, 115, 121, 127–29, 134, 138, 139, 144, 164, 165, 169–71, 208–11, 220n13, 224n16, 225n11, 226n17, 230n24

trace, 3, 8, 12, 13, 18, 20, 29, 30, 37, 38, 40, 45, 48, 52, 53, 63, 64, 66, 75, 78, 81, 82, 85–91, 96–98, 113, 120, 130, 137, 138, 147, 150, 151, 156, 157, 162, 163, 165, 168, 192, 209, 211, 224n10, 229n8

tradition, xii–xvi, 5, 36, 49, 62, 160, 162, 167, 230n22

transmission, xii, xiii, 12, 28, 35, 37, 42, 48, 94, 137–39, 141, 142, 144, 149, 150, 153, 166, 174–76, 181, 186, 190–92

transversality, 110

trauma, x–xiv, xix, 9, 10, 20, 24–31, 34–47, 50, 51, 53, 54, 55, 56, 57, 58, 62, 64, 68, 72, 73, 78, 81–85, 88, 97, 98, 103, 135, 137, 140, 162, 163, 169, 201, 207, 210, 222n18, 223n22

traumatic, xi–xiv, 1, 3, 9, 10, 24–30, 33, 36, 40, 41–45, 47, 50, 51, 53, 62–65, 72, 74, 79, 80, 83, 85, 91, 92, 94–97, 109, 156, 162, 177, 191, 201, 223n1

tribal, 38–41

unintelligible, 9, 54

universal, 4, 14, 57, 110, 113, 128, 142, 159, 161, 164, 165, 169

universality, xiii, xiv, 14, 17, 18, 57, 101, 128, 158, 165, 188, 198, 226n23

uprooting, 5, 73, 120, 133, 194

van der Kolk, Bessel, 28

vernacular, 4, 200, 205, 208–12, 217n2, 229n10, 230n24

victim, xiv, 29–31, 33, 34, 36, 37, 43–45, 73

violence, xii–xiv, 4, 9, 10, 12, 13, 16, 25, 30, 32, 34, 35, 45, 52, 58, 75, 76, 92, 93, 103, 113, 118, 120, 125, 134, 147, 158, 170, 194, 195, 199, 201, 202, 204, 217n2, 222n20

visibility, 13, 36–38, 42

volcanic, 54

Walcott, Derek, xvi, 38–41, 45, 48, 49, 62, 69–72, 97, 159, 166, 204, 212

West, the, xii–xiv, xviii, 9–11, 14, 63, 75, 80, 109, 122, 123, 145, 157, 161, 179, 185, 186, 187, 188, 200, 204, 205, 208, 209, 217n2

whiteness, xiv, 200

womb, 26, 49, 51, 52, 64, 65, 73, 76, 93, 96, 114, 148, 162, 175, 212, 222n20

wound, 27, 29, 44, 45, 51, 52, 53, 55, 57, 72, 133

wreckage, xi, 9, 32–38, 42, 43, 50, 66, 67

Wright, Richard, 2

JOHN E. DRABINSKI is Charles Hamilton Houston 1915 Professor of Black Studies at Amherst College. He is the author of *Sensibility and Singularity: The Problem of Phenomenology in Levinas, Godard between Identity and Difference,* and *Levinas and the Postcolonial: Race, Nation, Other.*